THE PHILOSOPHICAL PARENT

THE PHILOSOPHICAL PARENT

Asking the Hard Questions about
Having and Raising Children

Jean Kazez

OXFORD
UNIVERSITY PRESS

OXFORD
UNIVERSITY PRESS

Oxford University Press is a department of the University of Oxford. It furthers the University's objective of excellence in research, scholarship, and education by publishing worldwide. Oxford is a registered trade mark of Oxford University Press in the UK and certain other countries.

Published in the United States of America by Oxford University Press
198 Madison Avenue, New York, NY 10016, United States of America.

© Oxford University Press 2017

Library of Congress Cataloging-in-Publication Data
Names: Kazez, Jean, author.
Title: The philosophical parent : asking the hard questions about having and raising children / Jean Kazez.
Description: New York : Oxford University Press, 2017. | Includes bibliographical references and index.
Identifiers: LCCN 2016037115 (print) | LCCN 2017007841 (ebook) | ISBN 9780190652609 (cloth : alk. paper) | ISBN 9780190652616 (updf) | ISBN 9780190652623 (ebook)
Subjects: LCSH: Child rearing—Philosophy. | Parent and child—Philosophy.
Classification: LCC HQ769 .K346 2017 (print) | LCC HQ769 (ebook) | DDC 649/.1—dc23
LC record available at https://lccn.loc.gov/2016037115

1 3 5 7 9 8 6 4 2
Printed by Edwards Brothers Malloy, United States of America

For my children,
with mathematical certainty.

CONTENTS

CONTENTS

INTRODUCTION

Having children turns every parent and parent-to-be into a philosopher. The philosophical questions are right there in the many perplexing situations we confront in the process of bringing new people into the world and then raising them. Fortunately, we're also in a position to spend some time thinking about these questions. Becoming and being a parent is full of waiting, which means we have time to muse, grapple, wonder, and discuss.

There's waiting to get pregnant—why is it so important to become a parent? Waiting for morning sickness to end—why does nausea make all of life seem so dismal? Waiting for lab results—are there any problems that would make termination of a pregnancy a reasonable choice? And waiting for a fetus to become a baby—at what point has your child come into existence?

Later, there's waiting for the crying to stop so you can leave for work—is it okay that you're going to work? Waiting at the park while your child plays—why is your child so beautiful and brilliant in your eyes, and should you try to be more objective? Waiting in doctors' offices—must you vaccinate, even if there's a tiny risk of a bad reaction? Waiting for one phase to end and another to begin—does your child remain the same child, through all the changes? And waiting for college admissions decisions—why do you care so much? And many other reasons to wait and to wonder.

One of my favorite occasions for thought, over the nineteen years since my twins were born, has been The Performance, whether a talent show, a play, or a recital. Your kid is somewhere in the line-up, and there are twenty other acts to watch and applaud. Every child is charmingly gawky and innocent, and there are patches of true talent here and there. But these things can drag, so there's time to think. And also something interesting to think about. Can I go home after my own child performs? Or do I owe it to the parents who watched my child to stay and watch theirs? What social obligations do I incur by being a parent in a community?

There's time to wonder and reflect, but not long stretches of time. The baby will wake up, the exercise class will end. You only have ten minutes to read at bedtime, before your eyes are going to close. So the chapters of this book are fairly short. Big problems are broken up into chewable morsels. Long stages of life for parents are broken up into series of shorter stages.

The questions are arranged in chronological order, starting with three about why we want children and whether we're being good, bad, or neither by having them. Next is a question about controlling the sort of child we have—whether to be selective, or to accept whatever child comes our way. And then there are questions about pregnancy, the fetus, and birth. At long last, a child has been born, and there are some hard questions to ask about the basis for saying the child belongs to one prospective parent or another.

Halfway through the book, we turn from questions about becoming parents to questions about being parents. Chapter 9 considers just what, precisely, parents do for their children—what the parenting job consists of. After that, I tackle numerous questions about how we ought to treat our children: whether to circumcise a boy; when we may lie to children; how much to care about a child's gender; and to what extent we should pass on our own values and beliefs. There are also questions about what it means to be a socially responsible parent. Must we get involved with the PTA at our child's school? Do we have to go along with collective projects like vaccination?

Finally, what do we get out of being parents? Happiness? Meaning? Or in fact a reduction in well-being, especially if we're not only parents but primary caregivers? And what should children give back to us, in return for being cared for over many years?

We'll begin at the beginning. We affiliate with other people in all sorts of ways—friend to friend, spouse to spouse, brother to sister, teacher to student. What's so special about parent to child? And in the first place, what is it for another person to be *my child*?

Chapter 1

Children Come from Us

What's so special about having kids?

Parenthood can begin by accident, or with minimal effort. Even if there is some forethought, the desire for a child can be so primal that there is no real "why" phase, no deliberation. "Why?" is a natural question for people who have to work harder to become parents. The more effort goes into starting a family, the more one has to think about the basic question: Why is this so important to me? Or even more basic: What am I going to have, if I have a child?

Wanting to have a child is different from wanting other things. If you want to have a dog, you probably enjoy being with dogs, and often pay friendly attention to the dogs you encounter. Some of your dog-desire will be satisfied by being with other people's dogs, or visiting the dogs at the animal shelter. But you can want to be a parent without having the slightest interest in babies in general.

If you want to have a dog, you probably have some kind of dog in mind: big or small, long-haired or short-haired. But people don't start thinking "What kind?" after realizing they want to have a child. It's not just that we don't have much control over the kind of child we create. It's not terribly important to us to have this kind or that kind. We just want to have "my child."

That is the crucial thing: our own. Wanting to become parents is wanting to stand in a very special relationship to another person. Most of us want to have our own, come what may. Ordinary people try to conceive, to have "my child," no less than beautiful and talented people do. Simply having "ours" or "mine" matters when it comes to baby-making more than practically anywhere else.

CHILD OF MINE

Having a child of one's own is not a simple matter of sharing genes: our brothers and sisters, nieces and nephews, all share our genes to some degree, but "my child" resonates in a way that "my nephew" or even "my brother" doesn't. More central to being ours is the fact that a child simply comes from us, the parents. The fact that they come from us tends to make our children self-*like*: not *exactly* self, but also not entirely other. So says Aristotle in the *Nicomachean Ethics*, one of the seminal works of Western philosophy. Nearly 2,400 years ago he wrote, "A parent, then, loves his children as he loves himself. For what has come from him is a sort of other self." The sheer fact of coming from us elicits a set of attitudes that we rarely have toward anyone but ourselves: identification, pride, shame, inflated concern, noncompetitiveness. (I discuss these attitudes more in chapter 7.)

It goes without saying that children come from us in a particular way—*not* as a present comes from a box or a sculpture comes from an artist. A child comes from a parent in such a way as to share a certain amount of matter and form with the parent, as Aristotle might have put it. And of course a child is a whole person who shares matter and form with us, not some insignificant fragment of a person.

The reproductive way of coming from us—according to Aristotle—tends to make a child "a sort of other self" and make a parent "love his children as he loves himself."

It's not that Aristotle thinks nobody can ever see someone as a second self on any other basis. He's well known for saying that a friend is like a second self. But children becomes second selves more readily than other people do, and also for different reasons, and more persistently. We start seeing them that way quickly, before we could possibly learn that we are compatible and share values. By contrast, Aristotle thinks friendship has a basis in two people sharing a virtuous way of life. We don't have to know anything at all about our newborn baby to feel profoundly identified with him or her, and the identification lasts through thick and thin, for years and years. For most people, having a child is the surest way they have of getting into a relationship in which another person is permanently self-like to them.

Jump forward to the present, from ancient Athens to modern America, and you find parents expressing themselves in much the way Aristotle does. Elizabeth Stone, a professor, author, and mother, once said that to have a child is "to decide forever to have your heart go walking around outside your body." Most parents know exactly what she means (and she's been endlessly quoted). The late philosopher Robert Nozick is just as poetic in his book *The Examined Life*: "Children themselves form part of one's substance," he writes. They "form part of a wider identity you have."

There's both a terror to be found in having a "sort of other self" and a great pleasure. One of the pleasures is that focusing on your second self takes the focus off your first self. It might be hard to figure out what to do next, career-wise, or how to solve whatever problems in living beset you, as a twenty-five-year-old or thirty-five-year-old.

Often what a small child needs is obvious by comparison: food, water, a nap, a medical check-up. It's easy to be clear-minded and wholehearted about baby-oriented tasks.

On a grander existential level, parents often find their own mortality easier to accept because of the thought that their children will live on after they're gone. That's akin to personal survival (i.e., my own survival) thanks to the felt quasi-identity of my child with my self, at the back of our minds and amorphous, but still an important aspect of what it is to have a child. Having children gives us a kind of afterlife—more life after this life, right here on earth, not in some gauzy, ill-defined heaven.

When children are *not* other selves to anyone, we've often entered some imaginary dystopia. The earliest known author of a reproductive dystopia was Aristotle's teacher, Plato. At least to our modern eyes, there's something ghastly about the system of reproduction Plato proposes for the leaders, or Guardians, of *The Republic*. Guardian men and women are required to copulate with one another, and when they produce children, the babies are taken away to be raised in groups by well-trained nurses. This disconnection between parent and child is supposed to make the next generation of Guardians perfectly concerned with the city as a whole, instead of partial to their biological parents and relatives. Likewise, collective child-raising guarantees that nobody will be partial to these children—for no caregiver are they "a sort of other self," as Aristotle puts it.

We also see reproduction devoid of special connections between parent and child in science fiction. The babies in Aldous Huxley's *Brave New World* are concocted in laboratories and brought up in institutional nurseries and schools. The whole idea of each person having a special "mommy" or "daddy" is seen in this society as primitive, sentimental, or even disgusting. Adults don't view any child in particular as their very own. In sharp contrast with these fictional worlds, it's a deep-seated part of our understanding of parenthood that a child *is* someone's own child; we think it matters which children come from which parents; and we welcome the thought that our children are akin to our very own selves.

We want to have our own child, but of course that's not all. We also want to play a role in the child's evolution from tiny newborn to young adult, and beyond. And we want to share a life with our child, which will initially mean sharing our own particular life. Over time we will give a child the food we love, the books we love, the music we love. If we love soccer, we'll try to get the child to play soccer. If we love ballet, we'll try to get the child involved in ballet. Over time, though, it may be the child who's sharing his or her loves with us. His fondness for politics may get us more interested in politics. Her interest in medicine may get us interested in medicine. But all along the way, the fact that a child is a *sort* of other self will mean a level of sharing that's distinctive.

Of course, what we have, in having parenthood, will become much more clear to us in the fullness of time. But choosing parenthood isn't a leap into the complete unknown. We don't choose parenthood as if it were hidden behind Door Number Three (on the old TV show *Truth or Consequences*). One of the things we do foresee is the feeling of a child being "our own." The fantasies of the would-be parent are about shared times—hiking with your child if you like to hike, baking with your child if you like to bake. Or just blissfully holding a newborn baby. We have premonitions of the exceptional level of identification we will have with a child of our own. That's at least one of the things that motivates us, making us persevere if we find out that making a child isn't going to be easy.

WHAT ABOUT ADOPTION?

In ancient Greece, there was no such thing as adoption as we know it. Adoption was only used to secure an unbroken lineage for men without biological sons, according to a history of adoption by Peter Conn. Thus, Aristotle would not have been worried that his description of parenthood seems to bar adoptive parents from having the usual parent-child relationship with a child. It's a firm component of our contemporary view of parenthood that adoptive parenthood *is* possible and neither inferior to biological parenthood, nor flawed in any way. So we urgently need to see whether Aristotle's conception of parenthood excludes or downgrades adoptive parenthood.

Some adoption advocates think this is so, regarding any focus on biological origins with suspicion. But perhaps Aristotle's understanding of parenthood doesn't exclude adoptive parenthood after all. If the crux of the matter is that a child is a sort of second self, that sort of identification is possible without biological parenthood. And it's not even out of the question that adopted kids come from their adoptive parents in an important sense. There are many ways that one person can come from another. A newborn baby—a girl, let's imagine—comes from her mother in a different way than from her father. The mother has grown the baby in her own body for nine months; a father has contributed half of the baby's genes and (ideally) assistance to his partner during her pregnancy. This is a big difference, yet there's enough "coming from" for the child to feel like another self to both parents.

Adoptive parents are progenitors too. The care we give to young, dependent children is all-encompassing—a daily effort that gradually transforms helpless, squirming newborns into talkative toddlers, smart adolescents, and (hopefully) accomplished adults. To have a major hand in those transformations gives parents the same sense of miraculous creativity that biological parents have during pregnancy, when an embryo is gradually becoming a baby. My personal involvement in these transformations—first anticipated, then directly experienced, and then remembered—makes a child *my child* whether I am involved as a biological mother, a biological father, or an adoptive parent.

What about nannies, babysitters, and day-care workers? Anthropologist Sarah Blaffer Hrdy calls these caregivers "allomothers," making them out to be a sort of mother. A nanny who raises children does have a hand in the child's critical transformations over many years. There is a difference, though. Caregivers know their relationship with a child can end at any time, and will change drastically or end when the child is self-sufficient. They often have their own children, and take care to maintain the distinction between "mine" and "theirs." So the alchemy doesn't work: someone else's child doesn't become the caregiver's second self.

Adoptive parents can have the parental state of mind toward a biologically unrelated child, but the majority of people adopt after first trying to conceive or with the knowledge that they can't conceive. Compared to all women, women who pursue adoption are twice as likely to have "impaired fecundity," according to a 2002 US study. Those who adopt after using infertility services often use them for years and years, at huge expense (adoption fees are high too, but they are a one-time expense). Some of the preference for procreation has to do with the difficulty of adopting. Adoptable children are often in short supply, especially for prospective parents who want to adopt an infant—the majority. And the adoption process typically puts prospective parents under an unpleasant microscope. Many want to have the reproductive experience from start to finish—they want procreative sex, pregnancy, childbirth, breastfeeding, *and* a child.

Some are disturbed by the thought that their gain of an adopted child will be the result of a birth parent's loss.

All that being said, *some* of the preference for procreation does relate to the core of what it is to be a parent. When a baby is in your arms, as a result of procreation, the child *already* comes from you. Mothers, especially, are intimately aware of that fact. Adoptive parents hold a child for the first time with the awareness that their connection to the child is just then beginning. There's less certainty at the beginning of adoptive parenthood: will this child, born of strangers, seem to me as children normally do to their parents?

The answer, for people who pursue adoption, is almost always "yes." In his memoir *Baby, We Were Meant for Each Other*, National Public Radio journalist Scott Simon gives an extremely touching account of falling in love with his daughter, adopted in China. When he and his wife first laid eyes upon her, she was dirty, crying uncontrollably, and burping up a "geyser of phlegm," Simon writes; but he focused on her "downy baby duck's head," her "small robin's mouth," and tears that "fell like soft, fat, furious little jewels." The pairing of parents and *this* baby does not seem contingent and arbitrary to Simon—he sees it as "meant to be."

The very same phrase is used by Harvard lawyer Elizabeth Bartholet to describe becoming the mother of a baby boy in Lima, Peru. In *Family Bonds* she writes, "I am the complete rationalist, with no religious or mystical leanings, yet I find myself wondering at the miracle that after all the years of wandering I found my way to this particular child, this one who was meant to be mine." It may not be that everyone could feel deeply connected to a biologically unrelated baby, but some of us can and do. Though different in various ways, adoptive parenthood is clearly not pretend or inferior.

In the chapters that follow I will usually picture the parent-to-be as someone contemplating or undertaking biological reproduction, but I will come back to adoptive parents' parallel path to parenthood.

CHILDREN ARE NOT LIKE TEETH

Describing children as "coming from" their parents can mislead us, and in a dangerous way. Aristotle himself goes astray when he says, "A person regards what comes from him as his own, *as the owner regards his tooth or hair or anything.*" We'd better not think of children on the model of our teeth or hair, or we'll start thinking we have much too much power over them. We can cut our hair if we like, or even pull our teeth; there are much greater limits on what we may do to our children. All sorts of things come from our bodies, and they are not all in the same moral category. Of things that emanate from our bodies, only a full person seems like a second self at all, and something that complete is only a *sort of* other self, not literally an extension of me. The "second" in "second self" matters as much as the "self" part. Aristotle doesn't continually make the "tooth or hair" comparison; he also elaborates on the self you have in your child this way: "It is other because it is separate." Many qualifications have to come into play when we think about the ethics of parenthood: the otherness, completeness, and separateness of children, but also their being second selves of their parents.

Why does coming from us make a child self-like even slightly? It pays to first ask what makes my future self my *self*, despite the differences (older, grayer, more forgetful), instead of someone else entirely. If it's even a part of the answer that older me will come from me, a child comes from her parents too (though of course in a different way than future me comes from present me). If it's part of the answer that older me is continuous with me, in a variety of ways, there are also many kinds of continuity linking parent and child. If future me is still me because of physical parts of younger me enduring and becoming a part of older me, constituents of parents become constituents of their children. As philosopher Charles Fried puts it, "Parenthood is a kind of physical continuity, a physical continuity which is also bound up with spiritual and moral continuity through our influence on our children." I don't claim that all these things wholly explain why a child who comes from me is self-like, but at least they save us from having to think it's delusional or outlandish to see a child that way. It's with some reason that our own children seem much more self-like to us than other people's children; they are at least closer to being, literally, ourselves.

In contemporary advanced societies, newborn babies are generally viewed as whole, complete persons—ripe for being seen as second selves, though as separate. Likewise, gestating fetuses who are ready to be born, if prematurely. In some quarters, "complete and whole" are terms to be applied even earlier, possibly even as early as the first seconds after conception. However, there are societies in which even newborns aren't viewed as whole and complete persons. Whether whole-person status is accelerated or delayed doesn't affect the basic point here: *at some point* the child who comes from you starts to be self-like to you. (I will return to the question of timing in chapter 5.)

MY MOTHER, MYSELF

Children are self-like to us because they come from us. The reverse is true too: to some degree, and at least in the fullness of time, parents are self-like to their children. There are asymmetries, though. We are more comfortable with seeing our children as second selves than with seeing our parents as second selves. Aristotle also touches on this, making an attempt to explain the difference: he says that people typically relish being a child's parent more than being a parent's child because parents have more certainty about the connection and know about it over more time.

There are probably many reasons for the asymmetry, but one is that knowing your children come from you creates a sense of power and fecundity; it's natural for this to be a matter of pride. To see yourself as coming from your parents also has the potential to be a matter of pride, but the feeling could instead be one of dependence and powerlessness. Starting as adolescents, it's understandable that most of us would like to be like the Unmoved Mover of Aristotle's *Metaphysics*. We would like to think we are completely the author of our own selves and in full control of our own lives.

To accommodate this natural wish, parenthood must evolve. We start off with a powerful sense of our children as our own, as having come from us, and as second selves, but parents must let go over time. Not only do children insist on it, but in fact the continuities between parent and child gradually decrease over time. As other influences on them make them come from other people as well— friends, peers, teachers, the surrounding culture—percentage-wise, they will come from us less. And they will start to be inventors of their own lives too, striking out on their own in many ways.

At that point it becomes a fortunate thing that it takes only so many connections for a child to seem like a second self. Continuity can decrease as children go their own way religiously, or politically, or musically, or in myriad other ways, without parents feeling any less connected to them. If my son grows up to be hugely different from me, he will be my own son no less than before. The pleasure of having your own child continues for the rest of your life (usually) and continues even when the gap between parent and child gradually widens, for a whole range of different reasons.

FACTS AND NORMS

A child has a complicated status: self, relative to parents, but never more than a *sort* of self (mother plus baby makes *two*). It advances self-understanding to have a good description of the relationship between parent and child, but I mean to use Aristotle's insight to do more than describe. I will argue that the fact that my child is another self, but separate, has ramifications for the norms that govern parenthood. There are different ethical rules for how we treat another person who is entirely separate, and not self-like at all; and other rules for how we treat a person who is literally one's self, and not separate at all. Given that my child is another self, but separate, it's to be expected that my child is someone with respect to whom I have unique prerogatives, responsibilities, duties, and so on. This is an idea that I explore in many chapters to come.

One of the issues I will come to is custody. Having a child of your own, a child who seems like a second self, comes about on the basis of physical and psychological events. But custody is a social and legal matter. Courts must decide who counts as a legal parent, and who should have custody of a child. It can't be a simple matter of parenthood and custody being granted to anyone who regards the child as a second self, because multiple people can have that sense and have it on good grounds. Mothers and fathers can compete for custody; biological and adoptive parents can compete. There is also the scenario in which someone comes to have that sense after a bad beginning—for example, a kidnapper who raises a child for ten years before being apprehended. It's one thing to understand the parent-child connection in Aristotle's terms, but another to think that connection is the whole foundation of parental rights. No, it can't be that simple.

It's good to see the commonalities that unite all forms of parenthood—maternal, paternal, adoptive. We want to be egalitarians about parenthood, denigrating and stigmatizing no one. But the complexities of custody force us to pay attention to differences between contenders. We'll come to the topic of contested custody much later (in chapters 7 and 8), after we have covered much more of the ground that lies between the hope of being a parent and the actuality of a new baby coming into the world.

The fact that children come from us is central to our desire to be parents. It's also central to many of our prerogatives and to decisions we make while raising a child. All of that will be argued for and elaborated on in coming chapters (7, 8, and 9 especially), but for now let's back up a step, or two, or three. Characterizing a child as a second self helps us understand why anyone would want to have a child, but presuming the desire is there, should we act on it? Is it really *right* to bring a child into the world?

Chapter 2

Life Is Good

Are babies lucky to be born or just the opposite?

Once, for almost all, reproducing was an inevitable part of the life cycle, like getting old. You didn't ponder the rightness or wrongness of having a family any more than you morally evaluated turning thirty. Of course everyone was straight, not gay, and marriage had to come before having children. But now things are quite different. We have access to contraceptives, and a sizable minority prefers a child-free way of life. People can have marriage without kids and kids without marriage. No, not everyone is straight. And yes, gay couples can have children too. We aren't all on the same life trajectory.

Even when reproduction did start seeming like a matter of choice, it tended to seem like a private, intimate thing, like choosing your friends, and so not something for others to judge right or wrong. Moral scrutiny, if any, wasn't aimed at the act of adding another person to the world, but at the character of prospective parents. If you had too many kids, without the resources to take care of them, perhaps that demonstrated a character flaw like carelessness; if you had no kids at all, you might be suspected of selfishness. But adding or not adding another person to the world wasn't *itself* up for approval or disapproval.

Now it's different. The world population has doubled in the last fifty years, making it increasingly reasonable to ask whether it's right to make new people. Adding to the complexity is the fact that the population isn't growing uniformly in all parts of the world. In fact, some countries' populations are shrinking. You can wonder if a person is having too many children, but you can also wonder if a person is having too few. If *you* are in the middle of deciding whether to have a child, there's a self-interested aspect to your decision-making: will it be good for *me* if I procreate? But there's also a second component: is it bad (or good) to add a child to the world?

The second issue is partly about having a child given how many people already exist in the world, or in your region. But once child-bearing itself has started to be a matter for moral reflection, we're going to want to back up to something even more basic. There are ethical questions about the sheer act of making a new life, however many people already exist. These very basic questions have to come first, because they can color the way we think about the population-specific issues.

So set aside, for the moment, the staggering population statistics (or in some locales, the meager ones). As far as this chapter is concerned, we could be living in a world with one billion people instead of seven billion. The issue for the moment is the ethics of creating one child, abstracting from any issues of overcrowding or underpopulation. And we'll focus on the child. Your parent-child relationship is a fine thing—fine in the way discussed in chapter 1— but what about bringing a whole new person into the world? Is *that* a fine thing?

As simple and obvious as that question is, it's a hard one to answer. That's because it's very difficult to think about someone not merely going from one condition to another (hungry to fed, short to tall, ignorant to knowledgeable, healthy to sick), but rather *coming into existence.* Coming into existence is like nothing else, and resists our usual ways of thinking about change.

THE UNCONCEIVED

Let's begin with Richard Dawkins, the well-known evolutionary biologist, who has said he wants this passage from his book *Unweaving the Rainbow* to be read at his funeral:

> We are going to die, and that makes us the lucky ones. Most people are never going to die because they are never going to be born. The potential people who could have been here in my place but who will in fact never see the light of day outnumber the sand grains of Arabia. Certainly those unborn ghosts include greater poets than Keats, scientists greater than Newton. We know this because the set of possible people allowed by our DNA so massively exceeds the set of actual people. In the teeth of these stupefying odds it is you and I, in our ordinariness, that are here.

This is supposed to soothe the mourners at a funeral, and I think the passage would be uplifting, but if you think about it, what Dawkins is saying is perplexing. Should we really see ourselves as lucky and the unborn ghosts as unlucky? And what are those unborn ghosts anyway? Are they real enough to matter?

Imagine a young couple hearing these words. If they took the speech literally, it could inspire them to do something about some of the unborn ghosts. They couldn't do much, since the unborn are so numerous, but they *could* do something about a few. They could save the unborn child who would be formed out of the woman's next fertilizable egg and one of the man's sperm. That unborn child will be one of the unlucky ones if they decide not to have a child, and one of the lucky ones if they decide to do so. But is helping potential people really a cogent reason for prospective parents to procreate?

If it were, there would be an altruistic component to having children, a motivation focused on the good of our offspring. We'd have to admire people with large families for saving more potential people from the misfortune of never being born (remember, we are disregarding population issues). We would have to see them in somewhat the same way we see a person like the actress and activist Mia Farrow, who has adopted ten children, saving some of them from much less fortunate lives in developing countries. Is it right to give people with large families this sort of credit?

We are not (if you're starting to wonder) talking here about saving immortal souls or any such thing. Unborn people, as Dawkins understands the phrase, are also not fetuses at some stage of development. Potential people are purely potential; they are specific people who could exist, or at least could have. Some are permanently locked out of existence. They would have grown from eggs and sperm that never had a chance to meet. Some potential people could still be helped into existence—the ones that would come of eggs and sperm that could still meet. They are saveable, salvageable, helpable—*if* people decide to become parents.

If procreating saves unborn children from the misfortune of nonexistence, it's as if there were a cosmic orphanage teeming with potential existers, some capable of leaving it, but some not. Only *you* can help the would-be children formed from *your* gametes. The couple at the funeral hearing Dawkins's words can help a different unborn child. But does any of this really make any sense? Do we help someone when we make a child, or is bringing someone into existence entirely different from "helping"?

Economist Bryan Caplan seems to think we do help people by creating them. He says as much in an interesting book with the odd title *Selfish Reasons to Have More Children*. We ought to have more children for selfish reasons, he says, but also for altruistic reasons. "To deny the gift of life to a child who would have made your life better is a tragic missed opportunity," he writes. There are two different tragedies: you miss out (after all, the child "would have made your life better"), but the child misses out too (he or she is denied "the gift of life").

Speaking of a gift of life is taking the unborn ghosts awfully seriously. They exist first without the gift (the idea must be), but as mere potentialities. Then they receive the gift, and they're transported out of potentiality all the way to here—to the land of actuality. This is picturesque, but is it *true*?

Wittgenstein, in his later writings, warned against the way we can be bewitched by the superficial features of language. All noun phrases seem to refer to robust objects out there in the real world. "Tall people" refers to people who are tall, like the basketball player LeBron James, so you might think that "possible people" must refer to people who are possible—"out there" like James, though somehow less robust than him. If you think that way, you're being seduced by the superficial similarity of the two phrases. But "tall" and "possible" don't actually work the same way, logically. When we talk about possible people or things, we're merely saying this or that could have happened, not that the real world actually contains a domain of ethereal, merely possible entities.

We are particularly susceptible to thinking of possible *people* as if they were actual (though ghost-like and wispy) and therefore eligible to be helped or abandoned. We wouldn't be as tempted to think that artists rescue or abandon possible paintings when they decide to realize, or not realize, their artistic ideas. Possible people may seem more robust because their blueprints—encoded in the gametes of actual men and women—do exist. So they have something of a foothold in reality, before conception occurs. It's also true that possible people have just one chance to become actual, and success is against all odds, since they (or their originating gametes) have to win a race against millions of other competitors. So they're semi-actual, and they're underdogs.

All this may explain the temptation to think that procreation is a rescue operation benefitting unborn children, but should we really think of it that way? This seems like the truth of the matter: nobody is really unfortunate, if parents decide not to have a child; nobody is actually left languishing in some cosmic orphanage. You don't let down your possible progeny if you decide to remain childless, or if you limit the size of your family. Possible children are merely possible, and not "around" in the robust sense needed for them to count as unlucky when they don't come into existence. Since they do not exist, they are not unlucky—or anything else.

If you do decide to have a child, nobody goes from worse to better; nobody starts out without the gift of life, and then receives the gift. Procreating is in a completely different category from helping, rescuing, saving, aiding—things we do to ameliorate someone's condition. Procreation does not ameliorate at all, but rather it brings someone new into existence.

FUTURE CHILDREN

Unconceived children don't need any rescuing from their non-existent state. But you might say that we still have a child-centered reason to reproduce. The kids to be concerned with are not the unconceived ones, but future children—the ones who *will* exist in one, five, ten, or one hundred years. They will be glad they were born, so you do deserve some credit for procreating, because you'd be doing what those future people will want you to have done.

What? This reasoning seems a little weird, but why? We normally do give the preferences of others some weight. If your husband wants to go to the mountains, not the beach, that gives you *some* reason to go to the mountains. We also do give weight to the preferences of future people—and should. When we think about our impact on the environment, the concern might be about people living fifty or one hundred years from now. Should we use up all the resources, so we have plenty today, but people living in the year 2100 have none? They don't exist yet, of course, but it's not unreasonable to give them—*whoever* winds up being in that world—a say. Their welfare counts as a good reason for us to conserve resources.

What, then, is odd about giving kids a vote on whether we bring them into existence? Well, at the time when prospective parents are deciding whether to have children, there are two possible futures, only one of which includes their next child. They are at a fork in the road, trying to decide which way to turn. It's perverse to treat one of these roads—these futures—as the actual one, at the time of the decision, and give the child at the end of that road a vote. That is to treat the other possible future, the childless future, as a negligible possibility. Of course, if the childless future turns out to be the real one, no child is going to be at the end of that road, and no one is going to be voting for her own existence. To give a future child a vote on whether to create her is to act as if you have no real decision to begin with—as if the future-with-child were a foregone conclusion.

We saw before that it makes no sense to have a child in order to save an unborn ghost, a potential child who will be "one of the unlucky ones" if we don't reproduce. There aren't any unborn ghosts to be saved. And now we see that it makes no sense to have a child for the sake of your future child, taking into account her vote for her own existence. At the time that we are deciding whether to reproduce, if we are truly *deciding*, we can't take it for granted that there is a future child casting a vote. So what's the upshot? Is there no child-centered reason to have children—no reason having to do with them instead of us?

WORLD IMPROVEMENT

The reasoning so far about unborn ghosts and future children shows that we can't press child-making into a familiar mold: we don't respond to the needs or desires or problems or demands of a particular child—unborn ghost or future child—when we procreate. Bringing new people into existence is a different kind of thing altogether.

Creating a child can still be a good thing, even if it's not a one-to-one interpersonal favor that we do *for* someone. It can be a good thing if adding a child to the world makes the world a slightly better place. But does it? It certainly seems that way. (Remember, we're pretending there are just one billion people in the world.) There are lots of things that we can create. Trivial things like graffiti on a wall. Terrible things like weapons of mass destruction. Good things like works of art. And probably neutral things as well. We do commonly say a life is "infinitely precious." Even if this is somewhat effusive, and not meant quite literally, a human life is a valuable thing. This isn't because humans contain some magical, ultravaluable essence, but because of what happens in a human life. When you create a child, you start a "flow" of happenings, enjoyments, achievements, realizations, decisions. In the vast majority of cases, much of this is valuable, not negative, and not neutral. Just slightly (relative to the huge heap of good there already is), but in a perfectly real way, the world is better for your child's life being part of it. I don't mean just because of the impact the child will have on others. The world is a little better because people *themselves* add something good.

So yes, we do something good when creating new people, as far as the people created are concerned. We don't do a favor for unborn ghosts by procreating, and can't think of ourselves as respecting the wishes of future people. We're not aiding, rescuing, or helping someone, or heeding someone's desires or preferences. Nevertheless, the enterprise does have a positive valence, just in virtue of the value of human life.

Or so it seems. Now we turn to some skeptical voices.

JOYS AND SORROWS

Anti-natalists actually deny that child-making has a basically positive valence. They think that we always do something bad, not good or even neutral, by having children. Yes, there are anti-natalists, people who are opposed in principle to all child-making, and their arguments merit some attention. To grasp their case against reproduction, anti-natalists ask us to focus on the headaches and heartaches in people's lives. These, for one reason or another, are seen by anti-natalists as conclusive reasons not to reproduce.

Of course, there are plenty of headaches and heartaches, and some of the troubles start very early. Perhaps it's uncomfortable wearing your first pair of diapers, or even squeezing through your mother's birth canal. From the first day onward, a life will be marred by miseries and failures and mistakes to one degree or another. One way to go on is to say that the bad fraction of any life, however large or small, is problematic because you can't get a child's permission before creating it. A more subtle anti-natalist argument is made by South African philosopher David Benatar in his much-discussed book, *Better Never to Have Been: The Harm of Coming into Existence*.

Suppose you're thinking about creating a child. Some specific child will be born, if you go ahead: "Charlie," let's call him. If you do not have Charlie, one day you might think of him, your would-have-been child, and though it would be odd, it would make sense if you said, "It's *good* Charlie isn't suffering his headaches and failures" (or whatever bad things would have been in the bad fraction of his life). You might go on to think it's good that Charlie isn't having the terrible bout of gastroenteritis you (somehow) correctly guess he would have had at age six. Later you might think it's good that he isn't having the migraine he would have had at sixteen. Still later, you might think it's good that he isn't going through the emotional trauma of breaking up with his girlfriend, as he would have at twenty-six. Somehow you can picture the life history that would have been, and you are grateful for the missing bad times.

Now for the crux of the matter. Benatar argues that nothing counterbalances the good of those missing bad times. That's because the opposite can't be said: Charlie's missing pleasures aren't *bad*. It's not a bad thing that Charlie never got to eat a bowl of ice cream. It's not a bad thing that he never won a chess match. But why? Why is it good when nonexistent Charlie's pains are absent, but not bad when his pleasures are absent? Benatar says the asymmetry is due to the fact that absent pleasures are only bad when they are experienced as deprivations; and nonexistent Charlie won't be around to feel deprived. Absent pains, on the other hand, are good even if nonexistent Charlie isn't around to be glad of their absence.

If we take this subtle asymmetry seriously, then we have one score as the basis for judging the no-Charlie scenario: the *positive* score that we awarded based on the good of his missing misery. There's no negative score to be awarded, based on his missing pleasures and successes. It's all good if he doesn't exist; it's not at all bad. And there is nothing special about Charlie. You can run this argument on any would-be child, so long as he or she will endure so much as a second of misery in life. The point is *not* about how much misery and failure there is in people's lives, compared to the joy and success. The point is that the misery, however little, means a person shouldn't be created, and all the joys do not reverse that conclusion.

Affirming the asymmetry has enormous ramifications, but Benatar expects us to find it intuitively plausible. He also encourages us to accept it by trying to show that if we didn't, we would be forced to swallow some very unsavory implications of affirming the *symmetry* of absent pains being good *and* absent pleasures being bad. Given this symmetry, Benatar thinks people would have a duty to *avoid* creating miserable people and a duty to *create* happy people, in order to prevent all those bad pleasure-absences. Childless people would have to feel guilty for not procreating, and people with just a few children would have to feel bad about not having more. Another unsavory outcome of not accepting his asymmetry would be this: when we contemplate unpopulated planets in remote reaches of the universe, we would have to think it's not only *good* that nobody's in agony there, but *bad* that nobody is enjoying themselves there. That strikes him as absurd, so Benatar thinks we can't just comfortably disregard his asymmetry. And when we affirm it, we're lead to his anti-natalist conclusion.

So, is it time to wrap up this whole crazy business of human existence? Yes, says Benatar. His argument, if taken seriously by all of humanity, and acted upon, would lead to a lot of vasectomies and tubal ligations, and eventually to human extinction. And Benatar affirms that upshot. It would be good, he thinks, not tragic, if earth were devoid of human life. To the extent that animal life, too, involves both good and bad, it would be best if all non-human animals went extinct as well. Should we all just kill ourselves now? No, he says, his argument shows that lives are not worth beginning, *not* that they are not worth continuing.

These might seem like outlandishly radical views that only an ivory tower philosopher could dream up, but anti-natalism is an outlook not unheard of in the world apart from hyperanalytical academic philosophy. It's even prefigured in the ancient *Bhagavad Gita*. Says the lucky, never-born person, "I was never born and I will never die; I do not hurt and cannot be hurt; I am invincible, immortal, indestructible." Benatar's anti-natalist position has a bit of the same flavor. He also homes in on the absence of suffering as a plus for the never-born, and discounts the concomitant absence of pleasure.

Most people think it's worth going through their Monday headaches to get to their Tuesday joys. They think it's worth the pain of climbing up the mountain to get to the joy of standing on the top. Pains, though bad, are thought to be redeemed by pleasures. This is fine with Benatar, if we are thinking about our life choices as people who already do exist. In that case it certainly makes sense to manage our lives so that we put up with misery when it's worth it for later gains. Otherwise we'll later lament being deprived of enjoyments. But we have to refrain from this sort of thinking when we're considering whether to create a whole new person. There will never be any deprivation if we don't bring Charlie into the world, and there *will* be the advantage of his absent miseries.

Convinced? One reassuring thing, if you decide to have a child, is that it's almost guaranteed that your child won't be. If he exists, Charlie will often make "It's worth it" judgments—"It's worth it to break my arm falling out of a tree to enjoy a life full of exploring nature." And Benatar approves. Chances are Charlie will not appreciate the subtle distinction between this judgment being made during his life and *you* making it prospectively, before he exists. This life-affirming confusion will ensure that Charlie doesn't find fault with you if you go ahead and procreate. But we ought to say more than that. Perhaps he won't find fault with you *and* he actually won't be confused either—he'll be right to think you made a permissible choice.

Suppose we reject Benatar's asymmetry, which certainly isn't overpoweringly plausible. The two unsavory implications—about empty places and procreative duties—aren't as decisive as they may initially seem. Confronted with the right scenarios, we often actually do make symmetrical judgments about absent pleasures and absent pains. Imagine a deserted playground that was once teeming with life. Children ran around shouting and laughing with delight; they also occasionally fell and scraped their knees. Now nobody remains; the miseries are gone along with the joys. One could easily think it actually *is* bad that the fun is all gone—even though no child feels the deprivation. People who write books and make movies about the eventual end of life on earth, or imagine doomsday scenarios, generally think there is something very bad about a deserted world. What's behind this must be the intuition that an absent pleasure *is* bad, like an absent pain is good—even if there's no one deprived in the first case, like there's nobody glad in the second.

As for everyone winding up with a duty to create happy people, as well as a duty to avoid creating miserable people, unless we affirm Benatar's asymmetry, that's not inevitable. If absent pleasure is bad, there's something good about bringing more happy people into the world, but there's something good about a lot of life activities. We don't have the strongest imperative to do all of these good things, from making new people to planting trees to volunteering at the animal shelter. There can be something good about creating people without the imperative rising to the level of giving us a duty. And there could be a different sort of imperative at the two ends of the spectrum. The activity of creating happy people is very different from the non-activity of not creating miserable people: the two have different direct costs and also different opportunity costs. For many reasons, it's open to us to think the imperative to create more happy people is quite muted.

Though Benatar's argument is marvelously thought provoking, I think we can sustain the idea that creating a child can be a good thing to do, overall. We do something good by creating Charlie, assuming he will have enough good experiences in life, and other sorts of successes, and his life will not be relentlessly miserable. A world without him is better with respect to his missing sorrows, but also worse with respect to his missing joys.

WHY IT'S GOOD

It's important to straighten out *whether* it's good to have a child and also *why* it's good. If it were good to have a child for one of the reasons I've discarded, that would give us quite a strong imperative to reproduce. Forlorn unborn ghosts would have to be taken care of— we would have duties toward them. If they counted at all, I would have to feel guilty for not letting more of them out of nonexistence while going to college and graduate school; and for not having more kids after my first two. It would be good to create lots of kids even if you couldn't take good care of them or didn't want to parent them yourself.

If procreation did liberate forlorn ghosts, that would mean it's almost always a good idea to procreate, *even if* we know that the person born would have serious problems; after all, being stuck in the

closet of nonexistence—if you take it seriously that this is bad—
would presumably be very bad. Whatever the outcome of a pregnancy, we would be able to say "Ah, but life is a gift!" when the child
is born. We would be able to say we had done the child a favor, just
about however his life turned out.

But no, nobody is personally aided by being born, and nobody is
personally harmed by not being born. It's good to create new people
not because it's beneficial to a cosmic orphan, a potential person,
but simply because a human life is a (mostly) good thing. So in most
cases we add some good to the world by procreating. That makes the
pressure to have children very weak. No unborn or future individual *needs* me to procreate. And when it comes to doing good, there
are lots of other options—lots of ways to add some goodness to
the world. Not only are there other ways to be beneficent, but we're
not on call, full time, to be as beneficent as possible. We don't have
to run around planting all the flowers we can, writing all the poetry
we can. There is no reason to think we must be relentless world-
improvers. The "Life is good" commendation of child-making is
not to be confused with a pro-natalist rallying call. There's nothing
about it to suggest we must all get busy making more and more
babies.

If babies are a plus, the decision to reproduce should still involve
many other considerations. We don't merely make babies, like artists make paintings or factories make cars; in making a baby we usually become the custodial parent of a baby. So it's crucially relevant
to ask, "Can I function as a parent, regarding this child as a second
self?" We decide not only to add to the world's population, but to
change our status in an important way. We may play the parental
role badly, or do worse in some other aspect of life, if we make more
babies. If we only add children to the world, with no intention of
parenting them, there are hardships in the child's life we must be

concerned with. Were procreation genuinely a matter of rescuing hapless people from cosmic orphanages, all these other considerations would pale in comparison to the importance of saving them.

So much for looking at child-making in abstraction from population issues. Now we need to bring the rest of the world back into the picture. We make children in a world in which others also make children. How do the other child-makers affect whether it's a good thing for *me* to have a child? This is such a large question it needs a chapter of its own.

Chapter 3

Quantity Control

Must we care about population statistics?

Once human beings were relatively rare. There were only four million of us in the year 10,000 B.C.E. If life was good even in that harsher world, that's reason to think it was a net positive that the human population grew to five million by 5,000 B.C.E. Barring special reasons why not, it's fair to say that more of a good thing is a good thing. But now we're getting exceedingly numerous. By the end of the nineteenth century, the world's population was 1.6 billion and in 1960, there were three billion of us. It took just forty years for the human population to double again—making six billion of us in 2000. The rate of growth has slowed, but the total population may rise to nine billion in 2050, and ten billion by 2100.

People haven't stopped being good things, but the good in one new life has to be balanced against the overall impact of adding one more person to an already crowded world. A new child will use up resources (land, water, oil, minerals) and produce waste (garbage, greenhouse gases, pollution). Because of rampant human procreation and consumption, the planet is warming and biodiversity is threatened. Making a child is a good thing to do, as far as that one child goes, but considering the impact, must responsible people think twice about having a third or a fourth child, or even a first or second?

If you are on the verge of having your first child, you will want very much to have a reason to put aside environmental worries. As a philosophical prospective parent, you will want a *good* reason, not just an excuse.

PRO-NATALISM

Religion is one path to procreative abandon. In the village of Kiryas Joel, in upstate New York, the average woman has four children, two more than the national average. They have this many children because they are Hasidic Jews, members of the Satmar sect, and tend to avoid birth control. Mothers of young children rarely work outside the home, and many of the men work at Torah study—the result being that the average family income is lower than anywhere else in the United States. They're having so many children because they follow the biblical injunction to "be fruitful and multiply." Traditional Mormons are driven by a more complicated reproductive theory. According to the doctrine of eternal progression, human spirits are created outside this world by the heavenly father and heavenly mother. More of these spirits get to have physical bodies and to be raised in the true faith if Mormon couples have more children. So for this reason, and presumably others, many Mormons have large families. In a 2014 Pew Research Center study of Americans, Mormons between the ages of forty and fifty-nine were found to have 3.4 children apiece, on average. Catholics are not supposed to limit their fecundity with contraception, but few seem to follow official teaching; the same Pew study found this group had 2.3 children apiece. Among evangelical Christians the average number of children is 2.3. Jews—when all denominations are included—have 2.0 children, and nonreligious people have the least of all: atheists were found to have 1.6 children on average, and agnostics only 1.3.

A nonreligious case for extra procreation is made by Bryan Caplan, the economist I mentioned in chapter 2. Caplan counsels his readers: however many children you were planning on having, consider having more! He has three, but will consider a fourth. A family with six should consider a seventh. Kids bring us a great deal of satisfaction, he says, especially if we are laid back and not unduly worried about them. They particularly bring satisfaction when they have grown up. Caplan makes a point that will not have occurred to everyone: kids bring satisfaction for your whole lifetime. So you shouldn't think just in terms of the early years. If you'd like to have four adult children when you're eighty years old, but just two toddlers when you're thirty, a good compromise might be to have three kids.

One point in favor of big families is that they do more to support the elderly. If you bring up eight contributing members of society, they will contribute much more to the Social Security system than if you bring up two. Another consideration is that a larger affluent population is linked to even greater prosperity. If innovators are one in a million, Caplan writes, seven billion people yield seven thousand innovators. Eight billion people would yield eight thousand innovators. The quality of life goes up, on average, when there are more people, not down (he claims). Another pronatal author, the philosopher Toby Ord, suggests that we are in the middle of an exciting explosion of technology due to the surge in population since the mid-twentieth century. The standard of living around the world has improved in many respects thanks to there being far more people, and therefore both far more ideas and far more trade.

But what about the impact of seven (or eight, nine, or ten) billion people using resources and producing waste? Aren't we using up the earth at such a rapid rate that there won't be anything left for future generations? Caplan points out that many resources are becoming cheaper, a sign that they are not less plentiful. But wherever there is a problem, yes, he says, we should fix it—in a targeted fashion. We should have a carbon tax to tackle global warming. If there are too many people on the highway at rush hour, we should have electronically collected tolls. We should be seeking to control overconsumption, not to limit population. On the whole, he argues, "the good effects of population far outweigh the bad."

Many environmentalists adamantly disagree, and at an absolute minimum, they're right on one issue. One of the negative effects of a growing human population is the concomitant dwindling of wilderness and wildlife. There are now only three thousand tigers left in the wild, for example. Compare the remaining tigers to the 86 million domestic cats living just in the United States. Animals we eat are even more numerous. There are an estimated 1.3 billion cattle in the world today. As humans become more numerous, there will be even more cats and cows, and probably even fewer tigers—until there are none in the wild at all.

It seems like something very good is lost as a result of the crowding out of other forms of life. Though one human is a fine thing, a veritable Picasso, our world seems like a museum stuffed with too many Picassos. Gradually, all the other masterpieces are being crowded out. Where we ought to see ourselves as sharing a world with other sovereign species, we have become one world, under human domination. Of course, there is still vast wilderness remaining and still abundant wildlife, but biologists argue that we are in the middle of and responsible for one of the great historic periods of extinction—the Anthropocene, as they have started to call it.

We should reproduce responsibly, but how should we think about that? What does "responsible reproduction" mean, if you are a person who would like to have a large family?

SURVIVAL RIGHTS

Each society has an ideal birth rate, or at least a ballpark ideal. Some societies should shrink, some could grow a little, some ought to remain about the same size that they are right now. Collectively, at least, we should aim to reproduce at the ideal rate for our own society. But what does this mean for each individual or couple? That's much harder to say.

It's too crude to say that each family's birth rate should be the same as the ideal collective birth rate. After all, collectively a society is only aiming at an average, and that can be achieved equally well whether every couple has the same number of children or there is a lot of variation. A better first-pass answer is that individuals shouldn't knowingly contribute to making the collective birth rate depart from the ideal. If you know the actual collective birth rate is under the ideal, you should have a child (assuming you will be reasonably good at nurturing and providing for the child). If you know the actual birth rate is above the ideal, you should cut back, and not have a child you might have wanted to have. The Reproductive Idealist—as I will call someone with this view—says, further, that these are straightforward moral "shoulds." It's right to help your society attain its ideal birth rate and wrong to hamper that goal by having too many or too few children.

It all sounds pretty simple and irrefutable, but, for reasons I will explain, Reproductive Idealism is implausible.

Suppose Carlos and Maria live in Mexico and would like to have their first child. They know that their society's ideal birth rate is 2.1 per woman, though its actual birthrate is three per woman. They would be helping their society attain its ideal if they changed their plans, and they would be hampering attainment of the ideal if they went ahead and had even one child. So according to Reproductive Idealism, they would be wrong to have a child.

Perhaps you will agree with me that it's very odd to think that this couple is wrong to have one child. There's a certain logic to saying they're wrong, but something's amiss with that verdict. The deepest reason why we can't condemn having one child, whatever the local collective birthrate, relates back to one of the reasons why people want to have children in the first place. One thing procreation achieves for parents is "ersatz survival"—it's a way of recreating oneself, so that after death, your life continues. Not literally your life, but close enough so that mortality becomes far more bearable. Through reproduction, we project ourselves farther into the future. Of course, people don't decide to have a child with thoughts of survival looming large; these are amorphous ideas at the back of people's minds. But if they are there at all, they can be appealed to in a defense of procreation.

Because of the connection between reproduction and survival, the right to reproduce has strong ties to other rights of self-preservation. Suppose your life is threatened in some slow-moving way that allows you time for research and reflection. Perhaps you have a small melanoma on your leg that you can either have treated before it spreads, or not have treated. You rummage through population statistics and worry about future generations. It would be better in the grand scheme of things, you conclude, to make your exit.

Your treatment is going to use up lots of resources. Yes, you'll be missed, but they'll get over it, and there are too many people in the world and too few resources. Really, you think, you *ought* to forego the cure the doctors are offering you. It's the only environmentally responsible thing to do.

No, surely not! Your right to self-preservation isn't absolute (you can't kill other people to keep yourself alive, for example), but it does allow you to take the cure, and set aside the omniscient, hyperobjective perspective you're trying to adopt. And so it is with reproduction. It's a means of survival too—or at least, a sort of quasi-survival that transcends the boundaries between one person and another. If we're entitled to live out our own natural lifespans, then perhaps we're also entitled to make use of our innate capacity to live on into the future, in the person of our children and our children's children.

It's important not to go the whole distance here, and assert that my children are literally part of myself, as there lurks the problematic notion that children don't have their own rights, and aren't entitled to any protection at all from their parents. But if we state the idea with the proper care, it's true: just as I am entitled to live out my own lifespan, I am entitled to an even longer vector into the future, through my descendants.

It only begins to make sense to condemn childbearing as flat-out wrong in the most extreme scenarios. Imagine a grotesquely overcrowded world in which every extra child puts a strain on already scarce resources. You might reasonably think people really ought to voluntarily avoid reproduction in this setting. If there are vastly too many people or vastly too few, it might begin to make sense to say that people really do have an obligation to have or not to have a child.

But we are not in that situation, not yet. Green anti-natalists may insist we really are, if we extrapolate from current reproduction rates to the state of the world in one hundred years. To refuse to do so, they may think, is to discriminate against future people. But no—the fact that problems lie far in the future makes a moral difference, and not because future people matter less. It makes a difference whenever and to the extent that there is significant uncertainty about what the future holds. We are not obligated to reproduce now as if we were *already* in the dire situation predicted by some futurologists.

THE ADOPTION OPTION

But wait! The "child who comes from me" template can be filled through adoption (I argued in chapter 1), even though the adoptive parent enters the picture after the child's birth. Why, then, is anyone justified in creating a new child, rather than adopting one of the children already in need of parents? After all, the sense of survival through progeny is available without any change to the world's census.

There are various points to be made here. It *is* possible to have the sense of survival through adopted progeny, but is it possible for everyone? Perhaps not all of us are that flexible, that capable of seeing ourselves in another person, without a biological connection. In any case, adoption for all would be impossible. There aren't enough parentless children available for everyone to form families that way. And treating adoption as a duty would be expecting a great deal of prospective parents. The adoption process, whether domestic or international, is often an arduous thing, full of red tape, delays, and setbacks.

What we really ought to talk about is a societal responsibility for parentless children. *We* should do all we can so that they have parents. It doesn't follow that any particular person is obligated to achieve the sense of projection into the future—ersatz survival—through adoption rather than procreation. We can discharge the societal obligation by collectively creating incentives to adopt, by bestowing special admiration on adopters, by treating adopted kids just the same as anyone else, by removing any remaining stigma from adoption. We would be going too far if we treated adoptive parents as simply doing what they ought to do, if they want to be parents, and treated biological parents as doing what's impermissible.

MORE OR LESS

The "ersatz survival" defense seems to acquit the Mexican couple who want to have a first child, despite the local birth rate being too high. If they go on to have a second child, they are merely replacing themselves, plural, so the same rationale applies; but what about a third, a fourth, or a fifth child? If my first child in some sense adds to my lifespan, and so does my second, then why not a third or fourth? Granted, none of this is literal life extension, but it's close enough that it works in roughly the same way as a justification for procreative decisions. Would we really say that someone was wrong to take a miraculous pill that would add twenty or even forty years to their lifespan? At some point perhaps reproducers and life-extenders *have* gone too far: by adding two hundred years to your lifespan, for example, you use up more than your share of earth's space and resources. By adding twenty children to the world, you likewise take more than your fair share. But it takes a lot of life-extension and reproducing before these judgments seem warranted.

It's peculiar to say, of any given person, that she should not have another child. And equally odd to say that she *must* have another child. Shifting our attention from Mexico to Canada, where the birth rate in some provinces is lower than the ideal, imagine a couple who do not want to have any children. Jacob and Olivia wouldn't be bad at nurturing and providing for a child, if they wound up with one by accident. On the Reproductive Idealist's account, they're doing the wrong thing if they have no children, because they're not helping their province attain its ideal birth rate. Proponents of Idealism will observe that when the birth rate goes down, people can lose jobs. The Social Security system is put at risk. The elderly are under-supported. Despite all of that, it almost never seems appropriate to say that someone has an obligation to make a child.

The survival argument used to defend reproducers doesn't carry over here, but other considerations do. Reproductive obligations, if they existed, would entail that people ought to do many other things: have sex with someone, or abstain, or use contraceptives; go through pregnancy and childbirth, or not. Because of their intimacy and scope, these are things it would be very odd to see as morally required.

Reproductive Idealism is far too simplistic. Upon reflection, we must conclude that there is a prerogative to have a child if you want one, and a prerogative to not have a child, if you don't want one—in many, many circumstances. It can't be true that, morally, we have to do whatever it takes to help our society attain its ideal birth rate.

That being said, it can't be wrong for a society to send some message either encouraging or discouraging reproduction—a message more muted than "You must have a child!" or "You must not!" What kind of messages would be appropriate?

PERMITS AND INCENTIVES

One possibility is to send a legal as opposed to a moral message. Traffic laws could serve as a model. Morally, it's not wrong for solo drivers to drive in the far left lane on our local highway, but legally the lane is reserved for high-occupancy vehicles. That's how we achieve the social goal of making the highway run smoothly. We could similarly make laws that constrain reproduction, consistent with its being true that, morally, everyone is entitled to reproduce (or not) just as they like.

Economist Kenneth Boulding, in a 1964 book, suggested a system comparable to the "cap and trade" approach that would later be proposed as a way to reduce greenhouse gas emissions. Each woman would be "capped" based on the ideal birth rate. If that were 2.1 children per woman, for example, each woman would be given 2.1 certificates, or perhaps 21 "deci" certificates. Women could then give and receive these certificates, or perhaps buy them and sell them. Men could only reproduce with women who had the right certificates. Morally, you might be entitled to have a child whenever you like to (as I have argued), but legally, you would have to have the certificates. Not enough certificates? No child! (What would be the sanctions for reproducing without a permit? Boulding doesn't say.)

This is a system that tries to hold down the birth rate, but what if a society's problem is the opposite—the birth rate is too low? The permit system would have to give way to some sort of incentivizing. While you might say everyone has the moral prerogative to have no children, it's perfectly consistent with that position to encourage reproduction through tax breaks or even outright rewards.

In fact, many countries with low birth rates do take the tax breaks and rewards approach to encouraging reproduction, with some even offering outright baby bonuses. Western democracies incentivize procreation as much as less democratic countries. But nowhere, and certainly not in heavily populated democratic countries, is the permit system used. Despite the flexibility that comes with buying and trading, such a system would encroach too much on personal liberties. You can always ignore incentivizing schemes, going your merry childless way, but you can't ignore a permit scheme. A less intrusive approach to discouraging overpopulation is needed, but what would that look like?

SOCIAL RESPONSIBILITY

Some means of lowering birth rates have nothing to do with direct appeals to prospective parents. Around the world, birth rates drop quickly when women start to have more education and more opportunities outside the home. Women postpone childbearing until later because they have the option of establishing a career. They have fewer than the maximum number of children because there are other things they would like to do with their lives. Birth rates also drop when infant mortality rates go down, giving people the confidence to stop at two, instead of having more as an "insurance policy" against loss of their first children. Plus, birth control and abortion bring down the birth rate by enabling people to have better control over how many offspring they bring into the world. These sorts of mechanisms, not an ethics of reproduction, are the main drivers of population size.

If social messages also have some role to play, they are messages not so much about right and wrong but about social responsibility— that is, being aware of and concerned with the impact of one's actions on matters of broad social concern. What counts as socially responsible is forever changing. Once bottled water seemed innocuous, but then environmentalists started telling us that the cost of all that plastic and transportation wasn't worth it, considering our plentiful and clean water supply. Once flying to exotic locations seemed fine (if you could afford it), but then we started to be told about the greenhouse gases produced by airplanes. The messages we get about bottled water and travel are quite different from a black-and-white moral message. It's not outright wrong to drink bottled water—it's just something we should cut back on, if we can. We ought to think about travel and its environmental impact, but we're not wrong to fly to Paris.

This isn't just splitting hairs. Wrongs are not corrected by rights. If you break a promise to a friend, you can't make up for it by keeping a promise to another friend. But social irresponsibility can be made up for by social responsibility. If I don't slow down and let any drivers get onto the highway ahead of me, I can make up for it later by letting in more than usual, or opening doors for people, or giving money to the homeless man on the corner. If I buy bottled water, I can make up for it by cutting back on driving or remembering to use my recycled shopping bags. If I travel a lot, I can also pay for planting trees that soak up greenhouse gases.

I suggest, then, that having a child if you live in an overcrowded place is a water-bottles-and-travel type of civic vice, and not just plain wrong. Seeing reproduction in these terms represents a shift from tradition but not a radical shift. The civic virtues have traditionally been virtues like serving conscientiously on juries, educating yourself about the upcoming election, and taking the time to vote. Family size has seemed like a purely private matter, on a par with deciding whom to marry. But in fact, having a child is one of the most high-impact things we can do. The decision is high impact not only because a child uses up resources and produces waste, but also for a less obvious reason. Because a child is a *person* and not just a high-impact *thing*, bringing a child into the world alters the situation of every other human being. Forever more, everyone will have to treat your child as an equal member of the moral community, recognizing her rights and interests. And the same will be true of your child's descendants.

Making a baby *is* private in many ways, and has a variety of very deep meanings for prospective parents—in contrast to buying bottled water, but not entirely different from travel. Thus, it seems out of the question for laws to regulate it, and not even plausible that there are moral obligations to procreate (or not). But it's a public matter too, and it's reasonable for there to be collective goals where total population is concerned. Thus, as part of a larger picture of factors influencing procreation, it makes sense to acknowledge civic virtues that pertain to family size. A society could send messages fostering smaller family sizes (or larger) without the messages presenting citizens with moral dos and don'ts. It's a good thing for a nonideal family size to start seeming self-indulgent—like big cars, vast amounts of travel, and bottled water—but it would be unsupportable to transmit the stronger message that deviations from the ideal are outright morally wrong.

In the United States right now, the birth rate is 2.1 per average couple—the replacement rate—and it's been 2.1 since the beginning of the twenty-first century. Quite possibly, that's ideal, and total population should neither grow nor shrink; it's up for debate, but it may be better for us to reduce our environmental impact in nonprocreative ways than to opt for smaller families. If that's correct, we can all have the number of children we want and can support. If you have no children, enough people are having four to keep the average birth rate at 2.1. If you have eight, enough people are having none or one to make up for your fecundity. You're deluded if you think everyone could have eight children, with no ill effects (as some pronatalists do think), but your own eight are not a problem.

In other places, the situation is more complicated, because the collective birth rate is too high or too low. If it's much too high, chances are that many people are poor and women don't have equal opportunities. If it's much too low, the lifestyle of families has somehow come to seem unattractive. Perhaps housing is expensive, or women are putting off having children too late and encountering the problem of age-related infertility.

Ethics will not be the main thing that makes a society start to hit its reproductive target, but if ethics has some small role to play, there is an alternative to making strict moral judgments. We need not think anyone is doing anything outright wrong by having a too-large or too-small family. But we do need to cultivate the virtue of social responsibility, and we need to do so even in the sphere of reproduction.

Chapter 4

Quality Control

Should we mess with nature?

You've thought it through carefully and you want to make a baby. Time for candlelight and romance and then, nine blissful months later, baby will arrive. Congratulations!

That would be a wonderful way for things to go, but life is not usually quite so smooth for modern couples. Along the way to becoming a parent, just about everyone invites in some sort of medical intervention. It may take high-tech intervention to make a baby, especially if parents are older, or if they are both men or both women. But even if conception is easy, pregnancy usually becomes medicalized early on, to ensure the best possible outcome for mother and baby.

Intervention to achieve conception used to be much more controversial than it is today. In particular, there was once a major debate about in vitro fertilization (IVF). It seemed freaky and potentially dangerous for fertilization to take place in a lab instead of inside the body, and various moral authorities disapproved, but today, fifty years after the first "test tube baby," there doesn't seem to be much remaining worry about IVF, per se. What still causes concern has to do not so much with lab conception, but with whose eggs and sperm are used by the prospective parents (theirs or a donor's?), whose uterus will be used for gestation (will a surrogate be involved?), how many embryos will be implanted (should two, or three, or four be implanted to increase the chances of success?), and what will happen to any leftover embryos.

As interesting as they are, those are highly specialized questions, only pertinent to a pretty small minority of prospective parents. It's more of an Every Parent's question how much intervening to do for the sake of a better outcome, baby-wise. Though some have more options than others, and those already using assisted reproductive technologies have the most, prospective parents almost always find themselves with the chance to baby-optimize to some degree. Should we take *all* such opportunities, or none of them, or some of them?

PROTECTING, SELECTING, MODIFYING

Some interventions are obviously required: you eat healthfully during pregnancy, you don't smoke. Ordinary prenatal care *protects* one specific future child who's already on the way. A baby who could have been born with certain problems is instead born healthier. We ought, surely, to protect a child we are committed to bringing to term. Not binge drinking during pregnancy is no different from putting your child in a car seat on the way home from the hospital—in both cases you are doing as you straightforwardly should. There are hard questions to be faced about how *much* protecting we must do—what we must protect our children from and at what cost to them and ourselves—but there is no question that we should be protective.

Other interventions are more puzzling, because what they accomplish is quite different. Suppose you have acne, and a dermatologist prescribes isotretinoin (commonly known as Accutane—an obsolete brand). The thick "iPledge" booklet you are given urges you to use more than one form of contraception, to avoid getting pregnant while using the drug. If you do conceive, your child has a significant chance of being born with abnormalities, it says. For example, the child's external ears might wind up being malformed (for the sake of simplicity, I will focus exclusively on this risk). You won't be able to stop the drug on time to prevent the malformations, since they can be caused in the first few weeks of gestation, before the pregnancy has been detected.

On the face of it, avoiding Accutane while you're trying to conceive (or avoiding conception while taking Accutane) is just like taking prenatal vitamins—you must do it because you ought to protect your future child. When we look closer, though, it's clear the rationale is actually very different. If you avoid conceiving while on Accutane and conceive a year later, it's not as if you'll be helping any baby who would have been born with abnormal ears. *That* baby won't be born at all, as opposed to being born later with normal ears. Rather, you'll be switching to having a different baby altogether— a baby formed from a different egg and different sperm. You will not have protected one baby, but will have instead selected between the earlier-born baby with malformed ears and a later-born normal baby. If protection is mandatory, selection may *seem* mandatory, only because it's so easily confused with protection. *Is* it really mandatory to select the better off of two different babies? (Because it involves two nonidentical babies, this puzzle exemplifies what philosophers refer to as "the nonidentity problem.")

This becomes a more urgent question when we notice all the different ways we can be selective. Another way, besides optimally timing conception, is by getting advice from a genetic counselor or buying a genetic testing kit—they are even available online.

Information can be obtained simply by swabbing the inside of your cheek and mailing the sample back to a lab. The test will disclose your chances of having a child with hundreds of conditions. If you found out you were a carrier for a very serious condition, you might think it was worthwhile to opt for IVF and preimplantation genetic diagnosis (PGD); that would give you the chance to select among several embryos, discarding those with abnormalities. Once again, you would be selecting among several embryos, as opposed to protecting one—giving one already destined for existence the best chance in life.

Selection is also an option for someone who undergoes IVF simply due to infertility—with no particular desire to control which child she conceives. If conception is successful, there may be too many embryos to implant them all safely. A choice among them will have to be made somehow. PGD could be used to decide which embryo or embryos to implant.

Besides protecting one embryo (or fetus) and selecting between two, there is also the possibility of modifying an embryo, thereby altering the characteristics of a future child. So we have a total of three ways to optimize: through protection, selection, and modification. But each of those can take several forms. For instance, you can protect your future child from having abnormal ears, or protect the child from being deprived of stellar intelligence. Likewise, for selection and modification: they can be done to avoid unwanted traits or pursue desired traits. The literature on optimizing refers to avoiding the unwanted as "therapy" and pursuing the wanted as "enhancement," terms that I will occasionally use but with a warning: in cases of selection they're misleading. For in cases of selection, no one child is enhanced or receives therapy. Rather, the more advantaged of two possible children is selected.

At some point along the spectrum from taking prenatal vitamins, to timing conception auspiciously, to selecting better embryos, to modifying embryos, does the practice of optimizing pregnancy outcome become too meddlesome? At what point, if ever, do parents go from acceptable or even obligatory protecting to something more pernicious?

DRAWING THE LINE

You might say an important line is crossed when parents go from protecting to selecting (and beyond). Selecting draws more scrutiny, but it's not easy to say why. When we control which of many possible children come into the world before conception, we do no harm to the children "left behind." As we saw in chapter 2, there aren't any unborn ghosts in cosmic orphanages, waiting to get lucky and to be born. The potential child *not* conceived because you used contraception while taking Accutane is just that—potential, and not the least bit real. Nobody's literally excluded because of preconception selection.

If selection goes on in the context of IVF, the embryos left behind are only a few days old. In chapter 5 I will be arguing that these very early embryos are on a par with sperm or eggs. They are mere precursors of us, not "one of us." It will take another week or so of development for one of us to be on the scene, and even then, that being will not be a person yet, just as he or she will not be a child, teenager, or adult yet. If there is a problem with being selective, the problem doesn't seem to be one about destroying or never implanting unused embryos.

Still, aggressive selectiveness does seem troubling, at least to me. There is something worrisome about guarding the gates of existence too carefully. After all, most people who make it through, despite having suboptimal characteristics, are much loved and destined for perfectly decent lives. We might want to say that sometimes we should select and sometimes we should not—*if* we can draw the line in some principled and coherent way.

Perhaps we should say that selection is bad when it is bound up with discrimination. In the world of the superb movie *Gattaca*, genetic screening is used to select the "best" babies; after birth, screening continues throughout life. Those with the right genes (the "valids") get the best opportunities, while those with the wrong genes (the "invalids") are stigmatized and excluded. Selection is condemned by the movie's implicit "argument" partly on the basis of its awful social consequences. In the dystopian world of the movie, the exclusion of people with disabilities does a great deal of harm to people who don't measure up. (The movie also rejects the *power* of genes, by having characters' lives turn out differently than their genetic profiles would have predicted.)

In the real world, selection is indeed sometimes linked to discrimination. Take sex selection—one of the most commonly used forms of selective technology, and one that resists classification as either a therapy or an enhancement. Sex selection can involve using PGD to decide between available embryos in a lab, and discarding the "wrong-sexed" embryos. Sex selection can also mean detecting sex via ultrasound, and then deciding whether to continue the pregnancy or abort, depending on the outcome. Where sex selection is used frequently, like in China and India, more people prefer to have boys. The naturally occurring ratio of male newborns to female is 105 to 100, but in China it's currently 116 to 100 and in India 111 to 100. The result, eventually, is a larger number of unmarried men, and studies show unmarried men are less happy (on average), more prone to disease (physical and psychological), and more likely to commit crimes, compared to married men. They may also band together and perpetrate crimes—often against women. Beyond that, the fact that millions of girls are missing from China and India sends a terrible, sexist message, further lowering the status of women.

So, is it safe to say that selection should be avoided when and only when it might very well have negative social consequences? Some philosophers have argued that selection is more deeply pernicious than that. The harm in it is not just a matter of how the child will fare in society, eventually. There is something more immediately problematic about selectiveness *for* the parent who is selective and the child who is selected. They also claim that protecting and modifying can be problematic. But why? What's the problem?

MOLDING VS. BEHOLDING

Setting aside worries about social impact, many people think a high degree of choosiness would make procreation a little like the manufacture of a commodity. The Apple company certainly wants its next iPhone model to be the best it can possibly be. If a glitch is discovered during the design phase, it will be detected and eliminated before production begins. Appealing features will be added, provided the cost doesn't make the final product prohibitively expensive. We make baby-making more like product manufacturing if we use every selective option there is.

Proponents of selection say "Why not?" The higher quality we achieve leads to children existing who are actually better off than the different set of children we could have had, if we had opted for the "cheerful moral anarchy of the free range approach" (to use Jonathan Glover's phrase). So why think anything has gone wrong?

In his book *The Case Against Perfection*, Michael Sandel claims that designing the best possible new people is suspect, in so far as it goes along with an attitude toward life that is problematic in all of its many manifestations. Perfectionistic procreation involves striving for assets instead of accepting them when they come along as gifts; molding children instead of beholding them; trying to master the future, instead of having an "openness to the unbidden"; controlling our offspring, instead of being receptive to the unknown. The idea seems to be that perfectionistic procreation is just one aspect of a way of life that's worse on the whole.

The trouble with Sandel's objection is that in many avenues of life we do legitimately want mastery and control. Once a child is born, and we're trying to prevent him from choking or sticking his finger in an electrical socket, it's all to the good for parents to have mastery and control. Certainly I'm not overdoing it if I fastidiously avoid alcohol and smoking, and do my best to eat nutritiously during pregnancy (protection); or if I postpone conception while I'm taking Accutane (selection).

Sandel's main concern is with selecting and modifying for the purpose of securing the best assets for our offspring ("enhancement"), not for the purpose of preventing diseases and disabilities ("therapy"). The result of deliberate enhancement, he worries, is that assets will no longer qualify as *gifts*, because they will have been obtained through desire and effort. There's something unfortunate about that, admittedly, but the upshot isn't so clear. I may enjoy appreciating the sheer giftedness of the Beatles or Bob Dylan, but when it comes to my own life, it is not quite so satisfying to passively accept the presence or absence of gifts. I often strive to do my best, attempting to overcome natural ineptitude when it gets in the way of achieving my goals. We do the same once children have arrived. We don't settle for some children being gifted and others not; we help a child overcome his or her natural disadvantages. Granted, it's a virtue to accept our lot in life in some situations, but in others it's also a virtue to strive for mastery. If some types of optimizing are excessive, we still haven't figured out why, and which those are.

BETTER BABY, INC.

Reproducing is not just adding a child to the world. Instead, reproducing is making yourself a parent of a child—making someone else a sort of second self. Selectiveness *can* be in tension with the parental state of mind, or so I'm going to argue.

The usual forms of *protection* are certainly not inconsistent with the parental state of mind. Seeing my child as a sort of second self will tend to make me want to protect her—from cigarette smoke, poor nutrition, and the like. That's because of the "self" part: I aim for her good in the same way that I aim for my own good. But it's also because of the "second" part: a baby is a whole new person, starting afresh with none of the nicks and cuts we all accumulate over time. Of *course* we want our offspring to be protected.

Some instances of selection are also clearly consistent with the parental state of mind. Take, once again, delaying conception until you have stopped taking Accutane. As far as procreation's meaning goes, that really is innocent, just like we intuitively think. It's innocent because the drug is to be avoided both if your goal is to have the best-off child (having normal ears is desirable), and if you want your child to come from you in the usual way—the way that makes us think of a child as a second self. After all, the drug disrupts normal fetal development, stopping the child from having the traits dictated by her parents' genes or her mother's uterine environment. A fetus developing under its damaging influence in effect has another progenitor besides her two parents, and not a benign one. Selecting the baby who will *not* be conceived under the corrosive influence of Accutane is perfectly compatible with the parental state of mind.

We should say the same thing about many other possible motivations for postponement. Suppose right now I can't afford prenatal vitamins, but I will be able to later on. Or now I run the risk of being exposed to the mosquito-borne Zika virus, but later on the risk will be lower. Or now I'm living in an extremely stressful environment, but later on I'll be able to conceive and gestate a child in peace. In all these cases, potential parents are trying to eliminate nefarious intrusions on the normal process of conception and gestation, clearing the way for the child to come from them in the usual way. They are selecting between two babies, not protecting, but innocently so.

But now take another type of selection, one that could come out of a sci-fi movie, but isn't so terribly unrealistic. A couple opts for high-tech reproduction at Better Baby Inc., in order to be able to choose the baby's traits. Bella's ovaries are hyperstimulated, giving the couple ten eggs to combine with Ben's sperm. The resulting embryos are inspected for defects and four pass muster. Those four are enhanced, using a new line of Additions™ DNA. Genes for tall stature and blue eyes are added. So are genes for life-enhancing character traits like the ability to postpone gratification and high self-esteem. The couple only draws the line at the ultimate innovation, which is on the last page of the Additions™ catalog: Perfect Child™, a line of embryos contributed by extraspecial donors and then enhanced in the lab. That option they reject.

Finally, a selection is made among their four enhanced embryos, and two are implanted. Nine months later, Bellissima is born, a girl who grows up to be healthy and fit, tall and blue-eyed, and strikingly endowed with self-esteem and the ability to postpone gratification. Whether or not it's because of the gene insertions, no one can say for sure, but Bellissima becomes a great success in every way, and her success makes her exceptionally happy.

What should we think? Some ethicists think Ben and Bella actually do exactly as they *should* by being selective, if their decisions make for a better off child. Anything else would have been wrong. This is the upshot of an ethical principle proposed by Oxford ethicist Julian Savulescu. His Principle of Procreative Beneficence says we should choose, of the possible children we could have, the child with the best chance of the best life. Now, the possible children we could have are presumably the children we could have using our own gametes. Thus, we are permitted *some* bias in favor of our own. But beyond getting to use our own gametes, we must be optimizers. If the enhancements chosen by Ben and Bella give Bellissima a better chance of a good life, they are not just permitted to choose them, but obligated to do so.

Why don't they have to go even further and choose Perfect Child™ if the result would be a child with an even better chance of a good life? Apparently, Savulescu respects the desire to have a child who is biologically our own—up to a point. We may start with our own embryos, despite their not being the very best. But we should choose among them, and even modify them, to generate the child with the best chance of the best life, at least as long as this is not too onerous.

But does drawing the line at Perfect Child™ really make any sense? If Ben and Bella may draw the line there, then it seems to me they also *don't* have to optimize when it comes to their own embryos either. The less-than-ideal outcome is the same in both cases and so is the motivating thought: "I just want my own child, I don't have to have the very best." If that's an acceptable thought when Ben and Bella decline an unrelated Perfect Child™ embryo, it's also acceptable in couples who decline high-tech interventions that promise to deliver babies with better lives.

In fact, it's more than acceptable. It's positively good to see our children as wonderful, just the way they are. The tendency to see only good in our own is at its peak at the start of a child's life. Later, we may have to contend with toddlers who have tantrums and teenagers who don't do their homework or who total the car. But the sense of the child's original marvelousness persists. We love that perfect-seeming child and feel dedicated to him or her throughout years of sometimes arduous parental labor.

Aggressive optimizers like Ben and Bella would appear to have different attitudes. Having their own child does matter to them, as evidenced by the fact that they decline Perfect Child™ technology, but they feel compelled to have not just any child of their own, but one with the most optimal features. Now, they might defend this as an unselfish act. They don't care about having a child who is healthy, fit, and well endowed with advantageous traits. They might say they would see the child who comes from any of their embryos as equally their own, and equally perfect. In fact, they might insist, they would have found their child just as wonderful if the gene manipulations hadn't worked; they would have been just as loving to a less optimal child and just as dedicated to her well-being.

Some philosophers are prepared to believe you can pursue traits in a baby without caring if they wind up being absent. For example, in an article about Michael Sandel's book on designer babies, the philosopher Francis Kamm writes, "One can know that one will care about someone just as much whether or not she has certain traits and yet care to have someone, perhaps for their own sake, who has, rather than lacks, those traits." So optimizing doesn't intrude on unconditional acceptance.

I'm not entirely persuaded. Yes, we can know we will care about a child just as much, whether she scores high or low on the SATs, but nevertheless want her to score high (for her own sake). But decisions to pursue assets before a child even exists may be in a different class. It would be hard to know about something as mysterious as the besotted feeling parents have for their children, starting at the beginning of their children's lives and persisting through thick and thin. Would that love be threatened if parents essentially designed their own children, picking traits from a menu of possibilities? I don't see how anyone could know for sure.

My impression is that even the most hard-headed parents find something miraculous about their children, a response that's integral to the love and dedication they feel. I'm not sure we could find a child amazing and miraculous, while also knowing her personality was assembled using ingredients sold on page sixteen of a catalog. And so selectiveness ought to be considered at least possibly a threat to parental love.

Now, once parenthood gets underway, we don't accept the miracle of our child as is, ignoring all the child's flaws and shortcomings. We may very well help the child score higher on the SATs! But in all our endeavors to improve and develop, there's still an underlying sense of the child's being perfectly wonderful at the core. It's this baseline affirmation that seems potentially compromised if we start off adding a bit of this and taking a way a bit of that, to make the very best child. The core child could stop seeming quite so amazing and deserving of dedication, if *we* assembled him or her.

And of course, that would be bad. Parental dedication is crucial to parental satisfaction—which surely matters; and it's also crucial to the well-being of children. We should preserve that initial sense of a child being perfect just because he or she is ours, unless we have a very compelling reason to let it go. And it does not seem as if the traits being discussed here—height, eye color, and some personality traits—give us that sort of a reason.

WHEN TO OPTIMIZE

Like Sandel, I've focused on the state of mind of the person making procreative choices. While Sandel worries about the molding and beholding of prospective parents, I've focused on other attitudes. Savulescu, by contrast, is entirely concerned with the newborn's attributes. Decisions are good when they lead to better attributes, no matter whether the process involves protection, selection, or modification, and whether the aim is therapy, enhancement, or something else. Procreative beneficence involves too much concern with newborn attributes, I've argued, but we do have to have some concern. What needs to be added and clarified is that a good parent will care about securing or avoiding some attributes more and some attributes less.

Let's go back to the Accutane case. I said it was innocent to delay conception until you are through with the treatment. But that sounds too weak. It is not just innocent: you *should* delay conception to avoid a child having malformed external ears. At the same time, it seems problematic to insert genes for extra prettiness— doing so is inconsistent with parental receptiveness. How can this pair of assessments make sense? If we compare these cases carefully, I think we can see that they do.

Imagine you're taking Accutane and could have baby A (with abnormalities) now or baby B (with no abnormalities) in a year. Whatever you do, the other child will not wind up languishing, unborn, in a cosmic orphanage. You won't harm the child who doesn't exist. It's also somewhat reassuring that the relevant abnormalities are small; the child who exists, whether it's A or B, will have a good chance of a good life. So far it sounds like you don't have to select normal baby B, but is that right? Another relevant consideration is this: A would be a little worse off than B, and in a way that is bound to involve medical interventions and accommodations. If you decide to have A, you will inevitably work hard, after A is born, to get him to be as well off as B would have been. But what an absurd situation! Since you could have had B to begin with, without any significant effort or sacrifice, it's downright irrational to have A. It's foolish. And beyond that, it's also a harbinger of bad parenting. Since it's so easy to have B instead of A, the person who doesn't make the effort to have B probably doesn't have proper empathy for what A will feel as she deals with the inevitable interventions and the sense of being born with an abnormality. Worse, it's hard to imagine what could make someone do this, besides carelessness. All these points add up to the intuitive assessment: "You should wait and have B."

When the choice is between unpretty baby A and pretty baby B, and the procedure is PGD, with selection of traits from the Additions™ catalog, things look different. Being an unpretty baby isn't seen as an abnormality in need of medical remedy. Parents aren't going to intervene after birth to get baby A to be in baby B's better position. There's also much more effort involved in selecting traits from the catalog and inserting them using PGD. So where it does seem foolish, careless, and uncaring to conceive while on Accutane, it doesn't seem foolish, careless, and uncaring to throw out the catalog and let nature take its course instead of inserting genes for extra prettiness. The parents who throw it out are just feeling open and receptive—which is admirable.

How we look at any particular case of selection depends on many factors: the desirable attribute in question; what will happen after birth to a child without it; and the effort and sacrifice involved in pursuing it. One of the thoughts in the mix is a legitimate distinction having to do with sheer normality. Each of us would like to have a fortunate birth—a birth with all the normal human anatomy and physiology. Considering that this is a universal and rather deep-seated preference, it's worth more effort to secure simple normality than to secure extra talents and assets. But so much for relatively small things like normal external ears and extra prettiness. What about more important attributes?

Genetic counseling can reveal to prospective parents that they have a high risk of having a child with serious problems. Perhaps the most common risk factor is sheer age. Many women who postpone parenthood until their careers are established find themselves having to think about the risk of having a child with Down syndrome. Older women are also more likely to be using assisted reproduction, which increases the chances of multiple births. If you are a forty-year-old woman having twins, the chances that one or the other of the babies has Down syndrome is about 2 percent. Should you have pursued pregnancy to begin with? Must you opt for prenatal testing, to find out if you are carrying a baby with Down syndrome? What should you do if you find out that one of the fetuses has the syndrome, and the other does not? There are lots of hard questions here.

In this new situation all the stakes are much higher. I won't presume to offer advice or reach a verdict, but will just point out that we do not, out of consistency, have to reach the same conclusion as in the Accutane case. Now the choice is between possibly having a child with an abnormality, and having no child at all—the effort and sacrifice involved is much greater. The attribute is much more significant as well. It's certainly less clear than in the previous cases what we will do, if we are receptive, careful, and caring. I think reasonable, good people will avoid conception on Accutane and throw out the Additions™ catalog. But here, when the worry is about Down syndrome, and in many other situations, it's much less clear how to integrate all of the morally relevant considerations pushing us either toward procreation or away from it.

THE ACCIDENTAL OPTIMIZER

Some couples discover that only one partner can have a biological connection to their child. A sperm donor or egg donor is needed to make use of the gametes one partner does have. If they don't adopt, lesbian mothers need a sperm donor and gay fathers need an egg donor (and a gestational mother). If they turn to a sperm or egg bank, "quality control" is built in. Sperm and egg banks screen for diseases and disabilities. But there's more: surprisingly (to me, anyway), there are websites advertising gametes; and at these sites you can choose an awesomely talented sperm donor who looks like Keanu Reeves or an artistic egg donor who goes to an Ivy League university. If you came to the gamete bank just because you needed gametes—any gametes—is there anything wrong with optimizing while you're at it?

Then again—backing up a bit—what about the whole practice of using other people's gametes to make babies? Should the donor give gametes away and the recipient make use of them? Most people agree that nobody should deliberately produce whole babies for the sole purpose of helping potential adopters. It would be even worse if an infertility lab decided to implant leftover embryos in gestational surrogates, offering the babies to patients for adoption—and still worse if all of that were commercialized, with the babies advertised and sold. But most of us would go further. It's commonly thought we should use contraception to avoid a baby being accidentally conceived, even if chances are the baby could be transferred from biological parents to adoptive parents.

One good reason we think all of this is because it's terribly painful for most people to relinquish a child. If it's not painful, most likely the person is in extremely difficult circumstances that interfere with being responsive. Giving away a baby is giving away part of yourself—and these are exactly the words often used by relinquishing parents. If you care about yourself and respect yourself, you'll try hard to avoid the predicament in which that might be your best choice, all things considered.

Another reason we think baby transfers are to be avoided is because we think it's better to come into the world being wanted and loved by your creator—wanted and loved to the point of being kept and raised. A significant number of children given up for adoption do later wrestle with the fact that they were relinquished, suffering a "natal injury" of some size, from small to large. So we have two reasons to think giving up a baby is a last resort—a good choice in some cases, but to be avoided as much as possible.

What, then, of deliberately giving away sperm or eggs, as opposed to whole babies? It seems only consistent to have the same sorts of reservations to some degree. If you are thinking about the situation realistically and sensitively, there must be some pain involved in knowing you have a child "out there" whose life you are not involved in. It's not surprising that some donors choose distorted ways to think about what they have done. An egg donor discussed by a recipient in a *New York Times* magazine article describes egg donation as being akin to blood donation, as if there were no parent-child relationship at all between the donor and the future child. On the other hand, there is also a natal injury for the child to deal with, though again, perhaps a smaller one than when children are given up for adoption. (The child produced through gamete donation was never literally in the arms of one woman and then passed to another.)

Am I saying gamete donation is bad, all things considered, and should never be pursued? David Velleman does take that position in an interesting article called "Family History," on the grounds that the natal injury involved is too severe to be justifiably inflicted. Rivka Weinberg also worries about gamete donation, arguing that the donors are responsible for the resulting children, and cannot unproblematically transfer that responsibility to recipients. On the other side of the debate, it certainly would be unfortunate to conclude that there is no ethical way for some couples (gay and lesbian couples, infertile heterosexuals) to gain access to the very great good of procreation—that procreation, for them, necessarily requires misbegotten gametes.

Setting aside the hard questions about the morality of gamete donation, let's suppose a couple does use donor gametes. What about adding some oversight, or quality control, while they're at it? Why *not* select the taller sperm donor or the smarter egg donor?

This can't be problematic in exactly the way selecting between your *own* gametes is problematic, if my account of the problem is a reasonable one. The ordinary selector's choosiness is in tension with simply wanting a child, any child, who "comes from me". By contrast, the recipient of an egg or sperm donation isn't compromising openness to any and all of his or her own children. This may be someone who has tried long and hard to have children in the ordinary, haphazard, non-optimizing way. Or—if a same-sex couple—they are people who would be delighted if their two eggs could unite or their respective sperm could unite. They're seeking a gamete donation instead of adopting precisely because they'd like to use the sperm or egg supplied by one partner, come what may; they aren't choosy about the outcome of using that gamete. In fact, selectiveness about the *missing* gamete may not even stem from hyperconcern with the child's attributes. It may represent, instead, a desire for some level of control, a desire that exists only because control is already so diminished in the lives of people enduring all manner of infertility treatments.

What goes on here—on the surface, shopping for better babies, with catalogs, paid concierges, and high price-tags—sounds like a Neiman Marcus for reproduction. But the reality may be rather different. It tells us something important that the couples taking gametes from these banks would often give anything to just make babies in the usual free-range fashion.

Procreative ethics is complex territory, full of technical and vexing questions. I have barely scratched the surface here, and haven't considered any particular dilemma in detail. This has been no more than a brief visit to a very complicated set of issues. But let us move on, keeping our eyes on the big picture. One way or another, you've become pregnant (let's suppose), and in about nine months you will give birth to a baby. The philosophical parent will have lots of questions about what's going on in there—inside the uterus, where a tiny organism is changing and growing, hour by hour, day by day.

Chapter 5

In the Beginning

What's going on in there?

You are pregnant. You found out by taking a pregnancy test as soon as your period was late, so you know that fertilization took place roughly two weeks ago. In the bewildering official terminology of embryology, the product of conception is first a one-celled "zygote"; after division into two, then four, then six, then eight cells, and so on, the cluster of about thirty cells is called a "morula"; at about four days, it's a hollow "blastocyst"; once there is differentiation and full implantation in the wall of the uterus, it's an "embryo"; and at three months it's officially a "fetus" (although colloquially it's a "fetus" from start to finish). "Conceptus" is another term sometimes used for the initial product of conception. Whatever the terminology, now that you're pregnant, amazing changes are taking place every day.

As soon as I discovered I was pregnant, I became obsessed with fetal development, poring over every manual and website I could find. The whole process seemed so excruciatingly slow—one day followed another, and it seemed as if we were still an infinite distance from the finish line. Being pregnant with twins, I was particularly susceptible to morning sickness. The philosophical parent will notice a curious thing about morning sickness. Nausea isn't simply an isolated sensation; rather, it's intimately connected to cognition. In the throes of nausea, the whole world seems different—smellier, slimier, moister, more insidiously dangerous. Fortunately, all of that stops for most women around week sixteen. After a few months of relative calm, I went into premature labor and spent two months in the hospital enduring all sorts of medical interventions. At thirty-six weeks, my children were born at the staggering weight of seven pounds apiece—but I'm getting ahead of myself. There are plenty of interesting questions for the philosophical parent to think about during pregnancy.

WAS LARRY ONCE AN EMBRYO?

Let's talk about you—newly pregnant now, we will suppose. It has only been fourteen days since conception and you eagerly await the arrival of baby . . . Larry, as it might turn out to be. In a couple of weeks, you will actually be able to see the embryo in an ultrasound image. Now fast-forward to the day when you will be putting on Larry's first diaper, or walking him to school for the first time, or attending his high-school graduation. What's the connection between the embryo you will soon be seeing in the ultrasound image and five-year-old Larry? Are they one and the same? Do our children come into existence as early as the first weeks in utero?

This kind of question is often raised in the context of the debate about abortion. In thinking about the answer, we may find ourselves doing a lot of "look ahead" (as in a chess game) so we don't corner ourselves into a pro-life position if we're pro-choice, or corner ourselves into a pro-choice position if we're pro-life. In this chapter I will try not to engage in any "look ahead." Abortion isn't the issue, and furthermore, *whatever* we say about the point when our children's lives begin, there may very well be space to defend our preferred position on abortion. As a number of ethicists have shown, there is no simple, direct route from the status of the fetus to the permissibility, or impermissibility, of ending pregnancy. So for that and all sorts of other reasons, we ought to try and think about when our children's lives begin as a question in its own right, not as a prelude to debating abortion.

When does the lifespan of a particular child have its inception? At the very beginning of pregnancy, or later, or even much later? Or, putting it another way, when does the story of a person's life begin? Perhaps the best place to begin is with the "David Copperfield View" about the story of our lives. Here's the first paragraph of Charles Dickens's novel:

> CHAPTER I. *I am born*
>
> Whether I shall turn out to be the hero of my own life, or whether that station will be held by anybody else, these pages must show. To begin my life with the beginning of my life, I record that I was born (as I have been informed and believe) on a Friday, at twelve o'clock at night. It was remarked that the clock began to strike, and I began to cry, simultaneously.

David Copperfield must know he didn't come into existence ex nihilo. There was a fetus in his mother's uterus before he was born, and he is intimately related to that fetus. However, the story of his life starts at his birth, Dickens assumes. What comes before is a mere prequel.

That is a natural view, particularly from a standpoint within our own lives. When my children think about their lives, they do seem to have the David Copperfield view, reacting with utter boredom to anything I might tell them about the time when I was pregnant. When I think about their lives from my own standpoint, it's quite different. The stories of their lives include chapters that predate their birth. For example, I think of my son as having turned somersaults in his effort to get comfortable, north of his sister. I think of his sister as very quiet and stable, apart from periodic bouts of hiccups. I probably think of these early chapters in so much detail because of the daily fetal monitoring I had during the period of hospital bedrest in the third trimester, but I think of the story as having earlier chapters too. In fact, I think of their life story as beginning at the very beginning—that is, as soon as I became pregnant. The entities that they are seem to have had their moment of entry into existence long before the dramatic morning of their birth. This is certainly not because I think of them as having, on the day of their conception, souls, consciousness, an essence, or fully formed personhood. The thought is merely that the individual entities they are now are entirely continuous with the teeny-tiny clumps of cells that existed way back in July 1996.

So we have two initial possibilities for the beginning of your child's life story: the day of conception, or the day of birth. Setting aside all thoughts about the ethics of abortion (if we can), both possibilities have some appeal, though the conception story appeals more to parents and the birth story appeals more to children. But, do either of these accounts make sense—or should we shift to some third account of when your child's life begins?

VERY EARLY, VERY LATE

Let's get back to Larry, your future five-year-old. Can it really make good, sound sense to think that Larry-your-five-year-old was once a miniature embryo, the size of a coffee ground? Could the very same entity go from being coffee-ground-sized and primitive to having the size and sophistication of a five-year-old?

Well, yes. Nature is full of dramatic change. Baby birds are dependent and immobile, but then fledge and start to fly. Butterflies start off as caterpillars, and then undergo metamorphosis. Human babies are very small and dependent, unable to walk or eat solid food, unable to talk; they grow and change dramatically. Even if the abilities of mature birds, butterflies, and people are the ones we most identify with the species—birds fly, butterflies have colorful wings, and people are rational and talkative—we don't think maturity is an ontological turning point, a time when there's a shift in the individuals that exist. Adults are not whole new beings, replacements for immature creatures. Immature creatures *become* mature creatures: that is to say, one and the same thing goes through an immature phase and then comes to be mature and more typical of the species.

An embryo is arguably the extremely immature form of the very same thing that will later be an immature fetus, an immature baby, an immature toddler, an adolescent, and then a mature adult. Persistence of a single entity despite change will continue, as the mature adult becomes less physically capable and (in the event of dementia, especially) loses mental powers. In fact, you could think of the embryonic phase as the very earliest stretch of childhood, with the lines between embryo and fetus, as well as fetus and child, rather arbitrary. In humans, a twelve-month-old is a child out in the world, not a fetus any more, but only because mothers have narrow birth passages and their offspring have big heads. Immature humans develop a lot outside a woman's body because human anatomy doesn't allow a later birth.

The Very Early View of Larry's inception has many adherents, many with ethical and religious motivations. The advocate I'll be focusing on defends the view on strictly metaphysical—not religious, not ethical—grounds. The philosopher Eric Olson, in his book *The Human Animal,* argues that we run into some serious metaphysical perplexities if we suppose Larry's entry into existence comes later. But some do say it comes later. Much later.

A particularly tempting Late View is that Larry comes into being at the point when consciousness emerges. Scientists say different aspects of consciousness emerge at different points, with some aspects commencing as early as nineteen weeks and others many weeks later. At around twenty weeks, the fetus can probably smell, according to one team of researchers, and around twenty-six weeks the auditory cortex responds to sounds. The fetus fairly quickly looks quite baby-like: at twenty weeks it has a baby-like shape, it weighs about ten ounces, and its crown-to-rump length is over six inches. But what exactly is a fetus feeling? A relatively cautious assessment is that consciousness doesn't exist until between twenty-four and thirty-four weeks. Only then are there normal brain waves, as measured by an electroencephalogram; on the other hand, even at that point a fetus spends most of the time asleep.

Whenever, exactly, consciousness emerges, presumably what you're thinking, if you think there's no Larry until this point, is that Larry is in essence a conscious *self,* not just an organism. So he doesn't exist when we can't say any conscious self exists yet. Somewhere in the range of twenty to thirty-four weeks, Larry-the-self has come into being. And it so happens that by then he looks a lot more like Larry as a newborn and Larry as a five-year-old than any extremely young, coffee-ground-sized embryo ever did.

There are yet more positions on when Larry comes into existence. A Very Late account is supported by the philosopher Lynne Rudder Baker in her book *Persons and Bodies.* She thinks our personhood is essential to us: when we stop being persons we won't exist any more; when we aren't persons yet, we don't exist yet. Larry is a person at age five, and throughout his lifespan he is always a person. So he can't have entered the world before we can say he has the property of being a person. But what is that property?

Baker thinks to be a person is more than to be genetically human and more than to have simple types of consciousness. It entails having a "rudimentary first-person perspective," which includes consciousness but also two more capacities—the capacity to imitate and the capacity to be driven by beliefs, desires, and intentions. But even that isn't enough for personhood, on Baker's view. To be a person, one must not only have a rudimentary first-person perspective; one must also be on the way to having a full-blown first-person perspective, like older children and adults have. This is the sort of perspective you have upon gaining the ability to mull things over, decide what to do, copy the behavior of others, and the like.

The actualities and potentialities Baker focuses on mark us out as persons, because they lead to the powers we associate with personhood in the most honorable sense—reflectiveness, moral responsibility, reasoning, and so on. A human being has personhood for as long as he or she exists; by contrast, dogs, cats, and other animals never attain personhood. Though some nonhuman animals do have a rudimentary first-person perspective, none are on the way to a full-blown first-person perspective; so they don't meet all of the requirements for being a person.

We don't enter the world until we possess personhood, Baker thinks; we aren't persons until we have rudimentary first-person perspectives *and* we're on the way to having full-blown first-person perspectives; and that happens around the time of birth, she claims. Newborn babies do imitate others—for example, sticking out their tongues when others do—and do have very simple desires and intentions. And soon they will imitate and intend more often, and more deliberately. In essence, then, Baker supports the *David Copperfield* account of when Larry's life begins: "CHAPTER I. *I am born.*" His life starts at birth.

OLSON VS. BAKER

As much as the Late Larry and *Very* Late Larry views are intuitively attractive, to the extent that they save us from having to believe we were once little specks of unconscious organic matter, they're also quite puzzling. Eric Olson, who supports the Very Early View, points out how odd it is to suppose there was a precursor of Larry in your uterus all along, but around the time of birth, when a rudimentary first-person perspective starts to kick in, a new entity—Larry-the-self—emerges. How could that be? Why would that be? In his view, these questions don't have good answers.

One way that it could be is if dualism were true: if consciousness or a rudimentary first-person perspective resided in an immaterial entity—a soul. If a soul somehow gets connected to the fetus, one might think Larry *is* that soul. So a new entity exists at birth, roughly, because there is literally a new entity on the scene. Where there was once only a body (the fetus), there is now a body attached to a soul, and Larry is that soul, or perhaps that body-soul combination. Unfortunately (for this story about when Larry starts to exist), souls are deeply problematic. How do they latch on to physical things? How do the happenings in a soul have an impact on physical events? Where do souls reside before they latch on to bodies? What are they made of? None of these questions have good answers. For that reason, souls are part of the history of philosophy and religion and still present in the popular imagination, but have almost no fans among contemporary philosophers. Baker does not, in fact, endorse the David Copperfield view out of a belief in dualism.

Here is the story that Baker tells. As the fetus develops, the brain grows by leaps and bounds (on average, 250,000 neurons are born per minute over the nine months of gestation). At some point, the necessary physical changes take place so that the fetal brain can consciously feel sensations. After more time, the powers of the brain grow more sophisticated and there comes to be a rudimentary first-person perspective, one with the potential to become full-blown. At that point, which Baker sees as taking place around the time of birth, a new entity exists. Enter: Larry, who is essentially a person. Of course, the fetal organism that was developing for nine months doesn't vanish. Rather, Baker thinks that the organism persists, but begins to *constitute* Larry when it starts to have a conscious first-person perspective.

Baker explains what is meant by "constitution" by talking about statues and lumps of clay. A lump of clay could exist continuously for ten years, but constitute a statue of a cat only during the fifth year. Imagine the pliable clay is formed into a statue by a sculptor on January first of the fifth year and then squashed back into a pancake shape on December thirty-first. In the fifth year, we might say that a new entity exists—the cat statue—though of course it exists by courtesy of the lump of clay. The statue doesn't *replace* the clay, but it is rather *constituted by* the clay. Baker uses the same concepts to talk about the emergence of a new person. The fetus is an organism that continuously exists starting long before birth and will go on existing after birth. But Larry has a different entry point than the organism does: he exists beginning when that organism has the right properties to start *constituting* a person.

Olson's view is certainly far simpler. He thinks that Larry exists very early on and develops ever greater complexity throughout your pregnancy, until at some point he acquires the property of being a person. That's *not* an ontological turning point—not a moment when a new entity springs into existence. But a simpler view is not necessarily better, Baker implies. What's unacceptable to her is that, were Larry to exist early on, before he's a person, there would be a "not yet a person" phase of his life. That would mean that human persons are, at their core, mere animals or mere organisms. We are persons for most of our lives, but not for all of our lives. Our personhood is something that can come and go, like being a mother or an adult or a lawyer; personhood becomes, says Baker, "just an ontologically insignificant property of certain organisms." On Baker's own account, by contrast, persons are *always* persons, throughout their lifespans, and never mere organisms or animals (though they are constituted by organisms or animals). The view that Larry exists very early, before he is a person—says Baker—doesn't do justice to our specialness, which consists in our being persons with first-person perspectives (rudimentary or full-blown) *essentially* and therefore as long as we exist.

Some will share Baker's concerns about what we are, but I don't. I'm not troubled by the idea that I was once a nonperson, like I was once a nonadult, a nonmother, and a nonphilosopher. An attribute can be very important to me without my having to think I couldn't exist without it. And there is certainly specialness in being the kind of entity that is inherently programmed to *become* a person with a first-person perspective; most things are not that kind of entity. Larry is still pretty amazing if he is an organism that spends only *most* of its lifespan having consciousness, thoughts, desires, hopes, and dreams. If he is essentially an animal, he is a very special animal.

Of course there are far more points of debate between Olson and Baker—their books and articles should be consulted for the full picture. But let's now go on to a question about the earliest days of pregnancy.

THE VERY BEGINNING

If you think Larry was once a tiny embryo, is it inevitable that you will think his life started at the moment of conception? Olson says no, and Baker basically agrees; *if* Larry existed way back near the beginning of your pregnancy, his history couldn't go back as far as day one. The two agree that the fetal organism—whether Larry or not Larry—doesn't start to exist that early.

If you're willing to think of a very immature embryo as Larry (I'll go with Olson's view, to keep things simple), why stop there? In fact, there are some pretty compelling reasons *not* to think Larry's life begins at the very beginning of your pregnancy. I first encountered these reasons in a surprising source: a fascinating book called *When Did I Begin?*, published in 1991 by Norman Ford, a Jesuit priest. By closely examining the biological facts about embryogenesis, Ford casts considerable doubt on the Super Early Larry View—the view that he existed as a one-cell zygote and onward. Ford's views have been found convincing by Olson and quite a few other philosophers, but don't seem to have made their way into mainstream thinking about the beginning of life.

One reason for doubting a Super Early entry point for Larry has to do with the first few days of embryogenesis. The one, unified, continuous individual that is Larry can't have its beginning in the first few days if there is no single, unified individual in the first few days. And arguably there isn't. The rapidly multiplying cells (two, then four, then eight, etc.) are much like marbles in a bag, the bag being the zona pellucida that was once the wall of the egg. That's all the unity they have, says Ford: being together in the bag. The cells aren't part of a multicellular organism yet, because they don't work together to do the usual things organisms do, such as obtain nutrition from the environment. The cells divide, so there are more of them, but the collection doesn't grow in volume. Philosophers Barry Smith and Berit Brogaard point out that the collection also has no defense system to maintain stability. If one cell is plucked out, it's simply gone.

As it turns out, the cells may actually have a *little* more unity than a bag of marbles. Recent research in embryogenesis (see Pearson in the Bibliography) suggests the dividing cells may not be quite so jumbled. In fact, the collection of cells may even have axes—a top and a bottom, a back and a front. One researcher has suggested that the axes are determined by the exact point where the sperm penetrated the egg. However, this sort of unity may not be enough to make the collection of cells count as a unified organism. At this point the conceptus has the spacial unity of a flock of birds, not the functional unity of an organism that gets nourished, grows, and maintains its stability. And perhaps that's not really surprising. After all, the cells are very special. Each one of them, just like the original one-cell zygote, can initiate a separate fetus. If this happens when there are two cells, you will have twins; if when there are four cells, you will have quadruplets, and so on.

In fact, when there is actual twinning, instead of only potential twinning, the case against the Super Early Larry View becomes especially compelling—even irrefutable. Suppose Larry has an identical twin named Barry. We can imagine the twinning happening at the two-cell stage, though most twinning happens later. Two processes of embryogenesis ensue, one starting from cell A and one from cell B. A is a distinct entity from B, and Larry at one month will be a distinct entity from Barry at one month. But then, that means Larry doesn't start life as the zygote, because if he did, Barry would have too, and we'd get a contradiction. Larry is not Barry. But suppose Larry was the zygote and Barry was the zygote too. Then Larry would be Barry. He would be *and* he wouldn't be. That being impossible, we have to conclude that when actual twinning takes place, each twin does not start life as a zygote. The zygote is merely a precursor of Larry (and a precursor of Barry), but doesn't *become* Larry (or Barry).

Most of us don't have monozygotic twins, so we shouldn't make too much of the argument from twinning. But let's return to singleton Larry. There is a pretty strong case that he doesn't exist as a two-, four-, eight-, or sixteen-cell conceptus, because that's a collection of things, not a unified individual; and so he also doesn't exist any earlier, as a zygote. But what about a little later, on days four, five, or six, for example? To think about this question, we need a few more facts about embryogenesis.

The cluster of cells keeps dividing within the zona pellucida, which is the outer shell left over from the egg, and can't expand much. Thus, the cells get progressively smaller. Then, on about the fourth day after conception, the outermost cells (about one hundred of them) start to become compacted, so that there's an outer layer of flattened cells, the trophoblast, and a fluid-filled cavity in the middle. Within the cavity, at one pole, the embryoblast or inner cell mass (a mere twelve cells) forms. With these changes, the conceptus has become a blastocyst. Then, on day five, another major change takes place: the blastocyst hatches out of the zona pellucida. Without that constricting sac, the blastocyst immediately starts growing, and the inner cell mass starts differentiating. Some of it, in combination with the trophoblast, will become the placenta, amniotic sac, and other support structures, but most of it will go into making the fetal body. On about day six, the blastocyst completes its journey through the fallopian tube and implants in the uterine wall.

With that general picture in place, take the blastocyst on day four, with its outer trophoblast shell and its inner embryoblast. If the collection of cells that existed earlier was a mere collection, and not Larry, is the blastocyst enough of a unified system to count as an organism, so that it could be the earliest incarnation of Larry? Certainly it has much more unity than a bag of marbles, but it doesn't have *all* the earmarks of an organism. It still doesn't grow (because of the constricting zona pellucida), and still doesn't have a way of maintaining its own stability. But there's another reason to wonder whether the blastocyst is the beginning of Larry. The blastocyst contains the makings of *both* the later embryo *and* all of its support structures. In fact, 85 percent of the blastocyst will turn into support structures and just 15 percent will turn into the fetus. If the blastocyst at four days continues on as *something*, it continues on as the totality of the fetus *plus* its support structures. It doesn't continue on as the fetus alone. If Larry your five-year-old traces back to the mature fetus on its own, and the mature fetus on its own *doesn't* trace back to the whole blastocyst, then Larry doesn't trace back to the whole blastocyst.

But couldn't we say the fetus traces back to a *part* of the blastocyst—the embryoblast (also known as the inner cell mass)? No, we really couldn't, for reasons that have to do with the geography of the embryoblast. The embryoblast will develop partly into the fetus, but also partly into the fetal support system. What's missing from the embryoblast on day four is complete differentiation. There's partial differentiation, but that's all. With only partial differentiation, the rudimentary fetus and rudimentary support structures are still somewhat merged together; thus, there is nothing that can be singled out and identified as the earliest incarnation

of the mature fetus; and consequently, nothing that can be identified with Larry your child.

Now, this reasoning assumes Larry your five-year-old traces
back to the fetus *alone*, and not the fetus-plus-support-structures.
And that's at least initially quite plausible. It's natural to think he was
once just the *resident* of an amniotic sac, nourished by a placenta,
much like as a five-year-old he'll be just the resident of your house,
and nourished by the refrigerator. But you might think differently
about this. To defend a Super Early View, on which Larry starts off
as the blastocyst, you might say that Larry traces back to the fetus
plus its support structures. He was once an entity with an amniotic
sac and placenta as parts, in contrast with how five-year-old Larry
will never have your refrigerator as a part. Pressing the idea further,
you could say that the organs of mature mammals are "under the
skin," but the organs of immature mammals are not. These external
parts of Larry are shed at birth, like later in life he will shed finger-
nails, hair, and dead skin cells. It's not common sense that we have
an amniotic sac, a placenta, and so on, as parts of ourselves when we
are very, very young, but it's not out of the question.

Around fourteen days after conception, when the primitive
streak develops (the first sign of an emerging spinal cord), full differentiation has taken place: a distinct part of the embryo is fetal and
other parts are support structures. The later fetus, taken as separate
from support structures, can thus be traced back to the fetal *part* of
the fourteen-day-old embryo. If you regard Larry as *just* a fetus, and
believe the support structures are *never* a part of him, you can trace
him back as far as about fourteen days, but no earlier. Before then, the
conceptus is a fusion of fetal and support structures, so there is no
part of it that can be identified with Larry in his most primitive form.

So it looks like there are two coherent stories here: one where
Larry begins to exist as a whole blastocyst at about four days and

later has the placenta, amniotic sac, and so on, as temporary parts, to be later shed; and one where Larry begins to exist as *part* of the implanted embryo at fourteen days, and never at any point has the placenta, and so on, as parts. But there is no coherent story where Larry is the conceptus on days one, two, or three. I conclude that Larry starts to exist as roughly a four- to fourteen-day-old embryo, but certainly not as the zygote on day one. In the style of Charles Dickens, Larry's life story would begin: not "*I am born*," but rather, "*I am a slightly developed embryo.*"

PREGNANCY LOSS

Our topic is not abortion, since I'm presuming that you, dear reader, are deliberately pregnant and eager to become a parent. But miscarriages happen, and miscarriages can make us feel both devastated and puzzled (though mostly devastated). What have we lost, when we've lost an embryo or fetus? Well, we've lost the future we hoped for, at least temporarily; that much is clear. But what was the nature of the entity that is gone? This chapter's theoretical perambulations have a bearing on that question.

If there was no fetal organism before day four or perhaps day fourteen, then some extremely early miscarriages (many happen before we even know we're pregnant) stop a life from beginning, as opposed to ending a life that has barely begun. A very early miscarriage of a very young embryo is not literally the loss of a child-to-be, because a child-to-be didn't exist yet and thus couldn't be lost. An extremely early miscarriage can be mourned to the extent that it dashes hopes (at least temporarily), but it's not the loss of a life that has already started.

Of course, most miscarriages occur after the first fourteen days of gestation. According to the Early Larry view, these miscarriages *do* involve the ending of a life that has already begun. Yet in the first weeks of the first trimester, it has barely begun. Larry, at that point, is certainly not yet a baby, child, or adult; in fact, he is not yet a person (on a definition of personhood anything like Baker's) and not yet a conscious self. But yes, a life has begun—a being already exists who will *later* be a self, a person, a child, an adult, if the pregnancy continues.

With such a mixed description of an embryo or fetus, you would clearly need to do much more to arrive at a view about miscarriage or the ethics of abortion. All I have tried to do here is address a very basic question we find ourselves thinking about, as we go through pregnancy. What am I seeing in that ultrasound image at eight weeks; who or what is kicking at eighteen weeks? Is it merely a fetal organism, or is it the child I will later hold and cuddle and walk to school? A full defense would take much more space, but the best answer may very well be: the child—but the child prior to entering that special phase of life when he or she will have become a self or a person.

Fast-forward now to nine months after conception. It's time for baby to be born. Would a philosophical parent prefer natural childbirth, even at the price of greater pain? Or is that downright irrational?

Chapter 6

A Child Is Born

Is labor pain simply awful?

The philosophical parent isn't philosophical every moment of every day. As the day of a baby's arrival gets closer, expectant mothers and fathers are bound to be feeling many things: excitement, apprehension, boredom, discomfort, impatience, joy. Before birth there may also be reflection about the events to come—the great unknown, for those who haven't given birth before. In fact, there needs to be reflection. Parents-to-be have to make decisions about the birth process that involve first-class philosophical questions. One of these unavoidable questions is about pain.

According to a very simple view of what has value, pain is bad and pleasure is good; they're bad and good because of the way they feel. So far, not so controversial. But the account of value I'm referring to says something more exciting: it says pain is the *only* thing that's intrinsically bad, and pleasure is the *only* thing that's intrinsically good. On this view of value, the ideal delivery is not only painless for the mother, but joyous—mentally pleasurable—and will have no negative impact on the baby, in the present or the future.

For the majority of women, painless delivery does seem to be the ideal. Most elect epidural anesthesia, hoping to reduce pain as much as possible while remaining alert and involved throughout the delivery. A minority, however, see it otherwise. They think there could be something amiss with a perfectly pain-controlled delivery, even assuming mother and baby came out of it healthy. These are women who opt for natural childbirth and would *still* do so even if *all* worries about infant health were wiped away. (Let's set aside concerns about infant health, which must enter decision-making, of course.)

What about these women? Can their priorities be reconciled with the view that pleasure and pain are all that matter? Are these women irrational? Do they deliberately subject themselves to more bad and less good than necessary? Or do those who favor natural childbirth want things worth wanting, but things other than having more pleasure and less pain?

These questions about value are important ones that philosophers have explored for a couple of thousand years, but as the big day comes nearer, *you* have decisions to make. You must formulate a "birth plan," letting your doctor know how much pain relief you want to be offered. For you, then, it's urgent: What really matters, when it comes to having a good birth? Does it make sense to care about anything besides the best possible outcome for your baby and the most enjoyable possible experience for yourself?

WHAT IS IT LIKE?

I have framed the birth puzzle in terms of pain avoidance, but in fact, for the longest time I wasn't quite sure whether labor was actually painful. As a child I asked my mother about it many times, and got a rather hard-to-follow story about a frantic rush to the hospital and the feeling of a powerful vacuum cleaner sucking me out of her body. "Yes, but did it hurt?" I would ask over and over again, but I never got a plain answer.

In the movies, women scream their way through childbirth, but is that just a cliché? Following natural childbirth, my friend Susan spoke of an amazing experience. "Did it hurt?" I asked. She steadfastly refused to say that it did, though she let on that the experience was a challenge. On the other hand, a close friend called from Atlanta, still traumatized the day after her first child was born. After fourteen hours of fruitless labor, Jenny had needed to be "induced" with the drug Pitocin, and she eventually had an epidural. The tale of the lead-up to pain relief so consumed her twenty-four hours later that she was still talking much more about the ordeal than about her baby.

After a few months of pregnancy, I was still open to the possibility of natural childbirth, but my ob-gyn set me straight. I would have to have an epidural to be ready just in case anything went wrong. If the delivery became problematic, the epidural would allow for a quick C-section. Many obstetricians insist on Caesarean deliveries for twins, so I was grateful I was at least going to attempt a traditional birth.

At twenty-seven weeks (two months early) I went into premature labor and was ordered to check in to the hospital—for good. Two weeks later, my contractions started up again and I spent the morning in Labor and Delivery receiving a cocktail of powerful labor-inhibiting drugs to stop the process. My doctor kept making trips between my room and the adjacent one where someone was giving birth. Unfortunately, she forgot to close the two doors in between.

The woman in the next room was an Orthodox Jew and this was Saturday, the Sabbath. Earlier she had thought her baby was on the way, so she and her husband had come to the hospital on foot, because of Sabbath rules. Unfortunately they had come too soon and had been sent home. When the woman returned to the hospital, she took a taxi, but her husband didn't have a medical problem himself, so he had had to walk to the rabbi's house to ask if he could take a taxi as well. Unfortunately, the husband hadn't made it to the hospital on time. So there was special stress involved in this birth.

I have never heard a more harrowing sound than this woman's screams. It was the howling of an animal, the scream of someone being cut in two with a saw. In my childbirth class, which I attended only once before my incarceration, I had been introduced to the technique of imaging. Each woman was given a laminated photograph of a beach or a mountain scene. We were taught about relaxation and breathing. Could this woman's ordeal have been alleviated by a present and attentive husband, a photograph, and deep breathing? I would think not, and my doctor was skeptical too.

So yes, natural childbirth can be very painful. What does it tell us that people choose to go through it? That they don't anticipate the pain that awaits them? That they have made a rational calculation that they will enjoy the greatest balance of pleasure over pain even if they pass up pain medication? That people are irrational? Or that things matter to people besides pain and pleasure?

The woman in the next room was giving birth to her sixth child, so I don't think she opted for natural childbirth out of ignorance. Nor—to be clear—is there any religious mandate for Orthodox Jews to avoid pain medication. Do those who choose natural birth think the pleasures of unmedicated birth will exceed the pain, making them pleasure maximizers after all? This could be their thought, but I doubt it. Rather, they appear to attach value to things *other* than pain and pleasure. They put up with pain because they must, to secure something they regard as tremendously important. But what?

No, I wasn't pondering such questions at the time of my early labor; I was too agitated due to the drugs I had been given, and too preoccupied with whether I was going to deliver two extremely premature babies. And I was starting to be flat-out terrified of giving birth down the road—hopefully a long way down the road. But later on I thought some more about the pain question. Why would *anyone* put up with more pain, if they could have less?

THE GOOD BIRTH

Before taking a stab at an answer, let's consider a piece of evidence that people do care about things besides obtaining pleasure and avoiding pain. The evidence is provided by the way people would choose between ordinary life and a certain hypothetical life dreamed up by the philosopher Robert Nozick. Suppose that instead of going on with your life as usual, you had a chance to plug into an "experience machine"—a machine that "fed" your brain a virtual reality that induced extreme happiness. Though you would really be lying on a table connected to the computer by hundreds of wires, you'd feel as if you were climbing Mt. Everest, or winning the Nobel Prize, or swimming with dolphins. And these particular experiences wouldn't be foisted upon you: before you plugged in, you would have a chance to order up exactly the virtual reality that you desired. It all sounds quite enticing, but despite being given the chance to experience the life of their dreams, Nozick says most people wouldn't plug in. He thinks this demonstrates two things: that most of us *don't* just care about pain and pleasure, or happiness and misery; and that we *do* care about something else—namely, contact with reality.

In Nozick's thought experiment, pleasure comes from a computer-generated virtual reality instead of from real life. But Nozick could have revealed the same truths—that we care about pleasure but also about contact with reality—using a thought experiment involving drugs instead of virtual reality. Suppose you were offered a choice between going on with life as usual and going on while receiving a continual, steady dose of a drug I will call "Happy All the Time" (HAT, for short). HAT would keep you feeling good no matter what. On HAT, you would feel happy if you burned the toast; happy if your dog died; happy if your leg was mangled in the lawnmower; happy if your house burned down.

In Nozick's original thought experiment, your choice is between a happier life swimming with virtual dolphins and an ordinary life, where the dolphins are real but the water is painfully cold. In the HAT thought experiment, you get real dolphins and real cold water, but the cold water makes you happy, like everything else does. If you wouldn't opt for HAT, that shows you don't care only about pain and pleasure, happiness and misery, but it shows more. The best available explanation seems to be that we would reject HAT because we care about contact with reality. A person who is happy despite his beloved dog dying is not really in contact with his dog dying, or is at least in much less contact—he would probably think about the death much less and not notice as many features of it. You might even say the HAT user doesn't perceive the badness of the death, like a color-blind person doesn't see the redness of an apple.

What does this have to do with natural childbirth? Well, a perfectly effective epidural is a bit like short-term HAT—it's like HAT for the period of time when your child is being born. And like HAT, an epidural reduces contact with at least some aspects of the birth process. It stops a woman from registering every millimeter of cervical dilation, every inch of the baby's journey out into the world, every bit of pressure on surrounding organs and bones, every single tear. An epidural allows a woman to focus happily on her baby emerging and to be unaware of the various costs to her body of that emergence. The fact that some women do choose natural childbirth shows the same thing as Nozick's famous thought experiment: we care about more than just pain and pleasure; we also care about having contact with reality.

If at least most of us do want contact with reality—we wouldn't hook up to the experience machine or go permanently on HAT—and natural childbirth offers more contact, then why doesn't everyone choose it? The answer, I think, is that they actually do—up to a point. Most women choose a *more* natural type of childbirth than they would, if pain avoidance were the only consideration. I don't know of any women who would want to be knocked out for the duration of the delivery; and most would rather not be completely numb from the waist down. Many don't want to be draped so that the goings-on are concealed from view. Mothers want to experience childbirth in a first-person fashion; they want to experience it as happening in their own bodies, not in the third-person way their partners do. Since pain relief reduces the experience of the birth process, just about everyone is concerned to avoid excessive, contact-obliterating medication.

What's distinctive about the 10 percent or so who choose completely natural childbirth is not what they value—they value what everyone values—but the unusual way they weigh avoiding pain versus maintaining contact. They prioritize contact with birth realities over pain avoidance much more consistently than the other 90 percent do. Natural birth choosers want to be first-person aware of *every* aspect of the birth process, even if painfully aware, whereas others are satisfied to be first-person aware of the key events. Or at least this describes many of them. Others choose natural childbirth for health reasons, not to secure a certain sort of experience for themselves; they believe epidurals can have a negative impact on a baby's health (a possibility I am setting aside here).

Anesthesia during surgery obliterates all awareness that you are having surgery—you lose contact with the truth that your gall bladder is being cut out of your abdomen. Analgesia afterwards obliterates awareness that you have a fresh incision and discombobulated internal organs—you lose contact with those realities. An epidural during delivery provides an appealing sort of pain control partly because it preserves *some* awareness—but not awareness of every single thing that's going on. Gone is the perception of most of the pressure and stretching, the tears and abrasions. But what if a perfectly awareness-preserving epidural were available, one that obliterated none of the goings on, but merely converted pain to nonpain or even to pleasure?

When I was discussing HAT, I said you can't *really* be in contact with the fact that your beloved dog died, if HAT makes you happy about it. A happy reaction to his death is like seeing carrots as being blue—it's a misperception, a departure from reality. Can you really be in full contact with the fact that an eight-pound baby is coming out of your body if you're aware of every aspect of her emergence, including the rips and tears, but the awareness is entirely pain free? Arguably, perfect pain relief, even if perfectly awareness preserving, would have to rob a person of *some* contact with reality, like HAT robs you of contact when it makes you respond joyfully or neutrally to your dog's premature demise. So we should expect those who choose natural birth to reject not just real-world pain relief, which reduces awareness as well as pain, but also perfect pain relief, the imaginary kind that preserves perfect awareness but only eliminates pain itself.

OTHER VALUES

Is preferring natural childbirth all about valuing contact? No, it's more complicated. Some women want birth to be natural—vaginal, and fully experienced from beginning to end—because they value sheer naturalness. Granted, they don't prioritize naturalness always—they let the dentist numb them before pulling teeth, for example—but they think childbirth in particular is worth preserving in its most raw state.

Again, valuing "the natural" to some degree is common—even nearly universal. For all of us, there's *something* we'd reject for being excessively artificial. Most of us wouldn't want our babies grown in artificial laboratory wombs, even if that were just as safe for baby and mother. Women want to experience pregnancy, and it's hard to think of a reason besides the fact that for humans, pregnancy is simply part of the way nature works. We most likely wouldn't want to carry babies inside of us if the normal form of pregnancy for our species were spawning outside our bodies, like fish do. Men don't seem to be in any hurry to find a way to gestate babies, even if women value that experience. Why not? Maybe because it's natural for women to carry babies, but not for men.

There's a third thing that natural-birth choosers want. This came home to me after talking to a colleague of my husband's. A high-level executive, she exuded strength and competence when she talked first about being a runner and then about delivering her two boys without drugs. The pride and confidence in her voice when she told the story hinted at what it meant to her. Natural childbirth was an accomplishment for her, perhaps like running a marathon. Most runners wouldn't take drugs that blotted out all the experience of pain and struggle during a race, and likewise it was out of the question for her to opt for medicated delivery.

If you think of birth as something you will *do*, rather than merely undergo, and you want to do it well—if mastery of the whole thing is one of your goals—then natural childbirth may be what you choose, assuming there are no special circumstances like carrying multiples. And this is not terribly singular; there are times when mastery is important to us all. We want to make it through *some* part of life on our own steam. What's distinctive about women who opt for natural birth isn't the value they attach to mastery but the importance it has to them in this particular context.

BIRTH STORY (ABRIDGED)

In fact, the labor-stalling drugs did work, and I made it all the way to thirty-six weeks, which is considered full term for twins. My daughter emerged easily. My son was in line behind her, but he had spent the last two months of my pregnancy doing somersaults. I know this to be true because the daily fetal monitoring while I was in the hospital showed that his head was sometimes on my left side and sometimes on the right. He'd gotten himself tangled up in his umbilical cord, and my doctor couldn't get him untangled. Thanks to her foresight, it was a simple matter to ramp up the drugs coming through my epidural. It was only then that I did feel numb from the waist down. A screen was put over my middle so I wouldn't have to watch myself getting sliced open. Twenty minutes after our daughter, our son came into the world, just as big and healthy as she was.

The epidural did cause me to have less contact with all of the realities of the birth process. I didn't feel every single element of my daughter's arrival, and of course didn't feel my son's arrival at all—didn't even see it because of the screen. Some would say I missed out because of the epidural that reduced pain to such a low level during my daughter's birth. I had more contact than my husband did, since I experienced her birth firsthand and he experienced it as a spectator. But I had less contact than someone going through natural birth. I was aware of a lot less of the process. Then again, for the sake of more contact, I don't think I would have wanted more pain, nor would I have wanted a more risky delivery for my son. As much as I do care about naturalness and athleticism in some contexts, I didn't care much about them in that context—not enough to tolerate more pain or risk.

KAYAKS AND BOATS

I had the great pleasure of touring the waters of Resurrection Bay, in Alaska, several years ago. It was exquisite seeing glaciers up close, and whales, puffins, bears, and sheep in the distance. Sea kayakers in the area got even closer to the ice and the animals. I know what they were thinking of us on our comfortable boat. I know it because I've done my share of long-distance bicycling, backpacking, and canoeing. They were thinking we weren't really enjoying the scenery the way they were. On the other hand, from our boat, the kayakers looked like they were freezing to death in the steady drizzle. We on the boat knew we were having a lot more fun.

The boaters and kayakers are wrong in their assessment of each other, but right about one thing: they wouldn't want to trade places. Put a kayaker on the boat, and she will feel overly pampered and cut off from the thrills of being close to the water and the ice. Put a boater on a kayak, and she will feel so cold and exhausted she won't enjoy the calving glaciers.

It's the same way with women with divergent birth plans. The natural crowd imagines women going through an unnatural birth as missing out. Those who choose medication think women going through natural birth must be missing out. But women approach the birth experience with different priorities. It's not so much that they have different values, but that they assign different weights to their various values, and give them highest priority in different contexts. For example, athleticism and mastery pertain to childbirth a great deal for some, and not so much for others. Seeking authenticity and primordial experience matters to some when it comes to childbirth; for others this is as unimaginable as seeking primordial experience in the context of dentistry.

Undeniably, there are ways for things to go wrong. On the boat, some people were so preoccupied with their cameras that they didn't completely enjoy the glaciers. Some were too nauseated by the swells to look around. The tempting food inside the boat diverted attention from the gorgeous scenery. Closer to nature in a kayak, the headwinds can be horrid, the cold rain overwhelming. You can spend your time just wishing you were home and dry. You can choose a kayak when you should have chosen a boat, and vice versa. Obvious moral: you need to think carefully about where you put yourself so that you're in the place you really want to be. All the more so on the momentous occasion of your child's birth.

I have never met a woman who didn't love to tell her birth story. I would love to hear the Orthodox woman tell hers. I bet she would tell it completely differently than I have. Maybe it has comic elements in her telling—the two trips to the hospital, the consultation with the rabbi as she gave birth—and maybe her agony is heroic or operatic in the retelling. Maybe the birth didn't feel to her anything like it sounded to me.

Whatever birth was really like for her, it's her story, and I suspect she wouldn't trade it for any other. After all, that was the day when she got to meet her child, and that—finally having our new baby in our arms—is what matters most.

Chapter 7

Whose Child Is This?

Why do biological parents have prerogatives?

You've decided to have a child, conceived and gestated her, and given birth. Now what? You hold your child, gaze upon her in awe, feed her, kiss her—*her*, the child you gave birth to. It's so important that you do all these things with the right child that every baby wears an identification bracelet in the hospital nursery, and mix-ups are regarded as a total fiasco.

Are mix-ups really a fiasco? Most people think so, including the very rare person who is involved in one. Sue McDonald and Marti Miller were both born in Wisconsin in 1951, and raised in the same small town. Mary Miller, who gave birth to Sue, suspected a mix-up when she brought her new baby home from the hospital and found she weighed two pounds less than she did at birth. Mary Miller hadn't actually seen the baby that came out of her uterus because she had given birth under full anesthesia—a common practice at the time. The baby had accidentally been left in the delivery room when Kay McDonald gave birth—and was accidentally interchanged with the second baby. Mary Miller's husband didn't want her to make a fuss and embarrass their doctor, so he asked her to put her suspicions aside. Then Mary suffered a serious illness, which put the possible mix-up in the background. Blond, bouncy Marti didn't fit well into the large Miller family, who were all dark-haired, serious, artistic, and fervently religious. Dark-haired and introverted, Sue didn't fit well into the smaller McDonald family, who were blond, cheerful, and outgoing. It took Mary Miller over forty years to become convinced of her doubts and to reveal to Sue and Marti that their biological parents weren't who they thought they were.

As much as history took precedence by that point, and the parent-child pairings didn't change, there was emotional pain all around. Speaking to Jake Halpern, the journalist who reported this story for the National Public Radio show *This American Life* in 2008, Kay McDonald said this about Mary Miller:

> If I had as strong a feeling as she did that I had the wrong baby, I would have pursued it. I don't care whether my husband objected or not. I feel like I should have made a wrong into a right. I only had this one daughter. And she had five daughters. In fact, we weren't even sure we'd have another child. So, of course, we were elated when I did get pregnant. And then to think that I didn't get to raise the one that I had wanted so much.

The way she expresses herself makes it clear she didn't simply want *a* child, she wanted the particular child she had carried for nine months—and she says this despite loving the child she raised and being very clear in her mind that *that* one is now her daughter.

Some say no, such mix-ups aren't especially tragic. They think we only care so much about "the right child" being paired with "the right parent" because of spurious and harmful ideas about biological ties. If you take home a child you didn't give birth to, they say, nothing has gone seriously wrong, apart from the inevitable confusion about the child's medical history. They think attaching importance to biology has a multitude of negative ramifications, especially for parents who want to adopt and children who would be better off being adopted. Thoroughgoing skeptics about biological ties think children are basically interchangeable.

We will come to the skeptics in chapter 8, but here I'll assume that common sense is correct. Biological parents are the presumptive custodians of the specific children they bring into the world. It's with good reason that hospitals now take greater care to avoid mix-ups. Furthermore, I'll assume that biological parents have prerogatives even when they are in competition with other potential caregivers, and even when a case can be made that the others would make better parents. The very strong presumption is that children grow up wherever they land, not where it would have been better for them to land.

The idea that babies should be awarded to the best available parent, not left with their progenitors, has often been acted upon, either explicitly or implicitly. Often it has been young, unmarried mothers who were forced to give up their offspring, "for the good of the child." Heartbreaking stories of maternal loss are collected in Ann Fessler's book *The Girls Who Went Away,* an oral history of the thousands of young women who disappeared into homes for unwed mothers prior to the sexual revolution and feminist movement of the 1960s and 1970s. Pressure and deception were often involved in separating these women from their children, whether implicitly or explicitly. Recounting their loss, the biological mothers speak of an anguish that never completely goes away.

If you agree that biological parents are entitled to their offspring, you might think these prerogatives are so obvious as to be beyond explanation or analysis. It's simply natural and self-evident that a new mother is entitled to the newborn child who emerged from her body. But let's not abandon the stance of the philosophical parent, even here. What is the best explanation why it matters which baby goes home with which parents? Why do biological parents have the prerogative to raise the child they brought into the world?

In a nutshell, the best explanation seems to be this: children are second selves of the people they come from (a notion I first introduced in chapter 1). A mix-up would split you from yourself, or a part of yourself. If the babies get mixed up, you might nevertheless regard the changeling (so to speak) as a second self, but you would see yourself as mistaken, if and when the facts came to light. The baby you gave birth to is the one you *meant* to regard as a second self. Because of a particular baby's ties to you, that baby and no other should be brought to your room. And not only that—of course. Your desire to raise that baby must normally be respected, even if a potentially better caregiver is waiting in the wings. (We'll come back to "better off elsewhere" scenarios in chapter 8, looking at a number of examples.)

A lot rides on this notion of children being part of their parents' wider identities. Does it *really* make sense? Does it really help make sense of which children belong with which parents? To begin with, we need to get a grip on the talk of "second selves." A mother who has just given birth to a child sees that child as a self or as part of herself. Which means . . . what? We need to know in more detail, because the thought that a child is another self has many manifestations over time. It's relevant to which child you bring home and also to how we raise our children (as I will argue in chapter 9).

LIKE A SELF

So what does it mean for a particular child to be a sort of second self, to me? What is self-like about this child here, and not self-like (to me) about that child there?

One thing is striking, especially in the fullness of time: *parental generosity.* We don't hesitate to pay for our children's diapers, food, medical care, clothes, toys, school fees, and so on. Of course there are pathological and atypical cases—abusive and neglectful parents who do much less for their kids than for themselves. But it's fair to say that the typical parent does for the child what he would do for himself. I say "or more" because some children need more. This is abundantly clear in Andrew Solomon's *Far from the Tree,* a well-researched and comprehensive book about parents with special-needs children. The devotion of these parents is captured in hundreds of vignettes involving children with autism, blindness, deafness, and many other differences.

When I do things for my child, there is *no quality of altruism*—I don't glow with the satisfaction of giving to others. I vividly recall one afternoon helping to load a Salvation Army truck with used clothing after Hurricane Katrina (the truck would take supplies from Dallas to New Orleans). It's another thing altogether to spend the afternoon buying badly needed supplies for one's own child, which feels barely more altruistic than spending the afternoon buying supplies for oneself.

I expect that readers with children will agree. I even suspect that the hard-working, unbelievably devoted parents in Solomon's book will agree that they are not engaged in self-sacrifice when they care for their children. It's true that they give up a great deal—money, sometimes careers, sometimes personal happiness, sometimes their marriages. But from the way they talk about their children, I surmise that they experience their devotion as not so different from devotion to self; it's not like devotion to a complete other. Caring for one's own child with autism is not at all like being a hard-working volunteer at a school for children with autism. The volunteer is altruistic, but that is not the right way to characterize the parent.

Another part of the parental state of mind is that I am *anxious about the survival* of my child in much the way I am anxious about my own survival. It is common wisdom that nothing is so devastating as the death of our own child. We fear losing a child in at least roughly the same way we fear losing our own lives. I say "roughly" because of course there *are* differences. I once had a close encounter with a bear—a very large brown bear—deep in the woods of the Grand Tetons in Wyoming. I was closest to the bear, my husband was further up the trail, and furthest away were my two children. The primitive fear of being attacked was, in the first instance, a fear of *me* being attacked (I cannot tell a lie!), but all the effort I put into avoiding that fate was an effort to protect the four of us.

The flip side of being anxious about a child's death is being *gratified by a child's life*. My child's continuing to live after me makes my own death easier to face, giving me something of the feeling I would have upon learning I will have another several decades myself. Again, this is not a neat equation. Facing a terminal illness and eventual death, it's not true that all the terror is erased by the thought that your children will survive you. Not by a long shot. But knowing your children will go on living has some power to make you think you will not be entirely absent from the world. And this has to mean that a child has a sort of self-like significance, from his or her parents' perspective.

And then there is the fact that we *feel our children's feelings*. Anyone who has watched their child stumble in a school performance will know how close to true it can be that "I feel your pain." I say *close* to true, because the contagion isn't 100 percent, and it varies depending on the emotion. If *she's* the one in the dentist chair, getting a shot of Novocain, you may catch her anxiety, but you won't feel a painful prick in your jaw muscle. Then again, you will probably have all of the higher-order thoughts she has—the thoughts about that pain. You want it to end, you want it not to be repeated—and you can feel those desires as intensely as your child does. By the same token, we feel our children's happiness and excitement. A child's excitement over newly fallen snow quickly becomes our excitement. A child's enjoyment of a good storybook becomes our enjoyment.

The next central facet of the parental mindset is that, with the passage of time, it becomes striking *how little we compete* with our kids. If my daughter is prettier than me and scores higher on the SATs, I'm delighted! A man playing tennis with his son will take pleasure in the points he scores *and* the points his son scores. No doubt there are exceptions and degrees, but it seems for the most part true that we are noncompetitive with our children. This makes children self-like, because of course we are completely noncompetitive with ourselves, and at least competitive to some degree with most other people.

And then there is the parent's experience of *pride and shame.* Logically, we can only take pride in what is owing to our own efforts, or at least has a close connection our own selves. I can be proud of my lovely ears—they're my ears! I can be proud of how fast or long I ran this morning—it was my effort. Pride is in what is "self," not "other." That makes it something of a puzzle why parents are proud of their children—in fact, pride being one of the most sustained and pleasant parts of parenthood—even when their accomplishments are completely independent of parental effort. Why, for example, am I proud of my daughter's singing ability, given that I did nothing deliberate to create it and not even much to encourage it? It solves that puzzle to recognize that children are self-like, or part of our "extended self." Pride in our children indicates that the parental state of mind is an attitude toward a *sort* of second self. And in just the opposite way, we are ashamed of our children's failures in a particularly acute way. A child's "F" in math isn't just an "F," it's in some sense *our* "F."

Finally, there is the parental experience of *inflation*. Everyone thinks their own children are unusually attractive and remarkably gifted, in some way or another. This is one of the things that keeps us going through all the stresses and strains of parenthood—we are doing all this for such a marvelous five- or ten- or fifteen-year-old! Here we have something like the excessive love we feel for ourselves, but squared or cubed. Parents seem to inflate the virtues of their children even more than the virtues of themselves. Maybe egotism is at the root of it, but ordinary egotism—about oneself—is balanced by self-criticism. Egotism extended outward, to one's children, is mostly appreciative. "My child is amazing!"

All these feelings make the response to one's own child unique. We don't feel parental toward everything we love—our cars and plants, our dogs and cats, or even toward our friends and siblings. Notably, we are more competitive with a sibling and less proud; we feel a sibling's feelings less; we are generous with a sibling, but not usually *as* generous as we are with our own child or children. Doing something for a sister or brother does have a bit of the flavor of altruism, or at least more so than doing something for a child.

The parental state of mind is aimed at our offspring because children come from us in such a way that there are many kinds of continuity linking parent and child. No doubt it's also central to development of the parental state of mind that children come from us at a point in their development and ours when they are utterly dependent and we are capable of taking care of them. And it's central, as well, that the age difference between parents and children makes it highly likely that children will survive parents by several decades. Given the basic biology of parenthood—reproductive "coming from," dependence, and age difference—a parental state of mind is likely to develop. At least, this is the case in humans; I make no claims here about other species.

When a parent lacks the parental state of mind, there is often a specific reason why it's missing. In societies with high infant mortality rates, people may delay allowing themselves the attitudes I've just sketched. In societies that are sexist, parents may have these attitudes toward boys more than toward girls. Among the very poor in some societies, there's a tendency to exploit children for labor. Statistics show that in the United States, very low-income parents are vastly more prone to neglecting and abusing their children than low-income parents. Single parents are at greater risk of neglecting and abusing their children, and so are parents with many, many kids. Contraception is a factor too. Cultures that practice child abandonment, like ancient Rome, are cultures without reliable contraception. There is also more abandonment when it's considered a travesty to have children outside of marriage; famously, Jean-Jacques Rousseau abandoned five children he had with his mistress.

In all these settings where the parental state of mind doesn't fully form, it is nevertheless not altogether absent. Bad mothers are intermittently also good mothers. Rousseau had later regrets about his children, writing in *Emile*, "He who cannot fulfill the duties of a father has no right to become one." The Romans, who had no compunction about abandoning their children, loved plays and stories about parents being reunited with their children.

THE CONTENDERS

A child belongs to me, the parent, because she comes from me, making her a sort of second self—or so I have proposed. This is the heart of the matter—the main reason why a particular child is brought to my hospital room after delivery, and why I get to bring that child home. But there's more to it. It almost goes without saying, but needs to be said: when biological parents have a child, the newborn child doesn't come into the world from anyone but them—at least, in the way that makes a child self-like. Thus, the biological parent's claim to the child isn't in competition with anyone else's claim. Nobody else even begins to have a claim to the child. Furthermore, it almost goes without saying, you get to take the baby home because the baby needs a caregiver. When your child reaches the age of majority, your parental rights will diminish. Your child will be able to live where he pleases and make all of his own decisions. So there are three crucial factors here: you get to take home the baby you gave birth to because: (1) the baby is a part of your wider identity; (2) the baby is available; and (3) the baby needs a caregiver.

As frustrating as it can be for potential adoptive parents, this puts their parental aspirations in the hands of biological parents. Potential adopters certainly *could* come to have the parental attitude toward this child or that child, and actual adoptive parents *do* have all of the attitudes I have discussed. After all, biological conception and gestation aren't necessary conditions for the parental state of mind, as I argued in chapter 1. But no child is available for potential adopters to regard as another self until biological parents make their children available for adoption. A biological parent and a potential adoptive parent who equally see a newborn as a second self aren't in competition with each other, because the baby is available to the biological parent and not to the potential adopter, or at least not yet.

When two biological parents compete for custody, it's more complicated. In most cases, the child *was* available to both of them, and came from both, and constituted part of the extended identity for both. This accounts for each parent having any claim *at all* to the child—I am arguing—but isn't enough to establish an exclusive claim. To resolve disputes between legitimate claimants, other principles have to come into play, but our question is the most basic one: what makes someone even *begin* to have a custody claim? My answer is that those for whom an *available* child is a second self at least begin to have a custody claim. They are contenders. Furthermore, the way children come from their biological parents does have a powerful tendency to make children second selves to their parents. After all, the continuities that connect people to their future selves overlap with the continuities that connect people to their children. People typically *do* regard their offspring as self-like with good reason. This is not to say there's no other way to develop the parental state of mind; people do develop it through adoption, and children continue to "come from" from their parents, in many different ways, after they are born. But the biological connection between parent and child usually forges that connection, at least when certain facilitating conditions are in place.

This story doesn't tell us which *one* person should be awarded custody in case more than one person begins to have prerogatives, but that seems fine. The relevant considerations in family court are undoubtedly complicated. It wouldn't be fine if this story led us to think that custodial prerogatives were ubiquitous—that for every child, there can be dozens of people with prerogatives; and for every adult, there are dozens of individuals with respect to whom they have prerogatives. A bumper crop of prerogatives could be used to construct a reductio ad absurdum of the second-self account, a refutation based on the account's having absurd implications. But is the proliferation of prerogatives inevitable?

David Archard dismisses the second-self account of parental prerogatives in his book *Children*, citing just this worry about overabundance. If my biological child is part of my "wider identity" (to use Robert Nozick's phrase), Archard points out that other things are as well—"for example, friends, place of work and work colleagues, sports team, private club." He then asks, "My rights to choose for myself do not extend to these things, so why should they extend to my children?" Archard suspects the second-self story is really, beneath it all, just a "thinly veiled" version of the view that parents *own* their children (a view we will turn to in a moment).

But is the bumper-crop problem really a problem for the second-self account of parental prerogatives? We don't actually have to say that you get to take custody of your colleagues, not to mention your place of work and sports team, because they don't fulfill the third clause—they don't *need* a caregiver. For the most part, Archard's problem cases can be dismissed because of the need clause, but it's also open to doubt that people really have their friends, place of work, colleagues, and so on, as a part of their wider identity in the way they have their children. A child is vastly more self-like to parents than a colleague is, let alone an office. The various features of someone being self-like are either absent or much reduced, in the case of a colleague. For example, colleagues are competitive with each other in a way that parents and children are not; colleagues take *some* pride in each other, but not to the degree they take pride in their children; colleagues don't have an inflated view of each other's virtues—in some cases, in fact, just the opposite is true. It is only in an extremely rare case that anyone uses the language of second selfhood to talk about their colleagues, and when it happens it's noteworthy how interchangeable that talk is with parental talk: "He was like a father to me," we say, or "She is like a daughter to me."

If we say parents have prerogatives when it comes to their children because their children are second selves, we certainly can't be rigid about this. We have to allow that these prerogatives can be lost, if the parent fails to have the usual parental attitudes and doesn't treat a child well. The prerogatives can be absent from the start—as in the case of someone intent on abandoning or harming or exploiting their newborn baby. But the initial presumption, the starting point, is that parents have a privileged status with respect to their children—their second selves—like they do with respect to themselves.

OWNERSHIP

There are alternative accounts of a biological parent's prerogatives, of course—accounts that revolve around very different concepts. One thing you could conceivably say about parental rights is that parents have a child in something like the way they have a house or car. The child is sheer property: the baby I gave birth to is jointly owned by me and the child's father. And one story we could tell about *why* we own our children is rooted in John Locke's classic account of property ownership. Suppose you gather stones on a public beach and then labor for nine months, creating a statue of a baby. The labor would make Stone Baby yours, says Locke, so long as you left "as much and as good" on the beach for others. Applying Locke to real babies, the idea would be that we come into possession of our children as a result of our bodies contributing crucial ingredients and doing the critical work of growing a baby. (Though this story has Lockean elements, Locke didn't subscribe to it himself; he held the view that children are possessions of God.)

Clearly there are lots of problems with the ownership account of parental prerogatives. To begin with, this account will certainly not recognize much of an ownership right for new fathers. Even the most generous father bears a burden that is a tiny fraction of the mother's. A father-like figure would make an initial contribution to conceiving Stone Baby, but do little of the gathering or building; the statue wouldn't be his nearly as much as the mother-like figure's.

Furthermore, the entire analogy is forced. *You* build a statue, making a deliberate, conscious effort, and exercising your own personal creativity, but your body builds a baby. Would ownership rights really emerge out of both sequences of events?

And finally, in what sense is a baby *really* owned? Certainly a baby is not commercial property, to be exchanged in the market. If they are property at all, children belong to a rare category of property: the sort that *can* be transferred to others—as in adoption— but *can't* be bought and sold. Is there really such a category?

If we reject the ownership story, we are nevertheless looking for something that ties a child to his biological parents just about as tightly, and the second-self story gives us that. According to the second-self account, giving me the wrong baby is in some sense splitting me from myself. I am entitled to the self-like baby in the nursery, and no baby-hungry nurse is, no matter how well-qualified she is to be a parent. The ownership story and the second-self story converge on this assessment, but it's important to recognize that the second-self story isn't just the ownership view, slightly disguised. (As already noted, David Archard sees it this way.)

How are the two accounts different? One major difference involves symmetry and asymmetry. An owner is entitled to her property, but the property isn't entitled to its owner. The relationship is completely asymmetric. There is more symmetry in a self-to-self relationship: a child comes from, and is thus self-like to, the parent; the parent is source of, and thus self-like to, the child. Or at least, retrospectively, and in the fullness of time, the child will see the parent that way, and that is so partly because the child will attach significance to the parent's being her source. In the context of a hospital nursery, where parents are paired up with babies, it makes sense to speak of biological parents being entitled to their children and children being entitled to their biological parents. As sheer property, children wouldn't be entitled to one adult caregiver more than any other; all the entitlements would accrue to owners.

Considerable symmetry continues in the way the parent-child relationship works over time. To preserve an owner-property relationship, an owner just has to hold on to the property, keeping it in his possession. But to preserve a self-to-self relationship, two people have to preserve and refresh the continuities that bind them to each other. The sheer fact of a child coming from the parent creates an initial bond, but over time, more is needed. The two must share activities, interests, and concerns. On the property account, but not the second-self account, a parent will always impose his values and interests on the child. That will be as natural as homeowners imposing their tastes on their homes. In contrast, to treat my child as a second self, the most effective thing is often not to impose my own preferences, but rather to be open to a child's own activities and interests. If your child is self-like to you, you may be drawn into the world of Thomas the Tank Engine (for example) because you think that will be good for your child, but also because you're open to sharing your child's passions and interests. Sign of the latter: you find yourself working on the model train track even after they go to bed. Yes, parents will also pass on their interests and values to a child, but this direction of influence isn't dictated by regarding your child as a second self.

The ownership model and the self-to-self model converge on seeing parents as entitled (at least initially) to their biological offspring, but that's not because they amount to the same thing.

TWO MORE VIEWS

Is there no other way to explain parental prerogatives, besides making children out to be either owned by us or in some sense a part of us? In the book *The Ethics of Parenthood,* Norvin Richards offers a startlingly simple account. He argues that parental prerogatives stem from a general right to continue whatever we have started, as long as we have violated no one's rights in starting it. I started my daughter's life, not the life of Geraldine, who was born on the same day. So I'm entitled to continue that project instead of someone else taking over. It's up to me to bring my daughter home, if I wish to, for the same reason.

This is more straightforward than saying children are a part of their parents' wider identity—that they are second selves of their parents. But is it true? Is there really, in general, a right to finish what we've started? Richards has not convinced me that this is so. Suppose someone starts a day-care center, violating nobody's rights in the process. Parents place their children in the center, and the owner looks forward to the day when the first class will graduate and move on to kindergarten. That could reasonably be considered finishing what she started, with each child. The parents, though, find the day-care center not to their liking. You couldn't say the children's rights were being violated, but there isn't as much enrichment as the parents would like. Does the owner get to finish what she's started, keeping the children under her care until they're school-aged, despite the parents' preferences? Surely not.

Or consider the example of a music teacher who wants to shepherd children from earliest violin lessons to senior recital. Even if the teacher violates nobody's rights, parents are surely entitled to frustrate this teacher's ambitions, if they find the lessons inadequate for any reason. We *can* stop people from finishing what they've started. And so the prerogatives of biological parents are clearly not just extensions of some general prerogative to finish what they've started. There's no such prerogative.

Unlike day-care center owners and violin teachers, when we start raising a newborn baby, we do get to finish what we've started, but it can't be that we are entitled to do so merely *because* we started something. Rather, it must be for reasons that distinguish the parental case from the other cases. The difference is that biological parenthood makes me the first person the child comes from, the first to see the child as a second self. There could be others—a child comes from adoptive parents in many senses, and I may authorize such a transfer, but the prerogative to parent is mine because I was the first to have this very special relationship.

Now, two parents can disagree about a child's future, vying over custody and other matters. When they both have the same biological connection to a child, disputes have to be resolved on some basis or another. Looking at facts about how a child's life got started can be relevant, much like the best interests of the child can also be relevant. But the most basic thing—why biological parents have special prerogatives to begin with—is not just a question of some alleged right to finish what we've started.

Finally (and briefly), one more explanation for the special prerogatives of biological parents might go like this. When we create a baby, whether accidentally or deliberately, we cause there to be a situation in which someone is in a state of need nine months later— the baby. We are different from anyone else who simply notices the baby's being needy, like the person who causes a car accident is different from a bystander. More than anyone else, it's our fault the baby needs care, and so we (mother and father) have a duty to provide care. The next step in the reasoning says that someone who has a duty to do something must also have a prerogative to do the thing. The duty entails the prerogative. Thus, biological parents have a prerogative to care for their children.

It's certainly unattractive to derive our norms from such an unflattering description of becoming a parent—"It's like getting into a car accident!" But if we do take that description seriously, does it really lead to the desired conclusion? My duty when I cause an accident is not to aid the injured, but rather to make sure the injured receive aid. In fact, in some cases I shouldn't render aid, because others are more competent than I am. Likewise, if this were the right way to account for parental prerogatives, the only conclusion would be that biological parents have the prerogative to find someone competent to care for their children. Mere accountability for the baby's neediness wouldn't give them the right to take the baby home.

We must come back, then, to the simple idea that a child is an extension of self, a part of my wider identity. I get to bring home the child I delivered because the child is, in a manner of speaking, part of me. Although this wouldn't be decisive in every case (think of custody battles between parents), it *is* decisive the vast majority of the time. It's certainly decisive when the person vying for custody with a biological parent is an unrelated potential adopter.

The story I have told—involving "coming from" and children being second selves—gives us the best explanation available for the special prerogatives of biological parents. But wait. Do biological parents really have these prerogatives? I've assumed so throughout this chapter, but now we turn to some voices of skepticism.

Chapter 8

Nobody's Child

Does biology really matter?

I have assumed so far that biological parents do have the prerogative to keep and raise their offspring. The only question has been how best to explain why. My explanation leans on certain biological facts—facts about who comes from whom. There is a certain sort of adoption advocate who thinks even this much leaning on biology is too much. "Caveat biology!" (beware biology!) they caution: we shouldn't think that the facts about where children come from have moral importance. That's perniciously "bionormative," some claim, characterizing the error with a single pejorative term. It's time to hear from these voices of doubt.

INTERNATIONAL ADOPTION

Harvard law professor Elizabeth Bartholet takes a skeptical position on biological ties in her writing on international adoption. Since reaching a peak in 2004, international adoption has been in decline. The pattern, says Bartholet, is that a few irregularities come to light, and then sending countries shut down the adoption pipeline. Young children remain in orphanages too long, and fail to thrive in low-quality institutions, thus becoming less desirable to potential adopters. Red tape complicating the process often means a child is simply never adopted.

On the other side of the debate about international adoption, both journalist Kathryn Joyce and Samford law professor David Smolin claim there are serious problems when children are transferred from extremely poor countries to extremely rich countries. One problem is that adoption intermediaries make huge profits on the transfer, creating incentives for them to build more orphanages and seek out more parents willing to give up their children. The money flowing into these facilities makes it irresistible for some parents to seek better opportunities for their children by placing them there. The parents may think of the orphanage as essentially a poor person's boarding school. They may think a trip to America is only temporary—an enriching year abroad. It's open to question whether these parents really want to relinquish their children, as opposed to being in need of socioeconomic support. Their children are certainly not "orphans."

In other places (Joyce discusses South Korea), what motivates mothers to relinquish babies is very often connected to the "sin" of unwed motherhood. If social norms allowed it, these women would keep their children. This was the situation in Western countries as well, during the 1950s and earlier, before single motherhood became socially acceptable and abortion gave women more control over their reproductive destinies.

The adoption critics' concern for biological parents is largely misplaced, Bartholet seems to think. She sees it as rooted in "wrong ideas about children." One supposedly wrong idea is that children belong to their birth parents and to their community. She writes, "Those who believe in children's rights, in the idea that children enjoy

full personhood, should find it easy to reject claims based on ownership rights by birth parents and nations that treat children effectively
as property." Well and good—children are not our property. But are
they nevertheless "our own" in some other sense? That too she seems
to reject, since she disparages the "blood bias—the assumption that
blood relationship is central to what family is all about." It's because
of this bias, she thinks, that people work so hard to procreate, if they
face the problem of infertility, instead of immediately turning to
adoption. She regrets the ten years she spent undergoing infertility
treatments before finally adopting two boys in Peru.

How did we wind up with the blood bias? In her book *Family
Bonds*, Bartholet writes dozens of times that we are "conditioned"
to believe it. We are subjected to a barrage of messages about "natural" bonds and about how blood is thicker than water. Her own ten
years of wandering in the infertility desert were the result of all this
conditioning, she says.

In arguing that we are "conditioned" to believe in the importance of biology, Bartholet is not merely pointing out the surfeit of
reinforcing messages: rather, she is claiming that our belief is caused
by the messages, not by any reasonable response to the world as it is.
We are bombarded with messages about the goodness of romantic
love, but nobody says we are merely conditioned to value romantic
love. We value it at least partly because it has value! By speaking of
"conditioning," Bartholet is challenging the whole idea that biology
does in fact matter, that it really does make a difference who a child
comes from.

In contrast, Bartholet urges a child-centric approach, with the
emphasis on what's best for the children themselves. Children are
persons with rights, and are not mine or yours or anyone else's, she
insists. We are to imagine what an infant would want, if an infant
could rationally sift all the evidence about the various futures open

to him or her. And she thinks parentless (or seemingly parentless) infants in Peru, South Korea, Ethiopia, China, and other countries would want to be adopted by potential adoptive parents from places like the United States. That is what matters, not any alleged (but unreal, according to Bartholet) entitlement that parents have to the children they physically bring into the world.

Another adoption advocate, Peter Conn, is adamant that there is nothing special about biological parenthood. If you thought there was, you would have to be wedded to silly, outmoded ideas about the natural order. You would be susceptible to all the nonsense about the natural superiority of men in the history of thought, and open to what Aristotle says about the naturalness of slavery. All appeals to natural facts are suspicious, he thinks, because appeals to natural facts have sometimes camouflaged prejudice, custom, and emotional gut reactions.

BETTER OFF ELSEWHERE

About one thing, Bartholet and other "caveat biology" authors are surely right: "better off elsewhere" situations are a frequent reality. Social workers, adoption agencies, and would-be adoptive parents can sometimes see, for a particular infant, two futures. The child's local future with her biological family is pretty bleak. A much better future can be given to the child if she is transferred to a different parent or set of parents and grows up with all the advantages of affluence. Can biological parents justify keeping their children, when they would be better off elsewhere?

You could try to avoid the conundrum here by insisting that a child will actually *always* be better off with her biological parents. Even the worst-off kids are best off with their own parents, you might say. After all, there are built-in compatibilities based on shared traits. Athletic dads tend to have athletic sons, who can get the childhood they need from their biological dads. Introspective dads tend to have introspective sons. And beyond that tendency to be compatible, there is also the child's wish to know the people who brought him into the world, and to be embraced and loved by them. Furthermore, the fact that children come from us gives biological parents an edge because they are naturally disposed to have the parental attitudes to their progeny, many of which are beneficial for kids. From the biological parent, you can usually (though not always) count on devotion and investment.

All of these considerations should make us think kids are, in fact, often best off with their biological parents, but there are clearly many cases in which, despite all the very real benefits of biological parents raising their own kids, a child would nevertheless be better off elsewhere. The parents are *that* disadvantaged. So what about those situations? Do those disadvantaged parents have the right to raise their biological children, or should the best interests of the child be the decisive consideration?

It's all too easy to be seduced by the phrase "the best interests of the child." When two parents vie for custody, the best interests of the child may be the consideration that legitimately serves as a tiebreaker. In other cases, parents are abusive or neglectful, so the child's interests become a paramount concern. But in my view it is not up for debate whether children should remain with their biological parents whenever the alternative is adoption by a more capable and better off nonparent. Most of us think disadvantaged biological parents are entitled to keep their children and don't have to forfeit them to the best-equipped alternative parent.

Two fascinating, superbly written books, *Random Family*, by Adrian Nicole LeBlanc, and *Behind the Beautiful Forevers*, by

Katharine Boo, are full of "better off elsewhere" cases. Whether in the Bronx (LeBlanc) or in the slums of New Delhi (Boo), we surely don't want to abandon the assumption that desperately poor people are entitled to custody of their children. When intervention is warranted to help the children, it should usually come in the form of assistance, not removal of the child from the family. Likewise, parents were entitled to their children when Aborigine children in Australia were forcibly removed from their parents starting around 1909, and continuing for fifty-seven years. One rationale, among others, was to provide better care for the children, who were sometimes fostered out to white parents. If it could be proven that these children were better off, and went on to happier futures than Aborigine children raised by their biological parents, this wouldn't prove that the transfers were justified. They were not, most of us believe.

In another case of forcible child removal, children were taken from unwed mothers at Magdalene convents in Ireland, the United Kingdom, Europe, and the United States in the nineteenth century, and all the way through to the end of the twentieth century (the last one closed in 1996). A case of forcible adoption is dramatized in the movie *Philomena*, and the book by Martin Sixsmith on which it is based. Was it in the best interests of Philomena's son to be taken from her, in a country where "fallen women" were marginalized? He certainly enjoyed prosperity in the United States, and a level of success he probably would not have achieved in Dublin, becoming chief counsel to the Republican National Committee in the Reagan years. That surely does not make the Magdalene sisters' decision the right one.

Why are biological parents entitled to custody of their children even in many cases where the children would be better off elsewhere? There seems to be no better explanation than to say that the children we bear are *ours*—a part of our wider identity. My child—regardless of how disadvantaged I may be—is *like* a part of me; thus, I'm entitled to custody like I'm entitled to retain other parts of myself—my blood, my kidneys, my labor. Barring serious abuse and neglect, it's up to parents to raise their children if they wish to do so.

The prerogatives of a biological parent include being paired with the right child in the hospital, and rearing a child, but also deciding who else should rear the child, if he or she prefers not to. First parents get to choose second parents, and don't have to choose what is best, from some psychologically or sociologically approved perspective. This sort of prerogative is dramatized in the movie *Juno*, about a teenage girl who winds up pregnant while still in high school. After deciding against abortion, Juno chooses a single woman to adopt her child, without making any careful assessment of the pros and cons of different family structures. She simply prefers that particular woman. First parents are granted this power purely out of the belief that there's a very strong prerogative to determine the initial life course of one's own offspring. Children are *ours* in a profound sense, and there seems to be no better way to expand on that but to say they are a part of our very identity.

CHILD-CENTRISM

Bartholet's emphasis on the child seems morally admirable, but we should be alarmed when only children are taken into consideration, not the adults who create them. This child-only focus in adoption discussions on the political left is the mirror image of the child-only focus in abortion discussions on the political right.

Suppose each of us starts life as a zygote, and also that we are immediately full persons, starting at conception (I rejected both of those assumptions in chapter 5, so I'm *just* supposing.) Pro-life ethicists with those starting assumptions tend to say that they are conclusive. The child-centric approach to abortion requires women to carry their pregnancies to term, without consideration of how much sustenance the fetus has a right to, specifically from the mother, much like the child-centric approach to adoption puts the child first, and the mother far behind if part of the equation at all. The "caveat biology" stance on adoption is often taken by people who think of themselves as strong feminists—like Bartholet—but it's surely the furthest thing from feminism if we don't recognize mothers as rights-holders at every stage—both when a woman is pregnant and after she has delivered a baby.

Suppose we were to extend rights to both children and parents, but without taking biological relationships (that is, who comes from whom) into consideration. A recent book that approaches the right to parent this way is *Family Values*, by Harry Brighouse and Adam Swift. Adults, they say, have an interest in raising children, because this satisfies such a deep human desire; thus, adults have a right to raise children. To this they add the idea that "children come first": parents may only satisfy their interest in raising children *if* they can satisfy the interest children have in being raised. Biology is immaterial, on their view, apart from the way that shared genes tend to increase compatibility.

With only these principles in play, the parenting aspirations of would-be adoptive parents would be easily satisfied. They have a right to parent too, and many can presumably raise children as well as anyone else. That's all very well. The problem is how *much* adoption is sanctioned by these principles. Consider, again, some of the examples above. Suppose the unwed Irish teenager in a Magdalene convent and a rich American couple both want to fulfill their right to be parents by raising the teenager's biological child, and biology truly doesn't matter. Why *not* give the infant to the rich Americans, considering that it is unclear that the teenager can raise the child well enough, but more likely that the rich Americans can?

Why *not* build orphanages in destitute places, tempting poor biological parents to relinquish their infants, so that affluent Westerners can fulfill their right to be parents? Why *not* transfer kids from poor Aborigines to wealthy white people? If a child is nobody's child at birth, family courts need to peruse the various interests in question, and secure the best outcome. So much the worse for a birth mother who can't compete with what other potential parents have to offer.

Surely this is a reductio ad absurdum of dispensing with biological considerations. In my view, we shouldn't hesitate to make moral claims that are grounded in biological facts; we should just avoid making moral claims grounded in nonfacts or nonrelevant facts. Facts about origins, causation, history, and so on have a huge role to play in many areas of law and ethics. Imagine trying to have a law and ethics of criminal responsibility while dismissing natural facts about which murders originated from which individuals. Or trying to have a law and ethics of intellectual property without attaching any significance to who created what. No, natural facts are legitimately appealed to as the grounding for moral facts about prerogatives, entitlements, obligations, and rights. We merely must think things through carefully, focusing on the right facts.

By all means, let's do away with the idea that children are owned property of their parents. We can all agree that it shouldn't be possible to buy or sell a child. One of the ways that Irish unwed mothers were mistreated involved money: their babies were essentially sold to others (with convents reaping the profits). It wouldn't have helped much if the mothers had done the selling themselves, as the rightful owners of their children, pocketing all of the money. We all agree that children can't be owned in the way that animals currently *can* be owned. However, we do need a not-wildly-distant replacement for such property-based concepts. The replacement I am suggesting is the link between parent and child that makes one the second self of the other. We don't own our kids, but we can't split parents from their children—their second selves—without having very good reasons.

Even if biological parents' rights are recognized, we still should heed some of Bartholet's policy recommendations. When children are truly parentless and living in inhospitable orphanages, transfer to adoptive parents should be swift. Even if it's true that a community has rights on top of individual parental rights (I shall remain agnostic about that), it does a community no good at all to retain parentless children who are quickly becoming dysfunctional, and will become, over time, more of a community burden than a benefit. The true reason why some countries are closing the door on adoption is probably often national pride, the wish not to be seen as incapable of providing for the vulnerable and defenseless.

But if parental rights are recognized, we will also have to heed Smolin and Joyce's concerns about international adoption. Parents cannot give genuine consent to relinquishing their children when they're being offered unimaginable riches to do so: spots for their children in fancy orphanages and transport to "The American Dream." Orphanages need to be grassroots, community-based accommodations and not more. They need to be genuinely helpful to parents, without forcing them to choose between riches for their children, and preserving family bonds. The stigma of single motherhood should be lifted, so women can keep their own children, when that is their preference.

RHETORIC AND REALITY

The intent of Bartholet and others is primarily to elevate adoption, to remove any stigma attached to it, and to keep infants from languishing in squalid orphanages. You can't quarrel with those goals. But the rhetoric here, if taken seriously, leads in a frightening direction. Bartholet's approach, focusing as it does on what an infant would want, cannot explain what's wrong with taking babies from Irish unwed mothers, very poor Aborigine parents, and destitute people everywhere. These things *must* be just fine, if we liberate ourselves from the "biology bias" and adopt a child-centric perspective. But even Bartholet doesn't appear to think they're really just fine, in the final analysis. She does put forward "What would the infant want?" as the right question, but toward the end of *Family Bonds*, she says something entirely different.

> My point is not that adoption is the same as biologic parenting but that it should be recognized as a positive form of family, not ranked as a poor imitation of the real thing on some parenting hierarchy. I do not think we should jettison the biologic model of parenting and insist on a universal baby swap at the moment of birth.

In fact, Bartholet writes that there is "some presumption in favor of biologically linked parenthood." This is not based on the child's being "our own," for the parents, but on psychological facts. In some sense parents know their child during pregnancy, making relinquishment painful for them. Pregnancy, childbirth, and "the sense that a child is your genetic product" can create "a healthy bond between a parent and a child, and their absence may create a greater potential for problems." Furthermore, she concedes that "genetic heritage is an important influence on intellect and personality," and goes as far as to say that "for many parents some level of likeness is important and too much difference is problematic."

This is all perfectly sensible, but is it enough? The problem is that such concessions ground a rather weak presumption in favor of parents, not a strong presumption. If parents may keep their children *even* in spite of destitution or the heavy stigma of unwed motherhood (in traditional societies), or discrimination against their ethnic group, this can't be just because they are likely to be especially attached and especially compatible. That's a small thing, in comparison to the problems these children will face, if they stay where they are. And adoptive parents will no doubt be attached and reasonably compatible too.

The only thing that could justify parents in keeping children despite extremely difficult circumstances is something as powerful as ownership. And that's what I am putting forward: not ownership, but strong parental prerogatives based on the fact that a child is a quasi-self-extension. Only if that Irish teenager is permitted to assert "This child is mine!" can she demand to keep him, her socioeconomic problems notwithstanding; and that assertion is difficult to ground while denying the importance of where the baby comes from.

TIES WITHOUT STIGMA

I suspect "caveat biology" adoption advocates see it as more egalitarian to regard children as untied to biological parents. Taking biological ties seriously smacks of aristocracy and hereditary peerage, they think. Enormous privileges once attached to being an earl's or a duke's son, as opposed to just a commoner's son (and never mind daughters). It's in the same general realm to think it matters that you were born of one set of parents rather than another. We've done very well by eliminating aristocratic social categories, but would we be doing equally well if we thought of every child as just a citizen of a country, or even a citizen of the world, without attaching importance to each child's origin? *Must* there be a stigma attached to adoption if biological ties are given any weight?

There *can* be a stigma, if one thinks an adoptive parent cannot enjoy the sense of generativity that a biological parent has, and cannot have the full sense of their child as a second self. That was once commonly thought. Adopted children were seen as severed from their "real parents" and adoptive parents as pitiably worse off than biological parents. But those aren't inevitable consequences of taking origins seriously.

There need be no stigma associated with adoption at all, if we recognize that parenthood can be transferred from biological parents to others, and that people who desire parenthood are capable of finding much the same connection to children when the connection starts later on, and not at or before birth. I have argued that the first people with the parental connection to children are normally the biological parents but not that they must be the last people. If we are primed to have a certain kind of connection and attitude toward children we consider our own, we can have it whether we enter the picture as mothers do, as fathers do, or as adoptive parents do.

The way kids come from us, thus becoming second selves, makes being the first to parent a special case. It takes authorization from first parents for there to be a second set of parents (abandonment counting as tacit authorization). Second parents can have the sense of the child coming from them, because of all their innumerable interventions and their involvement in the child's transformation from baby to toddler, toddler to teenager, and teenager to adult. All this gives them, too, the sense of the child being a second self.

Could adoptive parents have that sense, could all of us have it, in a world where all children are redistributed as a matter of course, going to people based on their being willing to parent and well equipped? To what extent does the generativity of adoptive parents derive from their having internalized the model of the biological parent—perhaps, in part, due to their own earlier strivings to be biological parents?

"Caveat biology" adoption advocates typically reject the modeling hypothesis. "Adoptive parents need not model themselves on anybody, for what is specially valuable about the practice of parenting does not depend on a genetic connection between parent and child," according to Brighouse and Swift. I certainly agree that there needn't be any conscious modeling; what seems possible is that our tacit understanding of what it is to be a parent owes something to the "ur" experience of the procreating parent—in fact, perhaps particularly to a mother's experience (since children start off literally inside their mothers). That may be iconic for us all, regardless of our sex or fertility or preferred method of building a family.

On the other hand, the modeling hypothesis can be overstated. Edgar Page has argued that biological parenthood is not just a model, but a model adoptive parents can't live up to. In an article on adoption he writes, "For most people, I suspect, adopting a child falls short of being a perfect substitute for natural parenthood." This is not the impression I get from adoption memoirs like Bartholet's. She speaks of the pleasures of parenthood beautifully, discussing falling in love with her children and her sense of being "meant to be" their mother (recall the quote in chapter 1). The modeling hypothesis, carefully stated, doesn't denigrate this experience or stigmatize adoption.

Friends of mine struggled for years with infertility before turn-ing to international adoption. Armed with a suitcase full of presents for all the intermediaries in the Russian adoption system—as they had been instructed to do by the adoption agency—they headed abroad and returned with a son. The two doted on their baby like any parents would. When they later conceived a second child, it would have been not only insensitive but untruthful for anyone to speak of them only now becoming "real parents." They became real parents when they adopted their first child. We should insist that the adopted child's first parents did have the initial prerogative to raise, or not raise, the child, and at the same time celebrate and respect adoption. It's important for parenthood to come about without the violation of the initial parents' rights, but when it comes about ethically, adoptive parenthood is parenthood—nothing more and nothing less.

Once it's established that *this* parent is the parent of *that* child, we know where the child will grow up and with whom. But now the parenting must begin. Parents make vast numbers of critical deci-sions for their kids, and want to make those decisions as well as possible. What should we be thinking about when we make those decisions? What is parenthood's aim?

Chapter 9

Parenthood's Aim

What's a parent for?

As soon as children are born, there are decisions that need to be made. Should the baby be fed breast milk or formula? Should a baby boy be circumcised? Should a girl's ears be pierced? What about vaccination? Should a baby sleep with his parents or in a separate room? Should we let her cry herself to sleep, or should parents rush to her in the middle of the night?

Our initial prerogatives in the area of parenthood stem from the child being a sort of second self. This comes into play when we're thinking about why we're entitled to have children (chapters 1–3), how much quality control we should engage in (chapter 4), and why we're entitled to bring a child home, even if the child would be better off elsewhere (chapter 7–8). But now that we have established our role as parents (whether biological or adoptive), our focus starts to change. The child is a second self to you, the parent, but also separate from you—a whole human being who is totally dependent on you now, but will grow to full independence in about eighteen to twenty years.

What should we be aiming for, as parents? There's no particular reason to expect that parenthood has one purpose, or parents have one aim. We're not looking for "the essence of parenthood" here. The question is a looser one: What is the main thing that parents do for their kids, as parents? What makes a parent a special kind of caregiver, compared to the many other people who will help raise a child? How does the child's being a second self to a parent enter into the parenthood equation?

THE GOOD LIFE

It's so obvious that it's almost not worth saying: one thing we want, as good parents, is for our children to live good lives. But why not the best lives or the ultimate life? Of course the ultimate life would be terrific, but it's going too far to make that goal part of a parent's job description. Many parents don't have the resources to give their children the best conceivable life. Aiming that high would also inevitably turn the parent into a relentlessly self-sacrificing servant to the child. Our children's welfare matters a great deal, and their dependence on us makes us feel particularly responsible for them, but why should their welfare always be our paramount concern, and our welfare no concern at all? Surely we can be good enough parents while also carrying on with at least most of our established interests and passions.

It's a little harder to say what stage of life a parent should be concerned about. Some people think the main job of a parent is to prepare children to live good lives as adults, always assessing various parenting options in terms of their impact on children once they've grown up. These parents assess whether day care is a good idea, for example, based on whether it makes a measurable difference to how people turn out as adults if they spent time in day-care centers as children. These parents assess whether breastfeeding or circumcising a child is wise, based entirely on the measurable impact in later adulthood.

Why no concern with the newborn's current experience, or with the life experience of a two-year-old? Perhaps they think, consciously or unconsciously, that life doesn't really start "for real" until later on (around age eighteen). Childhood is merely preparation for adulthood, like the time we spend in the womb. Or perhaps they think that the times of our lives that we forget—and we do forget our first years and much of the rest of childhood—don't really count. Or they think the childhood years are formative, having an impact on the rest of life, and therefore *just* formative.

But all these patterns of thought are fallacious. There's no good reason to think that "real life" starts in adulthood. Forgotten hours matter, even if they matter just at the time, and not both at the time and during later moments of remembering. And "formative, therefore *just* formative" is obviously an illogical inference. Discounting childhood's significance is especially absurd in light of the fact that childhood is not only 20–25 percent of a person's life (depending on how you define it), but also the most certain part of life. We know children have lives to live now more certainly than we know they will go on having lives to live at age twenty, forty, or sixty. A parent's goal should be helping a child have a good life both as a child, and later on as an adult.

What, then, is a good life? Surely we want our children to answer that question for themselves when it comes to the details, but good lives do have some very basic things in common. On the view I favor and explore in a previous book (*The Weight of Things: Philosophy and the Good Life*), the necessary ingredients are multiple. People with good lives have enough happiness, enough of the time. Happiness makes our lives better, unhappiness makes our lives worse. So if we want our children to live good lives, we will want them to be happy.

Arguably, people with good lives also have an identity—a distinct "take" on life and a sense of who they are. "Being someone" makes our lives better; being like "Nowhere Man," in the Beatles song ("doesn't have a point of view, knows not where he's going to"), makes our lives worse. Identity is another feature of the good life that good parents will help their kids attain.

People with good lives make their own choices, where that is possible and appropriate. Autonomy makes our lives better and enslavement makes them worse. Add that to what parents want (and should want) for their children.

People with good lives interact with others, and have respect and concern for them, as opposed to living like solitary islands. Caring connections make life better and disconnection makes life worse. People with good lives grow over time, becoming more competent, more knowledgeable, more skilled, more wise. I would also say that growth makes life better, and stagnation or devolution makes life worse.

All of the ingredients we need to live good lives as adults are also needed to live good lives as children. Importantly, though, the details differ. Childhood happiness and adult happiness are not exactly alike. There is a kind of uninhibited, unselfconscious cheer that comes naturally to children. Kids are disposed to play, to have fun, to take great pleasure in make-believe games and fictions. A life that is happy enough on the whole seems to me to need childhood-appropriate happiness in the early years and adulthood-appropriate happiness later on. Something is missing in a child with an old soul, and something is missing in an adult who's as playful as a five-year-old. A good parent, then, will make sure childhood includes enough fun, by not overloading children with chores, schoolwork, labor on the farm, or paid labor outside the home.

We have to make sure our children have opportunities for the right sort of happiness, and also care appropriately about unhappiness. Of course, some suffering is unavoidable at every stage of life, but any that we deliberately impose has to be justified. The pain of a vaccination shot shouldn't be discounted in any of the usual fallacious ways—"He won't remember it," "It's just childhood," "Real life begins later"—but can usually be justified nonetheless (see chapter 13). The pain of circumcision can't be discounted—it matters, even if it's quickly forgotten. It can be justified only if there's some important advantage to circumcision (see chapter 10).

Good lives have autonomy as another essential ingredient. When does autonomy start to matter? Very, very early, it would seem. A baby trapped in swaddling clothes is missing the ability to make a very basic choice—whether or not to move her arms and legs! A baby trapped for hours and hours in a playpen can't make any choices either—like whether to crawl over there or over here. Autonomy matters throughout life, but the types that matter keep changing. For a teenager, it's not enough to avoid incarceration in a playpen; teenagers need significant mobility within their community.

We need autonomy, but sometimes less is more. Take a child who decides to drop out of school at age fourteen, so he can control what he does with his time. In and of itself, greater self-governance is positive, but in this case the child would have been better off with parents and teachers in charge. He will soon start to feel the negative consequences of not going to school, losing in the long term what he has gained in the near term. An adult stuck in a low-paying job for lack of earlier education will have much less autonomy than he might have had. He may also have less of everything else—happiness and growth, for example. Foreseeing this long-term impact better than a child can, it's a parent's duty to step in and make the child go to school.

Children have a sense of self, as adults do, but it's built out of different elements. It would be strange if a five-year-old's sense of self was centered on a political standpoint, but not if a fifty-year-old's was. Likewise, there is a degree of beneficence that makes little sense for kids, but more sense for adults. Kids don't make huge sacrifices, but adults certainly may.

ANOTHER SELF

Many of the people who come into contact with children—teachers, babysitters, clergy, and so on—try to help them live good lives. What's distinctive about a parent is that for the parent and not others, the child has a special status: my child is a part of my wider identity and not part of his babysitter's wider identity. This makes certain decisions easier. Your child will presumably come home with you and share your lifestyle. If you live in the woods, off the grid, your child will live in the woods, off the grid, even if by some objective standard it's better for kids to live in a town or a city. If you live in an urban area, your child will live an urban life, not a country life. If you live on a boat, your child will live on a boat. Parents don't have to study up on the best place to raise a child and immediately relocate to wherever that place may be.

Another thing that makes parents different is that parents simply do much more for their children than for others. Like we prioritize our own selves over others, we prioritize our children over others. We are advocates for our own children more than for other people's children. What does this preferential stance come to? May we do so much for our children that they wind up at an advantage, compared to their peers?

The average parent thinks the answer is "Of course." If you play soccer with your child every day after school, and she therefore thrives on her soccer team, you're to be commended, not criticized. Likewise if you maintain especially good discipline at home, so your child completes her homework on time and receives good grades. The second-self account offers an explanation for why parents may give their kids a competitive edge: doing so is just like having the prerogative to work hard at soccer and maintain work discipline ourselves, with resulting personal payoffs.

If you don't see children as part of their parents' extended identity, then you may have to depart from the standard view and not help with homework and soccer. While it's obvious that we can pursue our own advantage, and can pursue our kids' advantage if they're quasi-selves, it's not so obvious we can be boosters for entirely "other" people in the various competitive domains of life. Why should kids who are backed by more effective parents be at an advantage over other kids? In *Family Values*, Harry Brighouse and Adam Swift urge us to back off, so that all kids have equal opportunity, but not to back too far off. One of the key benefits children get out of being raised in families, according to these two philosophers, is a close, intimate relationship with their parents. Parenting activities can foreseeably confer advantage, but still be justifiable (Brighouse and Swift argue) when they are needed to create closeness. The bottom line is this, they say: if you're playing soccer with your kid just to help him make the team, stop. But if playing soccer is one of your only means of spending close, quality time with your child, then don't stop. Seeing your child as part of your extended identity (a notion the authors reject) gives you a greener green light.

It becomes very simple to say we can help our children compete, if we think we ourselves are free to compete, and we regard our children as self-like.

Once again, without seeing kids as part of a parent's extended identity, it's harder to see why parents have so much freedom to share their values. Why may we cultivate the love of art, music, sports, pacifism, or whatever it might be, in tender, impressionable youngsters? Without assuming a deep connection between parent and child, doing so looks overbearing—like parents are taking advantage of their power over their captive wards. As before, when conferring advantage was the issue, Brighouse and Swift sort things out in terms of family closeness. They think values can be shared when, and only when, the sharing is needed for intimacy. Then again, they think this is often the case. Children may very well have the best chance of enjoying family closeness when parents do allow themselves to pass on their values and interests. There is a problem with sharing values, according to Brighouse and Swift, when sharing values isn't needed for closeness or when sharing makes families more distant. Example (mine, not theirs): sending your daughter to a distant art camp for six weeks over the summer might reflect your values, but make her no closer to you, or possibly even more distant. Now there's no answer to the charge that sharing values is overbearing, on their view.

I'm inclined to think that sharing values with children is par for the course, and doesn't need to be justified in terms of an intimacy payoff. It's fine to pass on enthusiasm for art or sports or music even if you suspect this may not bring you any closer to your child. You can do so because the child isn't your student or someone you're babysitting for, but a part of your wider identity. Sport-loving parents are permitted to introduce their kids to Little League. Music-loving parents are permitted to make their kids practice the violin.

You can restrict your children to a vegetarian diet, teaching them that it is wrong to kill animals for food. You can teach them how to hunt, telling them that animals may be killed for food. Kids can be brought along to pro-choice rallies and to pro-life rallies. Parents don't have to emulate the professional educator who maintains neutrality or tries to strike a balance.

Understanding our children as second selves easily accounts for our freedom to operate out of our own values, passing those values on to them, but it's complicated. We have to come back constantly to the child's separateness, too. It may turn out that Little League makes my kid as happy as sports make me, but maybe not. Violin lessons may inculcate my values in my child, but she might hate them. Our initial plans for our children can legitimately be just the ones we would want for ourselves, but we must be willing to bend if these plans manifestly make our children's lives worse, not better. And we must bend all the more because autonomy is one of the necessary ingredients for a good life.

There's another way to bend besides ceasing and desisting so kids can do their own thing. If what I really want is a self-to-self relationship with my child, I can foster that by sharing my values with her *or* by letting her share her values with me. Philosophers often overlook this symmetry when they criticize the picture of the parent-child relationship that I'm advocating. It's easy, but wrongheaded, to quickly assume that having a second self is a lot like owning a piece of property, so that it's necessarily always the parent's values that get transmitted to the child.

In fact, at first transmission of values *is* one-directional, but over time this is less and less true. When my son was seven or eight, I liked the Captain Underpants series of children's books because *he* liked them so much. By the time he was fifteen, I started liking the music of Kanye West, Jay-Z, and Eminem because that's what he was listening to. More serious sharing has taken place over the years as well. I have become a little more liberal on some issues because my son has pushed me to be. And the same goes for transmission from my daughter—I do and like things now that I wouldn't do or like if it weren't for her. It's true that because kids need guidance, much of the influence will run parent-to-child, but not true that this has to be the case, or that it will always be the case over the whole duration of the parent-child relationship.

TYRANTS

The parents I'm holding up as a model are flexibly directive— they guide, but they bend, and they even allow themselves to be influenced by their kids at times. They contrast sharply with two other kinds of parents. One is the tyrannical parent. In authoritarian families and societies, parents reserve much more power over children—especially fathers, and especially when children are female. The parent dictates whom the child marries, what occupation the child pursues, where the child lives. Nicholas Kristof's books and his *New York Times* columns are full of examples of girls (and less so, boys) whose lives are controlled to a great degree by fathers and male relatives in countries like Afghanistan and Saudi Arabia. Wayward daughters are brought into line quickly and sometimes even violently, as the practice of honor killing horrifyingly demonstrates. Traditional parents are also obedient—to their own parents, but also to the community as a whole, to elders and religious leaders, to traditions and customs. The man who kills his daughter for kissing a boy before marriage or choosing a career as a fashion model (both examples are from real life) does as he is supposed to, according to some of the cultural and religious voices around him.

But to what end? In an authoritarian society, many individuals lack many of the essential ingredients of a good life. Living in a society in which so many decisions are already made for them, they may not be as happy as they would be if they were more free. Even more strikingly, people without choices don't develop their own identities, lack autonomy, and tend to stagnate, held down by the preconceptions of parents and community. But let's come back closer to home, where authoritarian parenting also exists, though usually in a milder form.

A rather tyrannical style of parenting is candidly described in the riveting book *Battle Hymn of the Tiger Mother*, by Amy Chua. As a Chinese-American Yale law professor, Chua had very strong ideas about the sort of life her daughters should live. They had to be not just A students, but A+ students; they had to be not just musical, but musical on the violin or piano (no other instruments would do); they had to be not just good at the violin or piano, but stellar. To accomplish all of those aims, the girls were required to spend long hours every day doing homework and practicing their instruments, with virtually no time off for the standard amusements of American kids—no TV, no sleepovers, no hanging out at the mall.

If all this had lavishly furnished the girls with all of the essential goods, both in the present and in the future, then "No harm done." You can at least imagine them enjoying all these activities, finding their identity in musical and academic achievement, and growing by leaps and bounds. You can even imagine this way of life not compromising the girls' autonomy, provided they were offered options, and actually chose to stay the course.

But life in this family was indeed a battle, as the book title suggests. When Chua first introduced her three-year-old daughter Lulu to the piano, Chua got her to stop smashing multiple keys at a time by threatening to put her in the backyard on a freezing day in New Haven, Connecticut. A few years later, she motivated Lulu to practice a hard piece by putting her dollhouse in the back seat of the car and threatening to donate it to the Salvation Army. As Chua tells it, these are success stories, because the child does become an extremely accomplished musician and an excellent student, but one has to wonder about what was sacrificed in the process. Fortunately, the family does eventually wind up bending to Lulu's preferences: Lulu stages a major rebellion at the age of thirteen and opts out of elite violin performance, finding passions of her own, including competitive tennis. A few years later she can be found at Harvard, so her parents did get the successful child they wanted, but that is surely not redemptive; the central question has to be whether Lulu succeeded in living a life that suited *her*.

We can encourage our children to move in directions that we value, but only as long as they continue having enough of all the critical life goods, *including* autonomy. Allowing them autonomy will mean backing off in many cases, admitting that the life we would have wanted doesn't suit our child. We have to be prepared to let a child quit the Little League, at least after a reasonable effort to give it a go; or quit violin lessons; or stay home from the hunting trips; or eat meat when the family is vegetarian; or become vegan when the family wouldn't dream of it; or develop a passion for conservative politics when the family is liberal; or be openly gay when parents find that foreign. If we are sufficiently flexible and receptive, our children will remain a part of our extended identity—second selves, but separate.

STEWARDS

The flexibly directive parent also contrasts with the "steward" or "fiduciary" parent. In this understanding of parenthood's aim, a parent is like a steward managing property for a landowner during a temporary absence, to use a metaphor suggested by the philosopher William Irvine in his book *Doing Right by Children*. The job of parents is to manage their young children on behalf of the adult children they will one day become. Much like a steward safeguards the property so that the owner has maximum freedom to develop it upon return, the idea is that we should leave as much as we can to our child's future self to decide. The steward parent is deeply opposed to thinking of her child as any sort of extension of herself.

A totally neutral steward would be a problematic parent, I think. She may very well produce adult children who lack the skills to succeed at music, sports, getting into college, or anything else that takes preparation in childhood. While a child could, in principle, choose football or the violin at the age of eighteen, sports programs and music departments won't choose *them*. Childhood training is not only traditional, but necessary for the highest levels of expertise.

What is more, growing up in the care of a neutral parent doesn't give children a chance to develop attitudes that will help them succeed—long-term dedication, persistence, commitment, passion. To wind up with these attitudes, it pays to be apprenticed to some full-blooded way of life—inevitably, in large part, the parent's life. This is for the best as long as the parent isn't the opposite of a steward—a tyrant. The child is better off as an apprentice as long as he is permitted to contribute to his future and resist the parent's plans, if it turns out they don't suit him.

Brighouse and Swift also have more or less a stewardship conception of parenthood (they prefer the term "fiduciary"), but soften it: they think a parent-child relationship ought to be close and intimate, which means a parent has more freedom to share his or her enthusiasms. The warm fiduciary parent and the flexibly directive parent will do many of the same things, but nevertheless diverge at points. My conception of the parent-child relationship explains why we may confer advantage and pass on our values in a different way than theirs does. The basic structure of the relationship makes this par for the course—to be expected and normally unproblematic. Brighouse and Swift, by contrast, see advantage-conferring and values-sharing as needing justification on a case-by-case basis. Again, it's okay when it's necessary for creating intimacy, but not otherwise.

To my mind, I can pass on my love of music to my kids even knowing—because I see it in my crystal ball—that doing so will make them retreat into their iPhones constantly as teenagers and run off to live music performances. I can do this without being able to say that any match between my music-loving and my children's will ever provide them with the good feeling of being close to me. What will inhibit the flexibly directive parent is just the child's reactions. It's one thing to try to share our values, but another to impose them on a resistant child with other ideas about what's interesting and important.

The stewardship model of parenthood is sometimes associated with the late philosopher Joel Feinberg, whose 1980 article "A Child's Right to an Open Future" has been enormously influential. The right he postulated is the right of children to have certain choices reserved for their later, adult selves. Out of respect for that right, Feinberg thought we shouldn't, for example, deny our children a basic education because we expect them to grow up and become menial laborers on the family farm. Advocates of the stewardship model take that basic idea and enlarge upon it, saying a parent's role is essentially to make sure the child's future is as open as possible, so that she can shape her own life.

We've already encountered one problem with that idea. If parents try to preserve every future as a possibility for their children, they will actually prepare their children for nothing and inadvertently narrow their possibilities. Another problem with invoking the right to an open future is that it's more important for our futures to be open in some ways than in others. By having me get braces as a teenager, my parents closed off the option of my ever being an adult with crooked teeth. I was also prevented from ever choosing straight teeth, or choosing crooked teeth—my smile is thus not my own doing. None of this seems bad at all, for two reasons: the road blocked off is not worth taking; and choice is not important in this area. It's not important for a person's dental situation to be their own doing.

And there's one last problem with parents continually limiting their influence based on a child's right to an open future. It would be odd if parents had to step aside in all things, considering that this would often clear the way not for the child's total freedom, but for other influences to have more power. Obviously, the surrounding culture has a huge impact on our futures, making anyone's future semiopen at best. Living in twenty-first-century America, my child will never be a knight, a serf, a chimney sweep, or a eunuch (thank God), because those social positions have been abandoned. But peers and cultural trends also make a huge difference. In the influential book *The Nurture Assumption*, psychologist Judith Rich Harris argued that we imagine parents making a bigger difference in kids' lives than they usually do. In reality, children are hugely shaped by their peers. Thus, if parents stepped aside constantly to honor a child's right to an open future, they would just be giving peers even *more* influence.

I don't think a parent must be constantly stepping back, in all areas of a child's life, but at times it's certainly important to step back. Roughly, parents ought to step back when there are multiple good options and the particular choice is one that there is good reason for the child to make for herself, whether or not other influences will play a role. Parents shouldn't be in control when an eighteen-year-old is choosing who to vote for, or, later, when that child chooses whether to marry and whom to marry, or which career to pursue. A doctor who puts great pressure on his child to become another doctor is giving too much weight to the child being a second *self* and not enough weight to the child being a *second* self—separate. That sort of excessive parental influence is worse than garden-variety peer and cultural influencing, because when parents have excessive control, they act as their child's puppeteer, and there is no comparable manipulator when lots of different forces blindly shape a child's trajectory.

When we think about narrowing a child's future possibilities, there are many things to think about. Are we excluding possibilities or only making them more remote? Is the future we are trying to prescribe for our child just arguably better, or obviously and objectively better (like straight teeth)? Is preserving choice in that area important, or is it just as well for parents to preempt later autonomous decision-making in that area? Reflecting on all these issues will hold us back from being tyrants, but will not turn us into mere stewards.

As I have argued, a child is like another self to us, her parents, which means we have far more freedom to transmit our lifestyle and values than we would otherwise have. That's a freeing conception, giving us the prerogative to go on with our lives, after becoming parents, and share our values, attitudes, and way of life. But a child is also a separate person, which means having to step back and adopt a more objective stance. We have to be at least ready to ask what is good for our child—what will give the child a good life not only in the future, but also now, during childhood. We have to be ready to take in evidence that our child needs something different, in order to grow and thrive, or needs to make her own decision, in order to have an age-appropriate level of autonomy. We also have to be ready to be the people influenced by a child, and not always the influencers.

So much for generalities. We now turn to some philosophically interesting moments in the lives of parents. As we are going to see, it does sometime help to bear in mind Aristotle's dictum that children are "second selves, but separate"—but there is more to being a philosophical parent than just having that thought. We will need that insight, but others as well, and also factual background, when we have to decide whether to circumcise a boy, how to deal with gender issues, whether to vaccinate, when to lie to our children and when we must be truthful, and whether to pass on our religious beliefs and customs. Onward, then, to one of the first decisions new parents have to make.

Chapter 10

First Decisions

To cut or not to cut?

All the generalities of chapter 9 only take us so far with any real-life decision. Now we need to get into the nitty-gritty dilemmas of the philosophical parent. New parents have to decide about vaccination. They have to decide about circumcision, if they have a boy. Mothers have to decide whether they will breastfeed, and if so, for how long. Decisions have to be made about whether the baby sleeps in the parent's bed, or in a different bed, or in a different room. There might be an issue about whether to pierce the ears of a baby girl. Even naming the baby could be perplexing. Is it fair to give a child a name like "God" or "Apple" or "Ima Hogg" or "Nutella"? (These are real examples.)

Though all these issues are interesting and some of them (like the last) are fun, I'm going to prioritize the questions that seem to have the most urgency and philosophical complexity: circumcision (here) and vaccination (in chapter 13). To remove a boy's foreskin or leave the boy intact? For some parents, this is an easy choice. One father I asked about it said he gave the issue absolutely no thought before having his son circumcised. Another father said he never seriously considered circumcision an option. Others think about this, and think, and think.

Parents, not doctors, decide about optional procedures like circumcision and immunization. We sometimes spin this as being due to the fact that parents know what's best for their children, but how could that be true? All sorts of people are parents, some with lots of ideological baggage and not a lot of education. Furthermore, it really can't be best for one newborn to be circumcised and another to be uncircumcised *just* because their parents have different views about circumcision. Parents are in charge not because they know best, but because medical decision-making, up to a point and in certain specific areas, is a prerogative that comes with being the mom or being the dad.

One question is who makes the decision. Another is about the content of the deliberations. What should parents take into account before making up their minds? The fact that the child is a second self might make it seem right to unreflectively decide, based on your own values or based on a gut-level preference; a father might quickly opt for "like father, like son." But the parent also ought to be thinking of the child as a separate being, and aiming for what's in the child's best interests. Foreskin reduction is a medical procedure that can have serious consequences—even death—if it's done, but also if it's not done. This isn't the time to act out of one's own values unthinkingly, as one might do if the issue were something minor, like what name to give the child or whether to pierce a baby girl's ears.

Before going on, we should notice something puzzling. In chapter 8, I argued that parents will sometimes permissibly keep custody of a child, even knowing the child would be better off elsewhere. It's legitimate for them to think "my child, myself" and hold on tight, like they'd hold on to their own right arm. The focus of parents, at that point, is on their own rights. A decision about circumcision might be made on the very same day, but now it seems inappropriate for the parent to simply assert his own rights. "I choose circumcision (or not) and so be it!" Taking on the parenting role can involve an insistence on one's own rights, but fulfilling that role competently requires caring about the child as a second self— but separate. And that means carefully sifting the pros and cons, so one can arrive at the choice that best reflects all the facts and considerations. Does this shift in stance make sense?

I think it does, if we consider that relinquishing a child is a gigantic loss for a parent, but making the less personally satisfying decision, out of concern for the child's well-being, is not a gigantic loss. Once a child is in our care, and we are confident of our role as the decision-makers, nothing stops us from thinking things through in light of both our own personal values *and* the best interests of the baby, taken as a separate human being who will have a long life, starting with but going beyond childhood. The fact that the child is mine *and* the decision is mine doesn't justify me in making the decision in a self-indulgent, unreflective fashion.

CIRCUMCISION 101

What is a foreskin anyway? In a heavily circumcised country like the United States, many people simply don't know. Basically, the foreskin is an open "sock" covering the glans of the penis and maintaining it as a sensitive, moist membrane. It starts off adhering to the glans but becomes fully retractable as a child gets older. A foreskin has an abundance of nerve endings, and winds up being erogenous tissue, much like the various parts of the female genitalia. Some men resent having lost their foreskins as babies, but some don't miss them in the least.

Of course, foreskins aren't merely lost or shed; they're cut off. Thanks to a video provided by Stanford University Medical School, you can see a state-of-the-art circumcision (http://stan.md/ 2gVRQsj) before deciding whether to choose the procedure for your child. The procedure demonstrated is used by the majority of circumcisers in the United States (67 percent) according to a 1998 survey (see Stang and Snellman in the Bibliography). The baby is first strapped down and then receives two injections of lidocaine anesthetic at the base of his penis. Next, he is draped with two sterile sheets, the little penis sticking up between them. Two instruments are used to stretch the foreskin up beyond the glans and to open it at the tip. A sharp third instrument is inserted in the opening and used to separate the foreskin from the glans. Next, a scissors-like clamp is inserted and used to make a vertical, one-inch "crush injury" in the foreskin. Then a scissors is used to cut to the base of the crush injury. The foreskin is retracted—peeled downwards. Remaining adhesions are cleaned off with gauze. The foreskin is pulled back up so it extends a few inches beyond the glans. Then a "Gomco clamp" is used to make the final cut in such a way that the glans is protected (watch the video if you want to know exactly how it works), and to insure that the cut is an even circle. There is some bleeding, but not a lot. The whole procedure takes about ten minutes, and afterwards the circumcised penis is covered with Vaseline-treated gauze and the child's diaper is put back on.

The majority of newborn boys in the United States are circumcised, though regional variation is striking: the rate is 80.1 percent in the Midwest; 69.6 percent in the Northeast; 64.7 percent in the South; and 34 percent in the West. Outside of the United States, only religion-linked circumcision is common. Of the 30 percent of males who are circumcised around the world, two-thirds are Muslim. In

Israel the vast majority of boys are circumcised. In Europe the vast
majority of parents don't circumcise their sons.

How, then, did nonreligious circumcision become so common
in the United States? According to Leonard Glick, author of *Marked
in Your Flesh: Circumcision from Ancient Judea to Modern America*,
American circumcision has its roots in Jewish circumcision, so the
story begins long ago. In chapter 17 of the biblical Book of Genesis,
God is described as establishing a covenant with Abram, promis-
ing to make him "exceedingly numerous" and to give him the land
of Canaan. God promises constancy: "I will maintain My covenant
between Me and you, and your offspring to come, as an everlasting covenant throughout the ages . . ."—but God makes demands
in return. Abram is now to be called "Abraham," and his descendants
must keep the covenant, sealing it through circumcision. "[E]very
male among you shall be circumcised. You shall circumcise the flesh
of your foreskin, and that shall be the sign of the covenant between
Me and you." It's also stipulated when circumcision shall take place:
"And throughout the generations, every male among you shall be
circumcised at the age of eight days." Even non-Jewish members
of the household must be circumcised: "As for the homeborn
slave and the one bought from an outsider who is not of your offspring, they must be circumcised, homeborn and purchased alike."
Circumcision is meant to function much like the signature at the
bottom of a contract: "Thus shall my covenant be marked in your
flesh as an everlasting pact." If you don't sign, you're left out of the
contract: "And if any male who is uncircumcised fails to circumcise
the flesh of his foreskin, that person shall be cut off from his kin; he
has broken My covenant." In the next two paragraphs of chapter 17,
Abraham is described as circumcising himself, his son Ishmael, and
all the slaves in his house.

Throughout the centuries, rabbis and Jewish philosophers have offered numerous interpretations of the practice of circumcision. According to one account, the point of it is only superficially to make a newborn baby a member of the community. In the twelfth century, the Jewish philosopher Maimonides suggested that the significance of circumcision is to serve as a test of the *father's* membership in the community of Jews. You won't circumcise your son "unless it be in consequence of a genuine belief. For it is not like an incision in the leg or a burn in the arm, but is a very, very hard thing." The modern ritual, known as *brit milah* (covenant of circumcision) does seem to be a challenge for many parents—both fathers and mothers.

It's certainly puzzling that the Jewish ritual gave rise to a secular procedure, which became the norm in the United States, especially considering that Jews have always been a tiny minority of Americans and Christians have always been a sizable majority. The apostle Paul established the unimportance of circumcision to Christians in the New Testament, saying that the procedure has no religious importance (Galatians 6:15–17). Furthermore, for centuries Jews were reviled for the practice. According to Glick, the tide turned starting in the nineteenth century in Germany and England, but especially in the latter. The idea was born that Jews had stumbled upon, or somehow anticipated, a procedure with significant benefits. Circumcising was touted as reducing masturbation, partly because boys without foreskins could more easily keep themselves clean without touching themselves. Circumcision was also thought to reduce sexual pleasure (an alleged plus, not a minus!). With respect to more strictly medical benefits, some doctors began studying Jewish communities that circumcised and comparing them to the general population. Some concluded that circumcision prevented syphilis and a host of other diseases.

Circumcision became popular in the United States for many reasons. Glick speculates that the many Jewish physicians writing about the issue were not prejudiced against the procedure in the manner of some of their European colleagues. In fact, some of them were beyond not-prejudiced; they were positively eager to defend a practice that had attracted the hostility of anti-Semites through the ages. In addition, circumcision became a favorite of creative physicians who saw it as a cure for everything under the sun. At the turn of the century, births started to take place in hospitals rather than at home, with a resulting medicalization of everything associated with childbirth: that was the beginning of a surge in popularity. By 1910, 30 percent of American infant boys were already being circumcised. In 1940 it was 60 percent. Over the course of a few decades, a practice that was once seen as peculiarly Jewish and in fact distasteful to most non-Jews had come to seem modern, medical, and mandatory.

As time passed, initial rationales were forgotten. Since circumcision was performed on infants, and in fact on most of them, men might grow up never seeing anything else. And women too. Because of the ubiquity of the practice in the United States, to many the circumcised penis started to seem normal and natural, and the uncircumcised penis started to seem deviant. In the United States (but not in most other countries), foreskin-docking became part of the aesthetic norm for the male human. And then there started to be skeptics who asked why newborn boys were being subjected to surgery on the first days of life. Was there really any good reason to continue the practice?

One thing that makes these questions hard is the difficulty of disentangling the various considerations. Do any of the main rationales—health, conformity, religion—withstand scrutiny?

THE HEALTH QUESTION

One thing is very clear: *if* you opt for the procedure depicted in the video, then you should also insist on the pain relief. It boggles the mind to suppose that the procedure could be anything but excruciating, if performed without the lidocaine injections. Granted, it was once thought that babies were incapable of feeling any pain, but that view is obsolete; and the sorts of procedures in question are generally assumed to cause pain. The American Academy of Pediatrics states that the newborn's age is not a reason to withhold anesthesia; newborns are not insensitive to pain or oversensitive to anesthesia. In fact, about 45 percent of circumcisers do use some form of anesthesia—far more pediatricians do than obstetricians—and of those, 85 percent use lidocaine injections. 55 percent of circumcisers don't provide any anaesthesia at all.

But should circumcision be done at all, for strictly health-based reasons? The medical benefits of circumcision are somewhat controversial. Circumcision is correlated with a reduction in penile cancer; however, penile cancer is rare, both in circumcised and noncircumcised men. Also, penile cancer is closely connected to the HPV virus, and there is now a vaccine that protects against some of the varieties of the virus most closely linked to penile cancer (and cancers in women). Condoms also help prevent HPV infection. Another well-established health benefit of circumcision is a reduction in the rate of urinary tract infections. That's good, of course, but UTIs are easily treated with antibiotics.

Circumcision is also correlated with a significant reduction (50–60 percent) in the risk of acquiring HIV–AIDS for heterosexual men living in high-prevalence regions such as South Africa, Kenya, and Uganda. High-quality studies have shown that this reduction really *is* due to circumcision, and not to concomitant factors. This should be a powerful consideration for parents who live in such places. However, it's not so clear to what extent circumcision will protect against HIV if you and your son live elsewhere. In the West, HIV–AIDS is far less prevalent and men who have sex with men are the subpopulation most affected. Circumcision has not been shown to reduce HIV risk in that group. With respect to heterosexual transmission in the United States, there has been very little research on the efficacy of circumcision. Extrapolation from the African studies may or many not be warranted, because there are many differences between populations with potential relevance: for example, there are differences in condom use, whether for cultural, educational, or economic reasons. Since condoms are extremely effective in preventing HIV infection, we would not expect circumcision to make the same difference in places where condoms are used at very different rates (the United States and Europe are at the high end, and some of the African countries most affected by the AIDS epidemic are at the low end, according to the United Nations). And bear in mind that public health experts do advise African men to use condoms after circumcision to prevent HIV infection or transmission. Of course, condoms are also valuable for preventing other sexually transmitted diseases as well as pregnancy. All that being said, it's reasonable to think that there is some HIV prevention associated with circumcision, wherever you live. And we should bear in mind that some of the benefit goes beyond men—women are less likely to be infected with HIV when fewer men have it, and thus also less likely to pass it on to babies during pregnancy.

Putting all three health benefits together, along with others, the aggregate is at least some reason to circumcise. But then there are costs, as well. Foreskins function in a way that's pleasing to those who have them (though rarely missed by those who lack them). The circumcised boy loses that functionality. He also runs risks from having the procedure. Though very rare, there are periodically deaths and injuries as a result of circumcision. The costs narrowly related to the procedure are pain during the procedure, especially if anesthesia isn't used (which simply seems inexcusable); and pain during the recovery period.

So where does that leave us? In 2012, the American Academy of Pediatrics (AAP) announced its new position on circumcision: that the health benefits of the procedure (for American newborns) outweigh the risks, but nevertheless are not great enough to justify recommending routine circumcision for all male newborns in the United States. On the other hand, they advise that insurance companies should cover the procedure. By contrast, in the United Kingdom, the National Health Service doesn't recommend circumcision and doesn't pay for it. Likewise, the Canadian national health service doesn't pay for routine circumcision. And even in the United States, Medicaid doesn't cover the procedure in eighteen states (as of 2016).

The AAP policy statement states that parents should decide "whether circumcision is in the best interests of the male child," but it also says this: parents "will need to weigh medical information in the context of their own religious, ethical, and cultural beliefs and practices." Putting ethics in a separate "context" list might make it seem as if health considerations don't involve ethics, but that's not so. It's an ethical matter how we should use the facts about health costs and benefits to arrive at a conclusion about what is medically warranted and what isn't.

One thing we must do, to make an ethical assessment of the health question, is to focus on health ethics rather than conformity or religion. I see no way to avoid these distractions except through the help of a thought experiment. So please imagine this: a world in which boys are born both with and without foreskins, like they are actually born with different skin colors or eye colors. Nobody stands out for having a foreskin or lacking a foreskin in Mixed World. Men don't care if they are foreskin matched with their sons any more than they care if they are eye-color matched with their sons. The average man would have seen both kinds of penises and the average heterosexual woman would have had partners with both kinds. There is no practice of routine circumcision, like in the real world we have no practice of routine infant tattooing, scarification, or ear-lobe removal.

Now imagine that you are going to have a baby boy in Mixed World, and then this happens: scientists start studying the two groups and decide there are certain health benefits to having no foreskin. The costs and benefits are exactly what they are in the real world, but there are no conformity or religion factors. What will you do? What should you do?

One possibility is to do just as the cost-benefit analysis suggests. If benefits are even slightly higher than costs, then we should have the procedure done. I think this would be the right approach if we were thinking about any number of other medical issues. Should the obstetrician put antibiotic drops in your baby's eyes right after birth? If the benefits exceed the costs, then yes. Should the pediatrician draw blood to check your baby for some possible problem? If the benefits exceed the costs, then yes. However, circumcision differs from drawing blood or giving eye drops. Unlike these procedures, it's the permanent, body-altering removal of a healthy, functional body part. Unlike other parts, such as blood, or the stump of the umbilical cord, the foreskin would be a permanent part, if it weren't for the procedure—a part on the outside, experienced as part of one's personal "surface." And the foreskin is a perfectly normal part, unlike a diseased appendix. Because circumcision is body-altering in this distinctive way, it seems proper to hold removing it to a higher standard than any of these other procedures—giving eye drops, drawing blood, and so on. We need more than benefits exceeding costs, we need . . . what? The higher standard might be that benefits exceed costs by a wide margin. Or that they exceed costs by a margin that's impressive to all thoughtful, educated people, so we've essentially reached consensus that the procedure is worthwhile. Or the higher standard might be that we can say for sure what our son would want us to do.

To my mind, these higher standards are not met, and I suspect that if we were in Mixed World, most parents would see that they are not met. It's *odd* to perform surgery on a newborn baby instead of leaving him whole. It's odd to make the judgment on a baby's first day of life that a healthy, normal part of him is dispensable—that nature made a mistake. When health considerations *alone* are our guide, we do surgery on newborns only for the most compelling of reasons, and the health reasons in support of circumcision don't seem to rise to that level.

THE CONFORMITY QUESTION

Suppose (either because you agree or for the sake of argument) that you wouldn't circumcise for purely health-related reasons. If that's your verdict about health matters, should you let conformity considerations move you? (We will turn shortly to religion.) To think about conformity considerations, we need to move back from Mixed World to the real world, and we need to choose some place to land. Let's land in the United States, where most people do circumcise. Could it make sense to go along with majority practice, so that your son will feel comfortable around his peers, or so that he will feel the same as his father, or so that his father will feel the same as him?

Certainly parents will do all sorts of things over time to help a child fit in, even making choices that they consider second best. You may not want your child watching stupid TV shows, but may let her do so anyway so she fits in with her peers. You may find girls' fashions too sexualized, but may bend so your child can blend in. You may have a vegetarian household but send a child to school with ham sandwiches, for the same sorts of reasons. In fact, it would be downright rigid and insensitive to make every single decision about a child's life with studied obliviousness to the world the child has to fit into. There are decisions we have to make about our children in light of what everyone else is doing, but we're talking about surgery here. When it comes to surgery, even minor surgery, there is a lot to be said for being conservative. Cutting for conformity is a lot different from getting cable TV for conformity—isn't it?

It can't be said that we should never cut for the sake of conformity. A friend of mine in graduate school had a sixth finger that dangled nonfunctionally on the side of his hand. It doesn't seem as if it would have been wrong for his parents to decide to have it excised when he was an infant. He grew up in another country and I'm not sure what he went through—it would have been awkward to ask—but in an American school you would probably have a rough time as a kid with an extra finger. If the dangers of surgery were small, I can see sheer social conformity as a reason to operate. On the other hand, even clear-cut abnormalities are not always grounds for intervention. I know of another child who was born with conjoined toes. Though this might result in teasing, the parents didn't intervene; a surgeon advised them that the procedure would be too complicated to be worth doing, if the child wasn't concerned about her toes. We can justify low-risk interventions to prevent a child being different from the biological norm in ways the *child* (not just the parent) cares about.

But there's something distinctive about removing foreskins for purposes of conformity, as opposed to removing a sixth finger or separating toes: the pressures to do it have everything to do with history and culture, not with a simple biological norm. Biologically speaking, a foreskin is more like a fifth finger than a sixth finger. It's owing to the practices of human societies, past and present, that a foreskin is seen in some places as something outside the norm. The parents who remove a foreskin so the boy conforms are acquiescing to very arbitrary cultural forces. In principle such forces could push us in any direction.

I do know some wonderful parents who did cut for conformity. One set of parents had no personal problem with the uncut penis—they came from a country without the practice of circumcision. They also weren't worried about father-son matching. (And health issues weren't a factor.) However, they made the decision at a time when most boys were being circumcised in the United States, and even more in the region and social class where the boy would grow up. It seems right to say that as a group, parents bending to that pressure are going along with an unfortunate and unwarranted custom. The more people rebel, the less likely that the custom will continue, putting future parents in the same bind and future babies under the scalpel. It's harder to say, of any particular individual parents, that they specifically should rebel and that their son should have to deal with the resulting non-conformity. Like in chapter 3 when the topic was population, there is a discrepancy between two levels—the collective and the individual, what we should do and what I should do. It's fair to ask: how much should one child have to sacrifice, to be part of a large-scale effort that's good and just?

I'm inclined to celebrate changes on the larger scale—the news, for example, that circumcision levels are decreasing in the United States. But because, as parents, we want to protect our own individual children, the clarity on the large scale does not make our personal decisions obvious. Hurray for mass rebellion, but I do understand parents worrying about their own individual child's experience of not fitting in.

THE RELIGION QUESTION

We asked if we should let ourselves be moved from an anti-circumcision position to a pro-circumcision position by considerations of conformity, and now we'll ask the same question about religion. If there were no solid health rationale, would Jewish parents nevertheless have an impeccable religious rationale? (I'm going to frame the question this way because of my own Jewish identity and because of the roots of American circumcision in Judaism; the religious question can certainly be raised in the context of other religious traditions.)

To some extent the religion question is a special form of the conformity question. Like the parents who want their son to be able to blend in in a school locker room, Jewish parents want their Jewish sons to feel comfortable in other social settings. But there is more to it. Being uncircumcised may make a Jewish boy feel different, but the religious rationale is not simply that. The argument, rather, is that it can't be wrong to meet the prerequisites of your own religion and religious identity. And many Jews agree on the centrality of circumcision. In Genesis 17, God does say an uncircumcised boy "shall be cut off from his kin." Throughout Jewish history, the Jews were known as a group who circumcised, and endured endless hostility and ridicule because of it. The popular Jewish writer Anita Diamant says this about circumcision in her book *How to Raise a Jewish Child*: "The most compelling answer to the question of why we do this to our sons is that if we stop doing *brit milah* we stop being Jews."

The Reform Movement within Judaism has at least been open to changing the "how," if not the "that." At a Reform *brit milah*, the circumciser can be a physician mohel instead of a traditional mohel. Some physician mohels use lidocaine injections, just like in the Stanford video, so the debate about religiously motivated circumcision doesn't have to be primarily about subjecting babies to pain for religious reasons. However, the pain issue can't be completely avoided. Orthodox Judaism rejects the use of physician mohels. Orthodox mohels can't use lidocaine injections and don't use other types of pain relief either (except as aftercare). The procedure they use is much faster than the one involving the Gomco clamp in the Stanford video, but it has to be painful. (An Orthodox circumcision can be seen close-up in the movie *Cut*—a critique of religious circumcision by Eliahu Ungar-Sargon, who was raised in an Orthodox family.) As the AAP says, the young age of a newborn shouldn't make us think otherwise.

Would Jews stop being Jews if they abandoned *brit milah*, as Anita Diamant claims? There are Jews who find this unconvincing, including Leonard Glick, the Jewish author of the fascinating book I mentioned earlier. Glick asks how it can be that Jews must circumcise to remain Jews, but (according to most Jews in the United States) they may violate so many other biblical commands and ignore so many of the traditions maintained throughout Jewish history. What is it about circumcision that makes it more essential than keeping the Sabbath or complying with the Torah's hundreds of dietary laws—practices dropped by most non-Orthodox Jews? Glick speculates that the perception of circumcision as being more essential has to do with the fact that *brit milah* is a one-day event, easily incorporated into a modern, assimilated lifestyle. Were the

Sabbath or a kosher diet given that centrality, Jews couldn't thrive in many modern occupations and couldn't live lives fully integrated with the lives of non-Jews. This may explain the perception that circumcision is critical for Jewish identity, but of course doesn't actually validate it. In Glick's view, circumcision really *isn't* central to Jewish identity.

There's one especially compelling reason to think circumcision isn't critical to Jews remaining Jews. Girls, of course, don't have foreskins, and so aren't circumcised. The covenant isn't marked in *their* flesh. I invite you to think once again about Mixed World, where half of all boys have foreskins and half, by nature, do not. In that world I think it's impossible to imagine Genesis 17 being taken seriously, much less written. The covenant couldn't be marked in the flesh of half of all Israelite men, but not the other half—assuming all of them do matter equally. Likewise, were women regarded as equal members of the community, it would seem preposterous to suppose the seal of the covenant had to be inscribed in the male half of the community, even though it couldn't be inscribed in the foreskinless female half. The implicit sexism of the Genesis 17 passage is one reason we should not treat it as sacrosanct, let alone as singularly sacrosanct.

There are Jewish skeptics about circumcision who are already raising sons who see themselves as Jewish, but haven't been circumcised. Then again, there aren't many, so the conformity issues become pressing again. A cultural tradition this deeply entrenched, but also this questionable, certainly puts parents in a bind. Circumcision has for centuries been the way boys are inducted into the Jewish community from the very beginning of their lives. One Israeli woman I talked to at my children's Jewish preschool long ago felt the bind so acutely that she expressed a wish about the child she was trying hard to conceive: just let it be a girl. But would it really be impossible to develop a successor method of induction, a ritual more symbolic and less surgical—and one that applies to both baby boys and baby girls?

The arguments of the Orthodox—that *brit milah* must not only continue but continue without anesthesia—are particularly unconvincing. If the argument is that Abraham didn't use anesthesia when he circumcised himself and his son, even the Orthodox have already adapted Genesis 17 to the modern world. Genesis 17 says that Abraham must circumcise his son, but modern fathers don't do the job themselves; they make mohels their representatives. In Genesis 17, it is written that all the slaves of the house must also be circumcised, but modern people, Orthodox or not, abhor slavery and would find it cruel and senseless if a Jewish slave-owner in the antebellum South had forced circumcision on his non-Jewish slaves. Pain relief is just another modernization, and not antithetical to the meaning of Genesis 17, as some interpret it. Even if we take seriously the interpretation of Maimonides, on which it's the parent's willingness to do a "very, very hard thing" that gives circumcision its significance, it's hard enough watching a newborn baby get cut with a knife, without having to see him suffer.

Putting the three considerations—health, conformity, religion—together, some parents will think three bad arguments combined just make a bigger bad argument. They will leave their boys intact. Others will think just one of the considerations is weighty enough, freeing them to ignore the other two. Still others will find enough weight only when two or three of the considerations are combined. While alone each consideration provides a weak reason to circumcise, together—these people think—they yield a strong reason.

In the final analysis, we probably need to agree to disagree when we do disagree about circumcision, but perhaps not too hastily. Discussing and debating the issue can help us clarify which considerations matter to us and which don't. We can become aware of reasons both for and against that may not have been apparent at the outset. Another parent's decision may seem alien at first, but can seem much less so after a full and frank discussion. Here as elsewhere, it pays to be a philosophical parent.

So you had a boy, I've been assuming. In fact, you may have had a girl. Do you care which it is? Does it matter to you? Will you do many things differently, depending on your child's sex? Our approach to a child's sex and gender is the subject of chapter 12. A more basic issue comes first. Who's going to take care of your newborn baby?

Chapter 11

Still Life with Child

Who's going to care for the baby?

Now that baby is at home, he or she needs to be taken care of. Parents are usually on the front lines of child care, but for some of the time they're bound to let someone else take over. Fathers can let mothers do the job or mothers can let fathers; relatives, nannies, babysitters, day-care workers, and teachers can be employed. The child can be an all-consuming first priority for at least one parent, or a parent can try to achieve some sort of balance between work and family. What should we think of the choice to put the child first, and to suspend, to the extent that it's feasible, whatever obligations may conflict with providing child care? If it's economically viable for you to stop or reduce work to care for your children, should you?

This is no idle question, as research shows that children do affect many parents' work-related decisions. Women without children participate in the workforce at a rate of about 80 percent, while mothers participate at a rate of about 70 percent. Fathers, in contrast, work *more* when they have children—86 percent of childless men work, compared to 94.6 percent of fathers. This doesn't mean there are no fathers at home with children; in fact,

3.5 percent of stay-at-home parents are fathers. But for the most part, parenthood pushes fathers to work more and mothers to work less. Stay-at-home parents are mostly mothers, and are also mostly married mothers. Stay-at-home mothers who are single (about 20 percent) tend to have distinctive motivations for staying at home with their children. Twice as many single mothers, compared to married mothers, have reasons for being at home other than caregiving; for example, they may be ill or disabled, unable to find work, or in school.

Despite all the media hype about professional women who "opt out" of the workforce, it shouldn't be assumed that staying home is only a privileged woman's option. In fact, only a small minority of stay-at-home mothers are affluent and highly educated (5 percent of married stay-at-home mothers with working husbands have a household income over $75,000 a year and an advanced degree). Leaving work is a choice made by parents at both ends of the economic spectrum. In a 2005 study, mothers with mid-earning husbands participated in the labor force more than mothers with either high- or low-earning husbands. At the low end of the economic spectrum, a second paycheck may not seem worth it, considering the high cost of childcare.

However a mother winds up at home with her new baby (and it is usually the mother), many people will judge her favorably. A 2012 Pew Research Center survey showed that 60 percent of people in the United States think children are better off with a parent at home. Others make just the opposite judgment—that it's disappointing when women leave the workplace. The philosophical parent will want to think through all the "shoulds" and "shouldn'ts" in this realm, deciding which to take seriously and which to ignore.

THE CALL OF DUTY

It used to be commonly thought that mothers—and only mothers—had a duty to be full-time stay-at-home caregivers for their young children. One could have that view out of the belief that once a woman has a child, the child's life matters and the mother's doesn't. In essence, the mother's old life comes to an end, and she must become nothing but a self-sacrificing nursemaid to her child. But no, this never made any sense. While I have described children as second selves to their parents, parents remain their own first selves. Of course they may go on caring about their lives apart from baby, at the same time that they also care about their new baby.

Some once thought (and still think) that mothers' own lives do matter, but that it takes a mother's care for children to turn out well. Today that's a minority opinion among experts on child care. It's only in the rare and exceptional case that it really seems mandatory for a parent, whether mother or father, to be the child's full-time caregiver. Granted, it's possible to imagine a case involving some combination of a child's special needs, a mother's or father's special abilities, and the absence of appropriate child care. But in the usual case, the evidence doesn't support the hypothesis that all the hour-to-hour work of caregiving must be performed by mothers or fathers. Studies of children in day care don't show they become very different from children raised by stay-at-home parents.

"Heroic" also seems like the wrong assessment of full-time parents, despite the popular adage that motherhood is "the hardest job in the world." Perhaps there is an occasional stay-at-home mother or father who really is a hero. A seriously disabled child will sometimes be better off with a full-time parent; there are cases in which a parent who gives up the pleasures of work deserves special admiration. On the whole, though, it doesn't make sense to super-valorize caring for children, especially on the account of the parent-child relationship I have developed in this book. However challenging it may be, parenting is not, at least in the usual case, a self-sacrificing activity, because children are so self-like to their parents. Making a child better off makes parents feel better off too.

It's also only in rare cases that we should consider it wrong for a mother to care for her kids full-time. We reserve that sort of full-throttle condemnation primarily for acts and ways of life that are harmful to others, and caring for your children is rarely that. Again, though, you can imagine disapproving in the occasional case—maybe a particular stay-at-home mother is the only obstetrician in the entire region and patients desperately need her skills. Maybe a mother is liable to become abusive if she spends long hours alone with an infant, so she really shouldn't do so.

We're not going to be able to make any generalizations to the effect that hands-on parenting is always required, or always wrong, or always heroic, but some additional types of cases do seem worth mentioning. The dramatic climax of the book *Into Thin Air*, by Jon Krakauer, is an account of one of the expedition guides—New Zealander Rob Hall—summiting Everest, and dying in the process, while his heavily pregnant wife remains at home, thousands of miles away. She is patched through to him on a satellite phone in his final moments for one last excruciating conversation. Considering that 20 percent of climbers die in the attempt to climb Everest, the father-to-be took a 20 percent chance of becoming a completely hands-off father—in fact, leaving his child fatherless. Do parents have a responsibility to live relatively cautious lives, so they can play some role in raising their children? What about people who reduce their role in their children's lives by ending their marriage, or by living far from their child's primary home, or by putting their children in boarding school, or by working seventy hours a week? What about soldier-parents who accept a tour-of-duty in a dangerous country? If we can agree that parents ought to have considerable hands-on involvement with their children, how much is enough?

While such questions are discussable, I'm not sure they're crisply answerable. So let's shift to a different, slightly more manageable set of questions. Our goal as parents is to help our children live good lives; so I said in chapter 9. But we aim to live good lives ourselves as well, and (if we are healthy and self-respecting) that will remain among our goals, after we've become parents. What of the person who does choose parenthood as a full-time occupation, whether for her own fulfillment, or because her entire income was going to be used to cover child-care costs? Is that a suitable way for an adult to fill her time? Can we leave work for full-time parenting and still live what ancient philosophy called "the good life"?

The impulse to be home with children—in those who wind up at home out of a preference, and not for economic reasons—can come as a huge surprise, even to the parent herself (or himself). To use the phrase of the philosopher L. A. Paul, having a child is a "transformative experience"—an experience that creates new and unpredictable ways of thinking and feeling. After a baby is born you can find yourself with new desires and priorities, ones that you didn't expect and others didn't expect from you. The situation is all the more awkward because there is an ineffable character to the new perspective. To the rest of the world a new baby is just a new baby, but to you, your new baby is your beloved, and your concern for him or her is profound. Some new parents feel inseparable from their newborns, or at least cannot imagine the long separations that would be required by a demanding, inflexible job.

Shifting to part-time teaching after my twins were born (for a multitude of reasons) was in fact transformative for me. Since work and achievement had been such a huge part of my life, I was fascinated by the rhythms of parenting and the very different way of life they create. Is this a good way of life? Is it enough? It was certainly a new thing for me that it did seem like enough; I had assumed it wouldn't be, from the external standpoint I had on the subject before becoming a parent. In fact, I had thought "couldn't possibly be enough!" many times, over many years.

EARLY DAYS

Many people get a taste of full-time parenting right after a baby is born, thanks to the family-leave policies in some countries and at some businesses. What is it like to be at home with a baby? Nobody does a better job of describing that experience than Anne Lamott, author of the bestselling book *Operating Instructions: A Journal of My Son's First Year*. At the time of her son's birth, Lamott was a single mother running out of money. On the other hand, she was on the brink of literary stardom and she had a support squad that couldn't have been more generous and reliable. Going back to the extra stressors: she was a person prone to depression and substance abuse. And going back to the positives: she had a religious faith and community that was a source of strength and comfort. She is just one person, of course, and one with a distinctive pattern of strengths and weaknesses, but I think she captures what many a new mother feels, and many fathers as well. What we feel is an absolutely overpowering mixture of desperate love and total exhaustion and irritation.

Lamott and her friends can't get enough of little Sam: "None of us could take our eyes off him. He was the most beautiful thing I had ever seen. He was like moonlight." But she is constantly sleep deprived and the baby is colicky. "I'm crazy tired. I feel as stressed out by exhaustion as someone who spent time in Vietnam." The intense love and enjoyment run throughout her journal, but it's mingled with fear.

> Before I got pregnant with Sam, I felt there wasn't anything that could happen that would utterly destroy me. . . . But now there is something that could happen that I could not survive: I could lose Sam. I look down into his staggeringly lovely little face, and I can hardly breathe sometimes. He is all I have ever wanted, and my heart is so huge with love that I feel like it is about to go off. At the same time I feel that he has completely ruined my life, because I just didn't used to care all that much.

When the colic goes on too long and Lamott can't take it any more, she knows to seek help, so her son will be safe, but she also puts her most horrifying thoughts on paper.

> The colic was very bad last night. Actually, it is bad almost every night now. Everyone is supportive and encouraging, but the colic still makes me feel like a shitty mother, not to mention impotent and lost and nuts. I can handle the crying for a long time, but then I feel like I'm going to fall over the precipice into total psychosis. Last night at midnight it occurred to me to leave him outside for the night, and if he survived, to bring him inside in the morning. Sort of an experiment in natural selection.

When postpartum depression is involved, the feelings evoked by a new baby are even more mixed and painful. Then again, at the opposite extreme, there are "good" babies who rarely cry and who sleep through the night, and "good" parents who have the fortitude and patience of saints. For the most part, the early days do tend to be intense—a mixture of the highest highs and lowest lows. Lamott's book is a classic not because her feelings are so bizarre, but because they're so bizarre and yet also so typical.

But those are just the early days. After a few months, Lamott's baby starts to sleep regularly and is no longer crying and fussing all the time. I also found that after a few months, even with twins, I could live, sleep, function, read, and resume a reasonable percentage of my former life. Let's focus, then, on childcare after the earliest days. Is caring for children the sort of occupation that can add up to "the good life"?

NOT ENOUGH

The "not enough!" view of full-time parenting is explicitly defended by Linda Hirshman—a philosopher, lawyer, and writer—in her book *Get to Work*, a manifesto that openly derides stay-at-home mothers and advises them to stay in the workforce. In her view, the full-time mother's life is the bad life, not the good life, because there isn't room for reason to flourish in the trenches of parenthood. This is the standard she considers the right one—a standard she draws from Aristotle and Plato. Hirshman writes, boldly, "Childcare and housekeeping have satisfying moments but are not occupations likely to produce a flourishing life." So what is the flourishing life, on her view? She says that a human life can't go well if we live like horses or dogs. We have speech and reason and must use them both to live good lives. We're not using those capacities if we devote our hours to vacuuming, repetitive childcare tasks, and talking baby-talk. Hirshman writes,

Although child rearing, unlike housework, is important and can be difficult, it does not take well-developed political skills to rule over creatures smaller than you are, weaker than you are, and completely dependent upon you for survival or thriving. Certainly, it's not using your reason to do repetitive, physical tasks, whether it's cleaning or driving the car pool.

Somebody has to do these repetitive tasks. If you're not taking care of your own children and your partner can't or won't either, then a nanny or babysitter or child-care worker is doing the job and not living the very best human life (Hirshman implies). But—the message seems to be—if *you* could keep working as a lawyer, teacher, or entrepreneur, because you have honed those skills and established one of those careers, then you would be harming yourself by shifting to full-time parenting. You would be making a bad choice. (I'm not sure what she thinks about women who leave menial, repetitive jobs to stay home with their kids; the objection to that, if she has one, must be quite different.)

But it's your choice! Hirshman isn't impressed with that response. Choice "doesn't remove decisions to a special realm where they can't be judged," she writes. Fair enough. If choices were shielded from judgment, then how on earth would we reflect beforehand on what we ought to choose? It's got to be legitimate to think about the case for and against a particular choice, and can't be out of the question for others, and not just the decider, to have those thoughts. There's also some question whether the choice to stay home is a free rather than a forced one, considering the options from which new parents have to choose. So yes, we should be willing to ask whether a full-time parent's life is stunted.

As for reason, or its absence, parenting certainly does use the brain differently than many an occupation. My full-time mother friends, when my kids were very young, were all refugees from challenging occupations. Roberta had been a math major in college and did statistical work for a phone company before her daughter was born. Now at home caring for her child, her days were certainly spent in a less brainy fashion. But what would ancient accounts of the good life really say about Roberta? Not exactly what Hirshman wants them to say. What they admire most is not the brainy competence of a professional. For both Plato and Aristotle, the consummate use of reason involves not just some peculiarly human endeavor, but the contemplation of timeless realities. The life of a leisured philosopher is the very best life. Roberta did nothing like that at the phone company and nothing like that at home.

The ancients did regard reason as having practical application: for Aristotle, reason makes us brave instead of overwrought or timid; truthful instead of boastful or self-effacing; liberal spenders, instead of spendthrifts or misers. Generally, reason enables a person to find the virtuous mean between extremes of feeling and behavior. Those virtues are best exercised on the battlefield and by political leaders, Aristotle believes—certainly not at home and not at the office either.

Mothers, or the workers who take care of children, certainly do important work, in the ancients' eyes, since they see the education of young children as critical to their development and needing to be done properly; but as a way of life, taking care of children isn't especially desirable. When Aristotle lists the virtues that are the critical ingredients of the good life, he leaves out some of those most needed in the course of childcare—virtues like empathy, patience, and compassion. And a parent's existence certainly lacks the sort of freedom and leisure that Aristotle sees as crucial for the very best life. But then, working for wages does too.

Rejecting the ancients' obsession with leisure and their exaltation of the virtues of philosophers, politicians, and soldiers, there's still something left that we might use to build an updated account of the good life: the idea that we live best when reason and virtue flower. But perhaps this can be a more inclusive theory, a theory more respectful of modern occupations. Ancient biases aside, reason and virtue actually can flower in the modern workplace. Roberta had use for a number of Aristotelian virtues on the job; for example, she had to interact temperately with managers and coworkers. But reason and virtue can flower at home as well. Once Roberta was caring for her daughter full-time, there were plenty of chances to be courageous, truthful, liberal, and the rest; to find a rational middle course; to keep appetites and passions in their place. And why not add more virtues to the list, including the ones most vital at home? Parenthood is actually a positively *good* arena in which to hone many of the virtues, especially if we judge by an enriched list.

In Aristotle's *Nicomachean Ethics*, reason at first gets its preeminent position from a supposed difference between humans and animals. Humans have reason, animals do not. Later on in the *Ethics*, Aristotle acknowledges that the things we strive for needn't be unique to human beings. The gods, he admits, have reason too. He writes, "We ought not to follow the makers of proverbs and 'Think human, since you are human.' . . . Rather as far as we can, we ought to be pro-immortal, and go to all lengths to *live a life in accord with our supreme element.*" Reason is one of these supreme elements, but there are surely others. It's fair to say that the best in some of us is a work-related skill: being a great veterinarian, a competent receptionist, an effective teacher. But can the best also be found at home?

Another one of my friends in the early days of motherhood was Christine. She was a Stanford graduate and had nearly completed a PhD in philosophy, but now her delightful little girl took up most of her time. Despite continual effort, her dissertation on the emotions never got done. But was Christine really not achieving her best? What, after all, is best? When we have worked extremely hard over many years to acquire a skill or a body of knowledge, it's natural for this to seem like the best thing in us. Looked at in this manner, the best thing in Christine was her expertise in philosophy. On the other hand, if what is best is her ability to be joyous, caring, committed, responsible, and nurturing, then she *was* living her life in accord with her "supreme element" in the years when she mainly cared for her daughter (and then two more children).

The ancients see the best life as one in which reason and virtue flourish, in which we reach for the best in ourselves. There are other things to aspire to, as I argue in my book on the good life, *The Weight of Things: Philosophy and the Good Life*. Besides reaching for the best, we want to fulfill the paradoxical-sounding Nietzschean adage "Become who you are." For many parents, the workplace is where they most fully develop and express an identity. Being home full-time would be a terrible loss for them. But there's no reason to think that nobody becomes who they are by doing the work of raising their children.

Sally was another woman in my circle of mother friends. Before her second baby was born, she had worked for a plumbers' association where she organized and ran conventions. As long as she had just one child, Sally was able to keep going full-time, with a nanny helping out. After having her second child, she left her job. Sally lost some kinds of autonomy when she quit working, but there was also a gain. Instead of spending her day doing someone else's bidding, she was spending her time as queen of her own castle. She was also discovering new things about her own identity and coming into a more complete sense of self. There had been growth at work, but also, in new ways, at home: she was discovering all sorts of new abilities in herself and becoming an expert on her children's medical and educational needs (which were sometimes complex).

Spending our time taking care of young children doesn't have to be a step down relative to whatever we were doing before. A year of caregiving may be a worse year of life than a year of college teaching, or lawyering, or working in a bank, or whatever it might be, but it also may be a better year. But a year is just a year. Now we must think about the bigger picture—the impact of caregiving on the rest of a mother's life.

KIDS GROW UP

Over time, there is less to do at home. Kids go to school, creating space for other activities. Mothers of elementary-school kids will point out that they're perpetually called upon to stay home with a sick child or bring the child to the doctor, so it's still difficult balancing work and family. But their free time keeps increasing, until eventually there is quite a bit of it. Many women go back to part-time work or try to resume the full-time jobs they once had.

Christine eventually did finish her dissertation, but with her husband's legal career more established, his employment took priority. Fifteen years after her first child's birth, her husband is a partner in a law firm, while she works as an adjunct professor. Sally now works part-time in an office—a job she loves—while continuing to be a stellar mother. On the other hand, Betty is a friend who spent many years mainly at home with her children, though teaching part-time. Once her kids were in high school and college, she got back to doing research, with the help of a National Science Foundation grant set aside for supporting women. A paleobotanist who studies climate change, she is constantly flying off to places like Iceland and

Ethiopia. Eventually she earned tenure, academia's coveted prize of a job for life.

Often, but not always, the full-time worker advances and the full-time parent falls behind. One study says that out of the 93 percent of American mothers who try to return to work, 74 percent will succeed in finding jobs. A large number, but not large enough. And the way in which women return is not always what they consider ideal. Just 43 percent will return to full-time, professional jobs. It's on this basis that a pro-work argument can be made most persuasively. The argument would be that if there isn't a road back to work, then a woman really had better not stay home to begin with. Even if the first few years are extremely satisfying or it makes financial sense at the time, eventually this choice may cost her in important areas in the long term. She may wind up less happy; if marital winds shift direction, she may wind up in dire straits, with little autonomy; and she may find herself stagnating, not growing. It's notable that the bored housewives Betty Friedan wrote about in her late 1950s book *The Feminine Mystique* were not caring for small children, but were mothers trying to fill time while their husbands and school-age children were away all day. Eventually we will be unable to reach for what's best in us, one might argue, if we make the decision to stay home with our kids. Mothers may miss out on the good life at the end of the stay-at-home road, even if they find it at the beginning.

So has a mother made a foolish choice if she spends some number of years outside of full-time work, and as a result can never rise to the status she might otherwise have had? Has she made her own life worse than it might have been otherwise? On the other side of the ledger, there is the possibility that those years may have been the best of her life. Later years may be pretty good too, despite the lower wages. There are a variety of experiences here, and not just one possibility. What I think we can say for sure is that some women will feel limited by their inability to get back on a full-time career track, and that this inability slows progress toward a world that many of us would love to see—one in which women make as much money as men and have as much power and responsibility.

On that basis, we should aim for significant change. Some women wouldn't leave work to begin with if there were options to work half- or part-time for a few years. An academic woman I know did have that option and now, twenty years later, her career is flourishing. Likewise, on-site day care could make it more attractive to continue working part- or full-time. For those who do shift to part-time or who leave work, assistance with returning could be offered. The assistance Betty received was unusual but could be more common. Another option is for employers to make a concerted effort to consider current part-time workers—often mothers—when new people are hired, instead of favoring the youngest applicants just coming out of school. Parental caregiving, by both mothers and fathers, is a profound human good that shouldn't have to be passed up so that people can hang on to their jobs. Family-friendly policies both accommodate that good and advance broad social goals, helping us toward a world in which women and men play more nearly equal roles.

But you, newly home with a baby, have to make your decision now, in the world as it is. For plenty of women (and most men) it's straightforward. Reaching for the best in themselves, and maintaining their identity, and contributing to a higher household income all point toward remaining at work. It doesn't even have to be a terrible wrench to part with baby in the morning. I have spoken with women who actually find it a relief to leave the home environment for work, exactly as I believe many fathers do. There's no reason to think these parents are ignoring the call of duty—there is no duty to be the hands-on full-time caregiver for one's children. And there's no reason to think these parents are making their own lives worse.

I would urge the same reading of parents who choose to be at home, whether for their own fulfillment or because they think it makes more economic sense. Rarely are they ignoring the call of duty—they're under no obligation to remain in the workforce. They're also not opting for the bad life for themselves. Yet there *are* risks in the long term. With a newborn baby in the house, it feels like you are beginning a whole new way of life, one that will last forever. But being a hands-on parent is one of the many occupations that we can't count on for a lifetime, like being a model or a rock star or an athlete, and it has the added problem that it's not remunerative, so puts us in a state of dependence on others. We can't be sure there will be paths back to the kind of work and income we want. Those uncertainties could be fixed to some degree by a workplace that accommodates parenthood better, but for a person making decisions today, there's no way to eliminate the uncertainties. Leaving work to be a hands-on parent is a risky business, but then again, so are many moves in life that we rightly respect and value.

And so we are now caring for children, whether also going to work or not. One immediate issue for new parents is that our children seem to come in two flavors: boy and girl. The philosophical parent will want to think carefully about what to make of that, and whether it's even entirely true. What should parents think and do about gender?

Chapter 12

Boys and Girls

Is it okay to prefer a girl or a boy?
Should parents reinforce gender?

Even people without much of a prior preference get excited when a child's sex is first revealed, whether during an ultrasound or at birth. To most people, "It's a boy" or "It's a girl" is big news. In the United States both sexes are usually welcome, like chocolate and vanilla ice cream are both welcome. Indeed, male and female are thought to be truly distinct, noninterchangeable flavors. We expect raising a boy to be quite different from raising a girl. So learning you're having a boy or a girl is learning quite a bit about what the future holds.

What is it you want, if you want a girl or you want a boy? Very likely, it's not only a matter of the physical features that distinguish boys and girls. You expect something inside to be different, but what? We're drawn to maleness and femaleness as distinct inner qualities without being able to say exactly what they are.

Pushed to explain, we might say there's a bit more social connect-edness to a girl, compared to a boy. And there's a bit more "rough and tumble" to a boy, compared to a girl. Of course, that's what our culture tells us about boys and girls, and we should be wary of cul-tural platitudes. Is it *really* different to have boys or girls? If there's any difference, how should we respond? Should we raise girls as girls and boys as boys, according to traditional gender norms?

For the most part, this is really a question not about ethics, but about the biology, psychology, and metaphysics of sex and gender. What are sex differences? How biologically real are they and how constructed or cultivated? How innate and how learned? The philosophical parent will have to think about these issues at many points as baby grows up. The early thoughts, when baby is at the very start of life, are just the beginning.

WHY WE WORRY

Second-wave feminists of the 1960s and 1970s vigorously resisted regarding typical gender patterns as natural and inevitable. They did so for the sake of their daughters, who were being held back by gender norms and stereotypes, but also for their sons. In the 1970s television special *Free to Be You and Me*, hosted by Marlo Thomas, kids were told girls can be competitive and independent, but also that boys can cry and cook. The message was that girls are hindered by stereotypes, but boys are too.

More recently, a second and quite different worry has surfaced, a worry about categorizing itself. If we accept that there are flavors proper to boys and girls, some children inevitably will be put at a disadvantage. Some girls aren't very girl-flavored and some boys aren't very boy-flavored. While there have always been tomboys, and many parents seem to take rough-and-tumble girls in their stride, boys are under particular pressure to be good at being boys. A boy with traits and behavioral tendencies typically associated with femininity can be worrisome to parents and to peers, and sometimes also to himself.

Binary gender expectations create problems for other kids, too. Not every child is born with a clear-cut, easily identified sex. Some children are born chromosomally male (XY) but their genes are missing something crucial for producing a complete biological male. For example, in cases of androgen insensitivity Syndrome (AIS), a chromosomal male lacks the receptors needed to respond to testosterone. These children are born with genitals that haven't been virilized during fetal development in the usual way. They look female externally and will acquire feminine curves during puberty, but they lack a female internal reproductive system and instead may have undescended testes. Other children are born chromosomally female (XX) but have genes that don't produce a typical female. Chromosomal females with congenital adrenal hyperplasia (CAH) produce an excess of various hormones, including androgens, so that their genitals and other body parts wind up being virilized to some degree.

These two conditions as well as various others put a small number of children between the two sexes (1.7 percent of children, by one estimate). Medical intervention often comes next, as parents and professionals strive to make these children more nearly look and feel like typical males or females. For example, AIS kids are typically raised as females and have their internal testes removed. CAH chromosomal females are typically raised as females, having their genitals modified. If the interventions are harmful at least to some kids, then it's not totally harmless to think that every child must be either a boy or a girl.

On the other hand, the male/female distinction can be a source of enjoyment. We—at least most of us—are drawn to masculinity and femininity and enjoy them in ourselves as well. Plus, the initial separation of the flavors makes for the possibility of flavor combinations, which some people also find appealing in their own way.

And it starts with children. We take a lot of interest in sex-associated characteristics of children starting when they are very young, probably because we're programmed to do so, but also out of a conscious desire to prepare them for life in the society we know.

So caring about and cultivating the boy-girl distinction involves both dangers and rewards. If it were a matter of choice whether to keep the male-female distinction going, we might "do the math" and decide whether it's an overall plus or an overall minus. On the other hand, if people simply *do* come in two flavors, we don't actually have the power to eradicate the difference, whatever the cost/benefit balance. But do they? The philosophical parent will find that an interesting but difficult question.

IS SEX REAL?

Feminist parents used to take it for granted that girls and boys naturally belong to separate groups. They advocated for both groups: both were being held back by stereotypes and traditional expectations. But they didn't question the reality of the groupings. Each child has a biological sex, they thought, though there was always some question whether sex entailed just bodily differences or brain differences as well, making boys psychologically different from girls.

More recently, a new brand of feminism has raised questions about the reality of biological sex. One influential argument has to do with kids with intersex conditions. Brown University biologist Anne Fausto-Sterling points out that the way doctors and parents choose a sex assignment reflects social norms. For example, there's the norm that boys must have a penis and girls must not. To adhere to that norm, there may be surgeries and hormone treatments, and ultimately the intersex child winds up being placed into one sex category or the other.

The way this works suggests to Fausto-Sterling that male and female are not two natural, biological classes after all. You could put it this way (though she doesn't): if more members can be added to the set of girls (or boys) at will, and out of adherence to norms, perceptions, and preferences, then how could that set have real, natural boundaries? Instead, sex must be socially constructed—not built into reality, but a result of choice, culture, and belief. Boy and girl are categories like cool and uncool, or, if a little more grounded in reality, then like ball and strike in baseball. Using terms suggested by philosopher Ásta Sveinsdóttir (author of the last two analogies), we might say these properties are conferred on individuals, instead of the individuals naturally falling into categories.

But does the intersex-based argument against the reality of sex really hold up under scrutiny? Even if the line between male and female may be drawn in multiple ways, the distinction could still be real. Surely there *is* a real distinction between children and adults, but the line may be drawn so that teenagers are categorized with children or with adults. At any given time, it's debatable who belongs in the set of children and who belongs in the set of adults. And yes, there are cultural norms pertaining to being a child or adult, and these do vary with time and place, but it would be silly to say the child/adult distinction is a *mere* social construction and not at all real. It's more accurate to say there's a real difference there, but one with unclear boundaries, and one that's given rise to a variety of beliefs and norms. We could quite plausibly say the very same thing about the male/female distinction.

Then again, there's another way to see things. Intersex conditions don't necessarily make for hard-to-draw lines between two groups, but instead create another category ... you might say.

Some feminists, such as Fausto-Sterling, believe we should construct more than two sexes (she suggests, a little bit tongue in cheek, five), but that's not exactly what I mean. I don't think (to take one example) a CAH child with virilized genitals can really be seen as a normal member of a third sex, because a third sex, by analogy with the first two, would involve some fully functional third way of contributing to reproduction. That's not what CAH produces; rather CAH is actually a bundle of health disorders that affect anatomy but can also affect urination, growth, metabolism, hair distribution, and body biochemistry. More plausibly, a child with CAH has an in-between sex, biologically speaking. The same goes for AIS chromosomal males who are raised female, despite having no internal female organs and sometimes having intact, undescended testes that are surgically removed. As a matter of strict biology, the classification here is "other" as opposed to male or female. Or at least, I believe that's the most plausible interpretation *if* we take care to think of sex categories as merely scientific, and not as honorifics or as personally or socially useful labels.

Regardless of there being intersex conditions, male and female do seem to be natural biological kinds, but how, exactly, are they defined? The definition should be broad, since there are male and female plants, male and female animals. Some biologists assert that it is extremely simple: males produce sperm (gametes that are mobile and numerous), and females produce eggs (gametes that are immobile and large). But maybe it's not quite that simple. A better, but only slightly more complex, definition might be this: a male typically has sperm and a body tailored to using them reproductively. A female typically has eggs and a body tailored to using them reproductively.

On this definition, an individual's sex is a question of gametes, but also a matter of other body parts and features. It would make sense to add one more qualification, in light of the vicissitudes of life. If we want to think of sex as a generally stable characteristic of individuals, then we've got to say being male is a matter of being equipped to use sperm reproductively at least for a part of the individual's lifespan. Male humans are male before they mature; they're still male into impotent old age. Female humans are female on the fertile days of their fertile years, but also on the other days, and before they become sexually mature and after menopause. On a definition like this, an individual *could* be both male and female. But being both doesn't occur in every case where an individual has a mixture of male and female parts.

Of course, in different species, which have evolved in different environments, sexual differences vary. Male gonads and genes boost male size in some species much more than in the human species; they make for colorful plumage in many bird species but horns or antlers in many ungulates; they cause all sorts of different instinctive behaviors in many species. The stage of life when gametes can be used varies as well (human females are among the few animals who go through menopause). But the underlying sameness is this: females are equipped to use eggs reproductively and males are equipped to use sperm reproductively.

What if the equipment has been modified or isn't working well? Is a gelding a male horse? What about men with low sperm counts or beta-males in a wolf pack who will always be prevented from using their sperm reproductively? Which individuals are anomalous or altered or subverted males or females, and which are "other"? Can an individual undergo a change of sex? A durable definition of "male" and "female" will need a little more work before it can yield a clear verdict on every single case. Should the definition allude to the way an organism could function, or is supposed to function, or stick to its actual (past, present, and future) functioning? Whatever we say, the hard cases needn't threaten the basic idea that, as a matter of plain biology, there are two major sex categories. They don't threaten the reality of the male-female distinction, any more than teenagers threaten the distinction between children and adults.

MENTAL SEX DIFFERENCES

If maleness and femaleness can involve the body as a whole—its size, plumage, horns, behavior, etc.—then what about the mind? To be female, must you have a female brain? To be male, must you have a male brain? And what would that mean, anyway?

Many neuroscientists who study sex and gender—for example Donald Pfaff, author of *Man and Woman: An Inside Story*—say that areas of the brain involved in reproduction take two different forms due to the different hormones produced by testes and ovaries during fetal development. Pfaff writes that the preoptic area and medial basal hypothalamus each take two forms. "Destroying the preoptic area greatly reduces male sex behavior almost to zero. Destroying the medial basal hypothalamus greatly reduces female sex behavior, almost to zero." Pfaff says this is the case in "a wide variety of vertebrate species," though what the behavior amounts to is species-specific. A great deal of research on brain sex focuses on the mounting behavior of male mice and rats and lordosis in female mice and rats—the way females arch their backs and raise their bottoms to accommodate a male. When it comes to humans, neuroscientists seem to have a better grip on male sex behavior than female; Pfaff says abnormalities in the preoptic area reduce the capacity for erection, penetration, and ejaculation. On the other hand, he admits that the effect of brain and hormonal patterns "in higher primates has been diluted by cultural and social effects."

In addition to those very limited sex-correlated differences, are there further differences between male and female brains, so that the male brain and the female brain are thoroughly different? Now we must restrict ourselves to one species, as there is no reason to assume the answer is always the same. It seems (but only seems) as if, in humans, the brain/mind is extensively sexed. After all, there are many aspects of the brain with respect to which males as a group differ on average from females as a group. According to psychologist Daphna Joel, "There are sex differences in the size of the brain and of specific brain regions, and in composition of neurons, neurotransmitter content, morphology of dendrites, number of receptors, etc."

Along the same lines, psychologist Janet Hyde has gathered and exhaustively analyzed hundreds of scientific reports on psychological sex differences, and found some consistent results. For example, in her meta-analysis, girls smile and self-disclose more than boys in 418 and 205 reports, respectively. Boys are more physically aggressive than girls in 111 reports. Consistent with Joel and Hyde, neuroscientist Melissa Hines notes that male and female toy choices are different: boys choose vehicles and weapons more often and girls choose dolls, dress-up toys, and household items more often. If you think this is simply cultural, consider that the same is true of male and female monkeys!

So why not simply embrace the idea that boys have thoroughly male brains and girls have thoroughly female brains? In fact, the data doesn't support that conclusion. First of all, many of these differences are on the group level only—as Joel, Hyde, and Hines all emphasize. Hyde's meta-analysis shows that the differences that exist are in the small range in 48 percent of published reports, and near zero in 30 percent. She writes that "within-gender variability is typically much larger than between-gender variability." Lise Eliot, author of *Pink Brain, Blue Brain,* says that out of 124 traits that are skewed by sex, 96 are only a little skewed, with over 76 percent of boys and girls being indistinguishable on that trait. Even the traits that are most skewed by sex are still not totally skewed. Males and females overlap in aggressiveness much more than they overlap in height. According to Donald Pfaff, "only the biologically-based more primitive behaviors related to reproduction are really convincingly sexually differentiated in humans." That is to say, beyond areas relating to reproduction, brains don't have parts that take two forms, with all males having one and all females having the other.

Furthermore, the traits don't all line up. If a boy is male-typical in one respect, he can easily be female-typical in another. An aggressive boy might be highly verbal, or a doll-loving girl might be very good at mental rotations. According to Daphna Joel, a picture of an individual's psychology, in gendered terms, would involve a mosaic. Some of the tiles are gender-neutral shades of yellow or green, and then there are the pink and blue tiles, with varying hues of pink and blue. Biological males don't have minds built out of all blue tiles, and biological females don't have minds built out of all pink tiles. The typical boy is a leaning-blue mixture, and the typical girl is a leaning-pink mixture.

So to count as female, do you need female gametes *and* the right body parts to use them reproductively, *and* a pink-dominated brain? Likewise, must a male have a blue-dominated brain? It makes sense to define biological maleness and femaleness in terms of gametes *plus* the bodily features that equip you to use them reproductively. And some of the machinery needed for reproduction is in the brain. However, not every weakly sex-linked mind/brain attribute is essential to being biologically male or female, because you really don't need them to use your gametes reproductively. The normal man who smiles a lot (pink!) can father children perfectly well, as can the normal woman who's physically aggressive (blue!). These are simply men and women, not semimen or semiwomen.

GENDER AND GENDER IDENTITY

Sex gets elaborated and amplified in every society, so what we think of as femininity combines biological facts and cultural ones. In the 1950s a woman was fully feminine only if she was kittenish, a little helpless, and highly focused on finding a mate and then having children. The very feminine woman could do certain things well, like serve drinks on an airplane and type reports, but couldn't do others, like present the news on TV or function competently as a lawyer or accountant. What we learn as we grow up is a complicated set of norms, not just the rudimentary facts about sex differences.

Children start thinking of other people in male/female terms early on—they start to notice biological sex *and* learn to deploy the socially enriched, culture-specific gender system. Gradually, they also start to think of themselves as having a gender. This is different from simply finding out their biological sex; in fact, kids who are biologically "other" usually come to identify comfortably as boys or as girls. And kids who are biologically one sex can identify as the opposite sex.

In the first year of life, kids start to distinguish between males and females in their world (psychologists can tell based on their reactions to various cleverly arranged stimuli). Later, children start thinking about their own gender identity. A girl usually has plenty of cues that she's a girl, based on self-examination, looking at her clothes, toys, and environment, or absorbing the way people interact with her, which is distinctive from day one. Her inner sense of herself may play some role too, and this inner sense may have some basis in the brain (you can't write honestly about this subject without using the word "may" a lot). That would be one way of explaining why some kids are fully cued that they are one sex, but nevertheless see themselves as another. The fact is, we don't fully understand how gender identity formation works—so says Fausto-Sterling, with admirable candor. It's usually, but not always, stable by around the age of three.

Having a gender identity consists of much more than merely believing something about yourself. A belief about yourself becomes an identity once it has gained a certain amount of centrality, persistence, and pervasiveness. An identity is something that comes to mind frequently and colors a fair amount of what you do. As an example of an identity, take being a hippie. As a teenager I dressed like a hippie, congregated with hippies, listened to hippie music, and decorated my bedroom in a hippie fashion. I would have wanted my hippiedom to be recognized by others; without others seeing that about me, I would have felt misunderstood. Then again, being a hippie wasn't literally a matter of numerical identity—I wasn't a different person back when I was a hippie, and I didn't become a second person when I stopped being a hippie. Identities do less than mark the boundaries between numerically different persons, but do more than reflect mere beliefs about our attributes, like (in my case) being hazel-eyed, or liking Beethoven, or living in Texas.

Having a sex, in every human society, and for most people, goes a long way toward creating an identity. We do a lot of what we do *as* boys or girls and then *as* men or women. Our gender plays some role in our lives, every day, as much as the role is hard to define. It may not be a matter of enormous conscious effort or attention, but our sex and our gender are very often a part of our experience. Does it have to be that way? Philosopher Georgia Warnke argues that it doesn't, in a passage from her book *After Identity*, which is worth quoting at length:

> [U]nderstandings and self-understandings as men and women . . . are incidental and recreational in the way that our understandings of one another as sports fans are; they are ceremonial in the way that our understandings of one another as Irish Americans are, and they are restricted in the way that our understandings of one another as siblings are. Just as one might understand oneself or others as Red Sox fans during the World Series, one might understand one's infant child as a girl in giving her a name, for example, or painting her room. And just as one might wear green on St. Patrick's Day to indicate that one is Irish, one might wear a dress or a skirt on certain occasions to indicate that one is a woman.

Is it incidental, recreational, and restricted for me to think of myself as female—a minor and optional part of who I am? As things stand now, that's how most of us experience our gender in some respects (perhaps getting a manicure is "ceremonial" in some sense) but not in every respect. With consciousness raising, we could move in that direction, but it seems to me it would involve considerable retraining to get all the way to this sort of minimalism and the retraining would go against the grain for many. When it comes to gender, most of us want to be recognized as the gender we are all or most of the time, and not just on special occasions. Gender is a much more central part of our identity than being a Red Sox fan or being Irish.

Most people put themselves in a gender category because *all* the data point in that direction—a person's body is male, they get lots of environmental cues that they are male, they are addressed using male pronouns, and so on. Occasionally, though, the data is mixed. Many intersex kids start off objectively "other," if all facts are taken into account, but nevertheless come to have stable identities as boys/men or girls/women, particularly if a sensitive choice is made at the outset. Other children are not intersex, but come to think they would rather be the other sex, or already are (inside) the other sex, often starting at a very young age. By an estimate cited by Fausto-Sterling, .9 to 1.7 percent of North American children feel this way. Some "desist" and some "persist," the persisters declaring themselves transgender at puberty or in adulthood.

A very common theme in transgender memoirs is feeling like a woman trapped in a man's body, or a man trapped in a woman's body. Some "brain-ify" the description: a woman's brain is trapped in a man's body, or a man's brain in a woman's body. That characterization remains to be confirmed (or disconfirmed) by brain science, but at least this much is true: the authors feel themselves to be one sex on the inside and another on the outside, and they are disturbed by the mismatch. They want their gender identity to be recognized by others, possibly with the help of clothing, make-up, hormones, surgery, voice lessons, and so on.

And then there are people who have a mixed gender identity, happily presenting themselves as male and female, man and woman. This may or may not be a stable, happy state for most people to be in, but there's no reason to think nobody can be happy with a hybrid gender identity.

WHAT ARE YOU, *REALLY*?

The biological male/female/other distinction is arguably a distinction in nature—sex is "there" before culture, social decision-making, and individual learning. Full-blown *gender* is a mix of the biological, the culturally produced and perceived, and the personally felt. Gender *identity* seems to be a still more complicated psychosocial stew. Some of it may come from inside, seemingly unbidden and unlearned; we just perceive something in ourselves— a masculine or feminine flavor, so to speak. But there are inputs from the outside too. A person thinks of himself as male based not only on introspection, but after looking around at the world and comparing himself to models of masculinity. What we see out there is not fixed and inevitable. Different cultures send extremely different messages. Likewise, the strength of our gender identity doesn't depend on inner feelings alone, but also on how much and in what way gender is stressed by people around us

If your gender identity is female, though a doctor would count you as male, are you *really* a woman or a man? If your gender identity is mixed, though biologically you're female, then what are you *really*? Perhaps "really" and "not really" don't matter so much here. What matters is choosing to handle sex and gender in the way most conducive to well-being. Many societies are deciding now that the best choice is to let biology create the initial categorization, but allow a person's experience of gender identity to supersede it. Gender-wise, we are as we persistently identify.

Does this make sense? A skeptic might point out that there are people who think of themselves as young, despite being old. We don't knock decades off their birthdays, to respect their self-understanding. We insist on objective, chronological age. Why acquiesce and accommodate so much more, when it comes to gender? This is not an easy question to answer, but there's this: age dysphoria is common and fairly shallow, whereas gender dysphoria is unusual and very deep. I would advise the skeptic to think first about intersex kids. If intersex kids ought to be counted as boys and girls, regardless of their "other" biology, then in principle there can be no objection to letting gender identity supersede biology.

RAISING BOYS AND GIRLS

Parents have to make many decisions that affect their children's experience of sex and gender. The first one is whether to let themselves care whether they have a boy or a girl. Should you think you've learned something significant when the obstetrician tells you your child's sex?

All of the issues I've touched on in this chapter come to bear on thinking this through. At the very least you've learned something about the physical child who will grow up in your house. You've also learned what kind of expectations society will have of your child. But have you learned more about your child than that? You could easily go overboard here. If "it's a boy" makes you expect an all-blue mosaic or "it's a girl" makes you expect an all-pink mosaic, you may be in for a surprise. Your girl could easily be a ruffian who likes dolls; your boy may be sensitive and squeamish, yet fond of trains and explosions. But the evidence does give us reason to expect a somewhat different creature, depending on natal sex. Boys are not from Mars and girls are not from Venus, but it's reasonable to expect differences of a much more subtle sort. Boys and girls are not as different as cats and dogs, but they're more different than black cats and grey cats. If we tamp down unrealistic and oppressive desires for pure femininity or pure masculinity (should we have them), then I think it's not misguided to care about the news that you're having a boy or a girl—it's not merely news about the social norm impositions and specific puberty experiences that lie ahead.

Some think that gender should not be read off of natal biology, but chosen by children themselves. We should respond to children neutrally until they have declared themselves—probably not until age two or three. That seems to be the view of Kathy Witterick and David Stocker, Canadian parents of three children who took an unusual approach to parenting a few years ago and attracted a great deal of media attention. Their first two children were given gender-neutral names—Jazz and Kio—and the freedom to dress as they pleased. In a picture, it's evident that Jazz, biologically a boy, likes to wear girls' clothing. Kio looks somewhat like a girl, but it's hard to know for sure. Taking gender-neutral parenting to another level, they decided to conceal the sex of their third child, Storm. That way, the world wouldn't be able to treat Storm like a boy or like a girl; and research does show people react to boys and girls differently from the earliest age, handling boys more roughly, for example.

The result? As of about age three, Storm sometimes said "I'm a boy" and sometimes said "I'm a girl"—a perfectly good outcome, according to the child's parents. Now five, the media lights have been turned off, and it's not clear what gender identity Storm has developed. No doubt the parents think it would be fine either way, or if Storm had maintained a mixed gender identity.

Storm's family doesn't see its approach as merely permitted, but rather as required. A California academic puts it in a way they find appealing: "Every child has a right not to be 'gender diagnosed,'" according to Jane Ward. Perhaps they would also want to appeal to the right to an open future. Gender identity, they might say, is something children must come to for themselves—like whom they marry and what career they pursue. And yes, it may be more a matter of "coming to" than choice. Nobody explicitly decides on their gender identity. But, the argument would go, people should freely and independently develop a gender identity, not have one foisted upon them by endless parental and societal training.

As I argued in chapter 9, we shouldn't think children must have open futures in every respect. It's okay to close off the future in which a child has crooked teeth, and the future in which a child suffers from vaccine-preventable diseases. We can say pretty confidently that straight teeth are better and very confidently that good health is better. Here, we can't say that a female gender identity is better than a male gender identity, or vice versa, but can't we say something else? Isn't it usually better for a person to have *some* stable gender identity? People who fluctuate between different gender identities—and some do—seem to experience the fluctuation as a problem, and sometimes as a very desperate problem. Coming into a new gender identity is not at all like changing your mind about who your friends are or even what religious beliefs to hold on to—it's a much more wrenching thing to do. Blocking off major inputs that may very well be involved in gender identity formation therefore seems unwise. Doing so probably slows down gender identity formation and makes it more of a focus for the child—to the child's detriment, considering that there are many other things a child needs to focus on, like playing and learning and making friends.

We can go further here. Isn't it better also, on sheer health grounds, for a person who is biologically one sex to have the matching gender identity? For people who persist in a nonmatching gender identity, the road ahead is difficult. According to transgender memoirs and sensitive third-person accounts like Andrew Solomon's in *Far from the Tree*, it is often a painful thing to feel oneself to be male, but to have a female body, and vice versa. Many people in that situation converge on the same negative description—they write or say they feel trapped in the wrong body. For children there are particular discomforts, like dreading the onset of puberty. Granted, mixtures don't bother everyone—there are people who will settle into a hybrid gender identity comfortably. But it's fair to assume most people will be happier being one sex/gender, in both mind and body.

But does parental behavior make any difference? I don't think we know for sure, but it might. Storm's family seems to provide data pointing in that direction. Gender nonconformity like Jazz's and Storm's is unusual, but two kids in the family display it. While there could be a genetic explanation for that, it's plausible to think the family's approach to parenting is at least part of the explanation. It sounds as if the children are encouraged to think it's particularly admirable to combine biological boyhood with typical girl ways, and biological girlhood with typical boy ways. We probably aren't helping our children live good lives if we positively encourage an identity/biology mismatch. And likewise if we withhold information from a child that might help them arrive at a match.

In short, there are good reasons to let our kids know early on whether they're a boy or a girl (biologically speaking). Clothing, hairstyles, and décor that gently remind kids where they fit on the gender grid are probably helpful. This is no different from what we do to teach kids about their place in the world in other regards. We do teach children many things about their identities, whether intrinsic or not: you're a child, not an adult, and this is how children are expected to behave—no swearing allowed. You're an American, not an Italian; please stop speaking Italian to the waiter. You're a twenty-first century suburbanite, not a twelfth-century peasant; so wash up and put on clean clothes. Gender, even if regarded as provisional, is another basic component of identity. There's no sense in hiding the most elementary gender rules from children, as much as we should challenge the more oppressive and restrictive rules. We may and should do away with "boys shouldn't cry, girls must be bad at math," but we ought to let kids know that boys don't wear dresses and girls keep their shirts on.

Minimal steering is not the same as demanding the "right" gender identity from a child. In homes where there is minimal steering, kids can still come to have unexpected gender identities. The intersex kid initially presumed to be more comfortable as a male may want to switch to being a female. The seemingly typical three-year-old boy may gradually start to think of himself as a girl. In another family, depicted in an Oprah Winfrey Network documentary, a biologically male child (also, coincidentally, named "Jazz") seems to have had the same upbringing as two older brothers, but started to identify as a girl very early on. Once gender nonconformity stabilizes, it becomes much harder to say that steering is helpful, or even how it would work. The time for steering is over, once it's clear that an older child, or teenager, or adult child, is in fact transgender. What's needed, and needed badly, is support and acceptance; parents must be willing to become allies for transgender kids trying to make their way in a society still full of hostility toward them.

Most parents go much, much further than minimal steering toward the biologically expected gender identity, whether consciously or unconsciously. Children are trained to have all sorts of beliefs about the difference between boys and girls—beliefs most of which go beyond the evidence. They're inculcated with whatever norms are prevalent at the time. They're also encouraged to make their gender identity a huge part of their lives. Being a girl is not permitted to be just one part of a child's identity, but must be a very big part, a constantly important, foundational part. Kids are trained to think it's bad to deviate from standard gender norms at all. This is the equivalent of not just letting kids know they are Americans, but encouraging them to develop their American-ness at every turn. Imagine worrying continually: but is this sport really American? Is this career really American? Typical parents encourage kids not just to recognize their sex, but to make it an omnipresent determiner of their choices.

The point of minimal steering is to help a child develop a gender identity comfortably and securely, but also to help a child manage, and in fact positively enjoy, the gendered aspect of life. Boys tend to feel boyish if they do whatever the other boys are doing. Girls tend to feel girlish doing whatever the other girls are doing. Steering a little doesn't mean boys and girls can never mix, and certainly doesn't mean they should be pushed to the most stereotypical end of the spectrum. In fact, pushing in stereotypical directions can just make kids feel uncomfortable. Some boys are not athletically inclined, so will hang out with the boys only if there are train sets and card games and blocks around. Some girls have no interest in dolls, so will join with the girls only if there are art supplies around. But it's probably doing children a disservice not to help them learn which group they're in.

We *can* go too far, steering aggressively instead of minimally. We're going too far if we assume boys are mentally all-blue or girls are mentally all-pink; if we refuse to accept and accommodate biologically surprising gender identities; if we think of gender identity as utterly central and all-important. It's fair to say that gender is part of identity for the vast majority of people—it's not just another feature, like having hazel eyes. But parents can raise kids to think their gender is their primary and most important identity. That creates pressure to be good at girlness above all, or good at boyness above all, and that can interfere with being good at other things.

This was strikingly apparent in an article about the Harvard Business School published in the *New York Times Magazine* in 2013. The author, Jodi Kantor, tried to find out why women comprise 50 percent of business students at Harvard, but are less likely than male students to land the best jobs after graduating. In interviews, one female student after another talks about her concern that assertiveness and combativeness are career-advancers, but unattractive in women (especially to male students). The concern gets in the way of class participation, which determines 50 percent of class grades. These women want to be feminine above all, partly out of a desire to find mates (expressed by some in interviews), but possibly also because in the gender training they received early in life, femininity wasn't just one identity element, but an all-important one. Of course, that would present a problem if femininity were generally perceived as compatible with assertiveness, as masculinity is. In the fullness of time, we can hope that will become true. But for the present, we can protect girls from being limited by gender if we discourage the idea that gender identities are preeminent. There's nothing that says they *have* to be, even if it's true that, generally speaking, gender is one aspect of identity.

We are not going to stop caring about whether we have boys or girls, and few of us will entirely stop nudging boys in a boy direction and girls in a girl direction. Up to a point this is both reality-based and in a child's interests. We enjoy being girls and having girls; we enjoy being boys and having boys. It's when we believe that all boys are "all boy" that we get into trouble, and when we believe that all girls are "all girl." It's also oppressive for kids to have predominantly gender-centered identities, as if gender was more important than anything else. Here as in many parental tasks we need to follow the Goldilocks rule. The amount of attention we pay to sex and gender should be: not too much and not too little, but just right.

Chapter 13

The One and the Many

When must I contribute to group efforts?

Parenthood makes us ask hard questions at every turn. Even something as simple as getting in the car raises questions: Must we put a child in a car seat every single time we go for a drive? Do older children have to wear seat belts? When should a child move to the front passenger seat, despite the back seat being safer?

These are all questions about how parents should treat their own kids. But parenthood also draws us into the wider world—the preschool, the playground, the public school, the community. We soon encounter groups of parents as well as larger groups who act collectively to create benefits that couldn't be generated one parent–child pair at a time. When do we have to join in on these collective ventures?

In the first sections of this chapter we'll think about some less serious variations on this theme, which will later help us with a much more serious issue: the ethics of vaccination.

THE TALENT SHOW

Little children are adorably innocent and guileless on stage, and fun to watch, whether talented or untalented. Parents come to a talent show primarily to see their own children perform, but this is not to be a private performance, like you could enjoy at home. You are there to see your child perform in front of an audience. That's supposed to give your child a chance to overcome stage fright and receive acclaim beyond what you could provide. The learning experience depends on there being a crowd watching, not just a few relatives. The parents benefit too, because they not only see their child performing, but get the gratification of seeing their child applauded. Plus, a bit less nobly, they get the chance to see how their child is doing compared to other children. This can actually be enlightening, whether the child compares favorably or unfavorably.

Anyhow, for a talent show to provide all the usual benefits, there does have to be an audience, and there's often a hitch. Some parents stay only until their child has finished performing, which may be very early in the show. At one of the first shows my husband and I attended as parents, this was understandable. It was the middle of a Dallas summer, and the air conditioning at the recreation center had broken. The first kids performed in front of a packed audience, and the last kids performed in front of hardly anyone. But I noticed this phenomenon at all the talent shows we attended over the years. Because of early departers, audiences gradually dwindle. The room is packed at the beginning and thinly populated at the end. Families of later performers serve as the audience for early performers, but families of early performers don't serve as the audience for late performers.

Is it wrong of the early performers' families to leave so early? I think so, but why? The simplest explanation would be that the early departers cause unnecessary harm to the later performers and their families. The late-performing children can see that the audience is dwindling. These children have their feelings hurt, and they also receive less of what performing in front of an audience offers: less acclaim, less experience dealing with stage fright. The late performers don't get an equal benefit from participation in the talent show. The parents of late performers also get fewer of the usual gratifications—it's less enjoyable to see your child applauded by ten people than by a hundred.

All that's true, but I doubt the simple explanation is the whole explanation, because it evaporates when the initial audience size is very large and an early departure is *very* early. If there are five hundred people in the audience and my child is the first performer, there will be no impact on anyone if we leave before the second performance—nobody will notice. And yet it still seems like there's something amiss with leaving. It's bad, even though it's not as bad as leaving later in the show, when there are fewer people left in the audience and every departure is obvious.

The badness has to do not only with impact but also with fairness. We might say this: you watched my child, the first performer, perform. Don't I now owe it to you to reciprocate, watching your child perform? I can't discharge my debt without staying until the very end and watching every child whose family watched my child. There's something to this fairness account, but it sounds a little too individualistic and transactional. Does each parent really do a favor directly to *me*, when they watch my child perform, putting me in their personal debt? Is it the same as when people set up babysitting deals—the couple who babysit Friday night being owed babysitting

Saturday night? The ethics of being part of an audience don't strike me that way. It's more that, back when you signed up your child to perform, you agreed to contribute to the audience, knowing that an audience is integral to a talent show. You then reneged on that agreement. You broke an implicit promise.

Perhaps most aptly, we should also say this: If you leave early, you and your child receive a benefit from the one hundred or five hundred people sitting in the audience at the outset, but don't pay for it in the way needed—by staying to the end and contributing to the audience yourself. You are thus not so much in debt to particular audience members but a "free rider" within the system as a whole. You're like someone who gets on a train without paying the fare. The fare evader should pay not because she's personally indebted to the paying passengers, but because it's generally unfair for some to pay and others to ride for free. For the same sort of reason, you should make your contribution to the talent show audience, instead of walking out and thus receiving the benefits of your child having a large audience for free.

THE PARENT-TEACHER ASSOCIATION

Our elementary-school parent-teacher association (PTA) planted flowers and shrubs in front of the school one year. Another year, the PTA raised money to build an environmental center—essentially a stone gazebo where students could enjoy outdoor classes. The person who leaves the talent show early, benefiting from the large audience but not "paying" for it by staying, is a free rider, like the fare evader. But what about the PTA evader—the person who doesn't participate in PTA projects?

There is a difference here that's noteworthy. The fare evader voluntarily got on the train. The talent show attender voluntarily entered her child into the talent show (assuming participation wasn't mandatory). But the PTA's endeavors come unbidden, if you are not an active member. A small group of intensely involved parents decides on the projects. Do the rest of us deserve to be castigated as free riders if we don't actively support what they do?

It would be strange to think that any and every beneficial project devised by a very vigorous PTA has the power to generate an obligation to contribute for every parent. It can't be that my time and labor is so easily someone else's rather than mine. The philosopher Robert Nozick once made the same point with an amusing example. This is about a neighborhood association, not a PTA, but the issues are much the same.

Suppose the neighborhood association came up with the idea of enlisting the 365 homeowners in the neighborhood in a project to broadcast a radio program from speakers attached to the telephone poles every day of the year. I have already enjoyed this benefit for one hundred days when my turn arrives, but I don't want to spend my day this way. Can I really be a blameworthy free rider if I don't pay for the radio service by making my own contribution? That assessment seems to empower the community too much, putting me at the mercy of their ambitious collective projects. Along similar lines, the philosopher Garrett Cullity tells this brief story about some enterprising elves:

> On the first day in my newly carpeted house, I leave my shoes outside. In the morning I am delighted to find they have been extraordinarily well repaired. I am less delighted when I receive the bill.

Nozick's and Cullity's examples certainly suggest that we are not always obligated to pay for benefits we receive.

But now imagine the elf story continues this way: as a result of the elves' work, I no longer take my shoes to my cobbler for repairs, as I used to do. Granted, I didn't request the elves' services, but since I clearly want my shoes to be repaired and now I am deliberately depending on the elves instead of the cobbler, I'm an active supporter of what the elves are doing for me. Because I meet this "pro" condition, I *am* a free rider, and surely it doesn't matter that I didn't explicitly request the elves' services.

The "pro" condition forces us to consider one more issue. We are "pro" on some projects as a matter of taste, but on others because rationally we should be. Some do care about the PTA gardening project, but all *should* care about the sensible new security system. This makes a difference. Suppose the elves serve as security guards one night, fending off a giant who tries to invade my house and kill me. In the morning they leave a bill. Whether I *feel* "pro" or not, the elves provided me with something I objectively did need, and ethically (at least) I ought to pay for it.

So—taking into account everything discussed so far—let's define blameworthy free riding like this. You're a blameworthy free rider if and only if

1. You receive a benefit;
2. You don't pay for it;
3. You're "pro" in one or both of two senses: (a) you do support the production of the benefit or (b) rationally you should support it.

Are those conditions jointly sufficient? What if (unlike me) some people relish participating in a PTA project—they enjoy gardening, chaperoning the school dance, or whatever it might be—and my doing so would merely deprive them of that pleasure? We'd better add another condition:

4. You could pay or contribute without gratuitously taking any joy of paying or contributing from other beneficiaries.

And then there's the person with special circumstances—someone who would love to garden but has terrible allergies, for example. We need one more condition, before we can say we have a set of conditions sufficient for being a blameworthy free rider:

5. You can't claim special reasons for not paying, beyond what anyone else would have.

Phew! We've worked this hard on defining "blameworthy free riding" not because the PTA conundrum is so pressing but because we'll need a good definition to contend with a much more important matter.

VACCINATION

Social ethics becomes particularly critical when public health is at stake. We are not under attack by giants, and defended by elves; we are under attack by germs, and defended by vaccines. We aren't so much asked to pay the *bill* for vaccines, but to "pay" for other people's participation by participating ourselves.

Seconds after birth, children start to be immunized: they receive the Hepatitis B vaccination, unless parents take steps to opt out. Later, with your consent, your child will receive dozens of vaccines over the years, with the exact list of specific vaccines determined by state mandate. There is no enforcement of vaccination until a child enrolls in elementary school; at that point, you will be asked for proof of compliance with state vaccination regulations. In Texas, for example, vaccinations against ten diseases are mandated, and this mandate appears to have a huge effect on vaccination behavior. The percentage of children starting public or private kindergarten who had completed the polio series in 2013–2014 was over 97.4 percent. The percentage completely vaccinated against chickenpox stood at 97.2 percent; the percentage vaccinated against measles, mumps, and rubella (the "MMR" vaccine) was 97.5 percent; and the percentage vaccinated against hepatitis B was 98.1 percent. There is much less use of the HPV vaccination, which is mandated in only a few states but strongly recommended by the Centers for Disease Control (CDC); by age seventeen, about 50 percent of girls and 23 percent of boys in the United States had completed the three-dose series, according to a CDC survey conducted in 2014.

Given the very high compliance rates for mandated vaccinations, it's surprising that Texas parents don't really have to vaccinate their children in order for them to attend school. Parents can declare their child exempt for "reasons of conscience" without saying anything at all about their reasons. The exemption can be made for specific vaccines, so a person could exempt their child from the MMR vaccine, for example, but not from the polio vaccine. Nobody is under any obligation to explain what specific "reasons of conscience" might lie behind such a declaration. Parents do have to sign a statement about the benefits and risks of vaccination in front of a notary public. There is also an option of exempting a child for medical reasons, but there are far more conscientious exempters than medical exempters. (For example, in 2013–2014 there were about ten times as many conscientious exemptions as medical exemptions.)

I met a vaccination refuser once when my kids were under school age—around two or three—and up to date on all their immunizations. I had taken them to a Dallas recreation center for an organized public activity. While the kids ran around, parents sat on the bleachers chatting—mostly moms and a few dads. I don't recall how it came up, but one mother announced that she wasn't vaccinating her children, as if this should cause no particular concern. It was a personal choice, in her eyes, like choosing circumcision or breastfeeding or using car seats or exposing children to secondhand smoke—all decisions that primarily affect your own child. Contrary to her attitude, decisions like this are not beyond public scrutiny, but it's true that we accord parents a certain degree of privacy and autonomy about them. If we judge, we do so quietly, so long as parental decisions don't descend to outright neglect and abuse. Nobody reacted vociferously to this woman.

The truth is, only one vaccination decision is, in fact, exclusively about your own child: the decision whether to vaccinate against tetanus. According to Paul Offit, MD, a vaccine advocate and author of the book *Deadly Choices*, tetanus is caused by a bacterium (*clostridium tenani*) that comes from the soil, entering the body through puncture wounds and insect bites; it doesn't travel between people. So nobody but your own child is affected if you decide to immunize against tetanus or not to immunize (apart from more indirect effects based on use of hospitals, ambulances, and other resources).

Some vaccination decisions are partly about your own child, but mostly about protecting other people. If you protect your healthy twelve-year-old by having her get flu vaccines every year, you could certainly make the case that the benefit accrues even more to the vulnerable elderly people she comes into contact with when she visits her grandfather in a nursing home.

For most childhood vaccinations, however, the motivation to opt in has to do with everyone. The MMR vaccine protects your child from three diseases with very serious potential consequences, but it also stops your child from infecting others with those diseases. On top of that, there's additional concern for vulnerable people who may be in contact with your child—people too young to be immunized or medically unable to be immunized, due to immune-deficiency problems.

There is one more fact about vaccination that's central in vaccination ethics: we each not only actively affect others, but are also passively affected by others. Simply by standing in the middle of the herd, my child can be protected by what other parents have done (except in the case of tetanus). This "herd immunity" is achieved when different percentages of the population are vaccinated, depending on the infectiousness of a disease. The more infectious the disease, the more people have to be vaccinated before the whole herd is immune, including the small minority who don't vaccinate. Other people can protect my child completely, even if I refuse to vaccinate.

May I refuse to vaccinate my child? People give lots of different reasons for doing so.

REFUSERS

First there's the "Medically Exempt Refuser," the person told by a physician that her child has a medical condition that makes vaccination inadvisable. Children like this depend on herd immunity, because immunization would put them at excessive risk.

A second sort we might call "Doing vs. Allowing Refusers." These people think harms are not all alike. It's worse when doing something to a child harms him, and different (not as bad) when something merely happens to a child. Giving a shot is active, so to be held to a higher standard. Better to be harmed by a disease, this thinking goes, than harmed by a doctor doing something to prevent a disease. If you take this attitude to the logical extreme, refusers of this sort will exempt their children from all vaccines, and from many other medical interventions as well. But in a more attenuated instance, the attitude is neither bizarre nor foreign to most of us. Suppose a vaccine called "Killsave" had this track record: it prevents a disease that's been killing 3 percent of the population but it kills one out of a hundred people inoculated. Though ultralogical to use Killsave, most of us would not. We'd rather allow three deaths than actively cause one. This preference for allowing fizzles out when the risks of causing harm are very, very low, and what we are trying to prevent is both far more common and far more severe.

A third group we might call the "Critical Refusers." Unlike those in the first three groups, these parents are critical of the science behind current vaccine mandates. For example, some Critical Refusers today believe that the MMR vaccine causes autism (despite overwhelming evidence to the contrary); others think that certain vaccine ingredients have very serious side effects (despite reassurance from medical experts). They have no objection to vaccines, in principle, but see the risks of using them as greater than the benefits—in sharp contrast to all mainstream medical organizations. It's certainly not always benighted to be a Critical Refuser. Sometimes vaccine science is flawed or in the early days, and critics are right to be skeptical. For example, in the early days of the polio vaccine, there had been insufficient testing, and parents would have been on solid ground to say no.

Fourth, there are "Conscientious Refusers," a type of refuser I'm naming by analogy with wartime conscientious objectors. People old enough to remember the draft in the era of the Vietnam War will remember Quaker pacifists being exempted from military duty. These were people who would not go to war under any circumstances, no matter how seemingly justifiable. They didn't object to the Vietnam War per se and wouldn't have been any more willing to fight in another war. They wouldn't have fought for the United States against Hitler or with Darfurians against the genocidal Janjaweed—they don't fight, period. The analogous refuser in the context of vaccination might be a member of the Church of Christ, Scientist, a church that frowns on all modern medicine, out of the belief that disease is always a mental problem, curable through faith healing. The church doesn't require nonvaccination as a condition for membership, but a particularly ardent member might see her religious duties that way. This sort of conscientious objector didn't vaccinate their children against smallpox in the 1940s, or against polio in the 1950s, or against tetanus in the 1960s. Today, this sort of refuser would reject all vaccines, but also all other preventative and curative medicine.

And fifth, there is the " 'Why Me?' Refuser." This refuser is happy to see other parents vaccinate their children—in fact, she wants as many children as possible to be vaccinated. Given how many do vaccinate, this refuser thinks there's no need for her own children to be vaccinated. By simply living in a society with very high vaccination rates, this parent procures all the protection for her child she deems necessary. She's all for herd immunity but refuses to immunize her own little calf.

Clearly the first group—the medically motivated refusers—have legitimate grounds for opting out. And just as clearly, the reasoning of the next two groups is dubious. You would have to have a highly inflated aversion to risks of doing, compared to risks of allowing, to think we mustn't "do" vaccines, despite their low, low risks. In some time periods, a philosophical parent might justifiably have been a Critical Refuser, but not today. There is no good science backing the various media-driven worries about vaccines—no vaccine–autism link, for example.

That leaves the Conscientious and "Why Me?" Refusers. True Conscientious Refusers are extremely rare and prone to behavior much more worrisome than not vaccinating; they also don't give their children antibiotics or allow operations and blood transfusions, and their children sometimes die as a result. If their freedom to dictate their children's medical care should be restricted (and surely it should), it would take us very far afield to spell out the details, so I'm going to focus just on the "Why Me?" Refusers. They deserve most of our attention because they are far more numerous, and also because behind the facade of refusal for other reasons, often there lies a "Why Me?" Refuser. It's far easier to scoff at science and mainstream medicine if you know that almost everyone else is complying with science and mainstream medicine, creating a community with a very low risk of vaccine-preventable diseases. It's far easier to creatively concoct the other rationales for not vaccinating, knowing your kind of creativity is quite rare. If we get a grip on "Why Me?" Refusing, we may actually be tackling at least a large part of the thinking of all the refusers.

So what should we say to the "Why Me?" Refuser? If I can protect my child enough by relying on herd immunity, why should I subject my child to the small risks associated with all those shots? Do I have to contribute to a society-wide immunization program, just because I can't help but receive its benefits?

"WHY ME?" REFUSERS

A popular book about vaccination, *The Vaccine Book*, by Robert Sears, MD, articulates and defends "Why Me?" refusing. Dr. Sears does so explicitly, but he also does so implicitly—by reporting the incidence of vaccine-preventable diseases in a certain way. When we consider the necessity of vaccinating, we have to think about the chances of our child being infected by a particular germ. We don't vaccinate against diseases that are rare in the United States, just because they still occur in Africa or Australia. Sears reports the incidence of vaccine-preventable diseases based on what's happening here and now, in the United States, *where there are very high rates of vaccination*. Thus, the incidence of polio becomes zero. Who would bother to vaccinate against a disease with an incidence of zero?

Tetanus is so rare, on his estimation, that only five people a year are hospitalized with it. Diphtheria is also nothing much to worry about: "This illness is so rare that I put the risk at close to 0 for all age groups." Measles led to just five hospitalizations in one recent year. There is no benefit to vaccines, looking at the data this way; to Sears and his adherents, vaccines ward off nonexistent threats.

Looking at it without taking vaccination for granted, the picture would be very different. It's hard to say how widespread polio would be today if nobody vaccinated, but there is no doubt that it would be far more prevalent than it is. Before vaccination started in the 1950s, children were being affected at a rate of 40,000 to 50,000 cases per year in the United States. In 1952, the peak year, there were over 57,000 cases; 21,000 children suffered some degree of permanent paralysis, and 3,000 died. In contrast, since 1979, no cases have originated in the United States, thanks to the inoculation of millions of children. But according to the Centers for Disease Control, polio would come back if people stopped vaccinating young children. In fact, there have been outbreaks in the United States in communities with low vaccination rates, including an Amish community. Fears about vaccination have resulted in polio resurgences in Pakistan, Afghanistan, Syria, and several countries in Africa.

Measles is now uncommon in the United States, but it has been making a comeback in communities with lower-than-average rates of vaccination. In the rest of the world, low rates of vaccination precede higher rates of the disease. The World Health Organization reported 158,000 deaths from measles worldwide in 2011, with deaths resulting from complications such as pneumonia. Likewise, diphtheria is uncommon to rare in places where people vaccinate, but on the resurgence where they resist vaccination drives. And the same goes for other vaccine-preventable diseases.

Suppose money is needed to repair a leaky roof at your child's elementary school. Must you contribute, so your child can learn without water dripping on her head? Sears's way of representing the need would presume the contributions of all other parents, which might be sufficient to pay for the repairs, considering that there are some parents who like to be especially munificent. Oh good, you don't have to contribute! But the more reasonable approach is to look at the bill for the repairs *before* anyone has contributed, and decide what's your fair share. The more reasonable approach to disease threats, likewise, is to ask yourself what the threat would be today if nobody vaccinated, and then determine how many need to vaccinate, to reduce the threat to a tolerable level.

But suppose you do think about risks in Sears's way. You know that 97 percent of kindergarteners in your child's school (four hundred kids, let's assume) will probably be vaccinated. That's enough for herd immunity against all the diseases in question. "My child would be number 401," you think, "so his being vaccinated is superfluous! Why take even the *low* risks associated with the shot?" Are you doing anything wrong to your own child if you don't vaccinate him or her? Are you doing anything wrong to everyone else?

Taking the first question first, it's not so clear. If the child's entire environment were homogenously vaccinated at a rate of

97 percent, then the child would be safe. However, the school is just a part of the child's environment. The child will be in doctors' waiting rooms, where he can be infected by sick children. He may come into contact with home-schooled children, on whom the state doesn't collect vaccination statistics. Immigrants from other countries can bring disease from other countries, as can travelers returning from abroad. So strictly for purposes of protecting one's own child, there's a case to be made for vaccinating. But maybe not a conclusive one.

The really interesting ethical question is the second one—whether the refuser does wrong to everyone else. Dr. Sears isn't worried. We are all entitled to put our children first, he thinks, even knowing that disease levels would rise if everyone thought that way. We have a right to hope everyone else vaccinates first, so *we* can not vaccinate at all. But there is an ethical problem here. The "Why Me?" Refuser takes it for granted that 97 percent vaccinate, treating that as a background fact. Thus, the other vaccinators, to her, are environmental conditions, like the amount of tetanus bacteria in the soil, or the amount of flu virus circulating in the population. What she's *not* thinking is that every other parent is in the exact same position that she is. If each thought of the other 97 percent as definitely vaccinating, each would have good reason not to do so either, and herd immunity would vanish. Her reason not to vaccinate cannot be spread around and made everyone's. And so she is privileging herself in a troubling way.

Now, *sometimes* it's alright to think in a way we wouldn't want everyone to imitate. One person's desire to have eight children cannot be spread around and made everyone's. That's okay. We don't all have to have 2.0 children, just because that's the only desire that can be safely generalized. You might say that, likewise, the refuseniks at an elementary school with high vaccination rates are just harmless stowaways on the ferry carrying everyone to safety; they want what very few people do.

I don't find this line of defense plausible, because I think *many* people would like to be the stowaways. In fact, I found it frightening to vaccinate my children—probably an irrational reaction, but a genuine reaction nonetheless. I believe many people feel this way. Vaccinators pay their fare because they think it's their obligation to do so, not because they want to. So fare-evaders really can't comfort themselves that their preferences are idiosyncratic, so nonproblematically impossible for us all to share.

FREE RIDERS?

It's starting to look like "Why Me?" Refusers *might* be guilty of blameworthy free riding, like audience members who don't stay to the end of the talent show and villagers who don't pay elves for protection against giants. That's the question we now turn to.

At least conditions (1) and (2) are clearly met.

1. You receive a benefit.
2. You don't pay for it.

But does a "Why Me?" Refuser meet the other conditions, which are also relevant to a free rider being blameworthy?

3. You're "pro" in one or both of two senses: (a) you do support the production of the benefit or (b) rationally you should support it.
4. You could pay or contribute without gratuitously taking any joy of paying or contributing from other beneficiaries.

5. You can't claim special reasons for not paying or contributing, beyond what anyone else would have.

The only real question is about (3). This is an important condition, because, as we saw above, we don't want to endorse the position that the wider community can devise just any old scheme, and command cooperation from all. I don't necessarily have to involve myself in the neighborhood radio program, I don't have to pay the elves in the simple version of the shoe repair story, and I don't have to plant flowers with the PTA. I have to do these things only if it can be shown that I either do implicitly support them or objectively ought to.

Does the "Why Me?" Refuser support public vaccination? Now, I think it's pretty obvious that the "Why Me?" Refuser ought to support it, because it is objectively valuable to her. Vaccination will reduce the amount of serious disease and death in the community and protect her child, at the cost of very rare side effects, most of them insignificant. But we would have an all the more compelling case that she's a nefarious free rider if she ought to, and tacitly does, support public vaccination.

And both, in many cases, are true. The "Why Me?" Refuser is typically someone who wouldn't put her child in a school environment, if she thought the other kids were unvaccinated. Or she would have her kids vaccinated, to protect them from germs carried by unvaccinated children. She would have had her children vaccinated, if the community had been only half way to 97-percent compliance. Whatever she says, she is a tacit supporter. She welcomes vaccination for others, wants it to be done, and puts her children in situations she deems acceptable only because other kids are immunized.

But what about the fact that 97 percent are vaccinating, and that's enough? Considering that a school is not an island, there is some benefit to additional vaccinators. But even if that were not so, it would be problematic to help yourself to an exemption. This is just like withholding money for school repairs on the grounds that everyone else will give more than enough. If somebody should be exempt, nobody gets to designate themselves the lucky nonpayer. There are fairer ways to avoid winding up with a surplus for the repairs, and fairer ways to avoid there being more vaccinated children than necessary, though of course the differences between the cases will require different solutions.

WHO SHOULD BE EXEMPT?

If "Why Me?"-ism is *any* part of someone's decision not to vaccinate, it shouldn't be. But in Texas and many other states, it can be. Parents in Texas can exempt their kids from vaccination for any reason. They get to call themselves "conscientious exempters" if they belong to an antivaccine church, but also if they have benighted ideas about immunology, and even if they're ready to fool themselves about doing vs. allowing—doing whatever they can with antiviral drugs after a child becomes ill, but doing nothing with vaccines beforehand. Most bizarrely, they get to be called "conscientious exempters" when they are really just "Why Me?" exempters, stowaways on the immunization ferry. Essentially, you are exempt for reasons of conscience if you say you are exempt for reasons of conscience!

Exemption from school mandates started, in the 1950s, with exemptions for people religiously opposed to vaccination, and not opposed for any of the other reasons. The idea was much the same as allowing conscientious objectors to avoid military service. If you think people shouldn't have to go into battle and kill others against the dictates of their own conscience, you might agree that they shouldn't have to hand over their child for an injection, against the dictates of conscience—at least not in circumstances where the child is healthy and not imminently at risk of life-threatening disease. State insistence on being part of a military or biological defense force, no matter what a person's objections, is worrisomely intrusive.

But exemption shouldn't be easy for everyone, no matter the basis for their reluctance. The "Why Me?" Refuser has no principled objection to vaccination; rather, he just wants someone else to shoulder the burden. This sort of parent is much more like the draft dodger of the 1960s, not the conscientious objector. The Critical Refuser is also on shaky grounds. These people are often critical out of sheer stubbornness, ideological rigidity, failure to read research, inability to understand technical matters, or poor critical thinking skills. Sometimes it becomes a matter of identity to be a member of the antivaccination movement, making it difficult for refusers to yield to overwhelming evidence. Critical Refusers don't have ethical principles that stand in the way of vaccination, like Conscientious Refusers do. And although Doing/Allowing Refusers do refuse as a matter of ethics, they have an ethical theory they are not always committed to: they know we can't just stand idly by while germs kill our children, on the grounds that anything we actively *do* to them must be perfectly safe.

So, should there be exemptions only for bona fide Conscientious Refusers, or not even for them? Ending all exemptions would not totally take control from parents, because they do have a way out: if they refuse to vaccinate, they can keep their children out of schools. They are in the same position we are all in with respect to airport security. We all have to go through it, if we want to fly. We can't be exempted because we favor prayer as the sole method of terrorism prevention. It wouldn't be politically impossible, either, to eliminate all nonmedical exemptions. After all, in Mississippi and West Virginia there are none, and there seems to be no insurrection on the horizon in those states. Religious citizens seem to tolerate the situation, and can always rest assured that an all-good, all-fair god would not hold *them* responsible for vaccinations they have to accept, so their kids can go to school.

Ending all nonmedical exemptions would make a lot of sense, but this would be an uphill battle. In 2015, forty-eight states allowed religious exemptions, and twenty also allowed nonreligious "personal belief" exemptions. In these latter states, there are 2.5 times more exempted children, according to a study by the Pew Charitable Trusts. And most of the growth in exemptions over the last ten years seems to be due to personal belief exemptions. For example, in California nonreligious personal belief exemptions doubled between 2007 and 2015. But there is hope for change: as of 2016, California became the third state in the nation with neither religious nor personal belief exemptions, and Vermont eliminated its personal belief exemption.

If most refusers are blameworthy free riders—essentially, cheaters—we could make some headway by saying so openly. I am not saying refusers should be forced to wear a scarlet "R"; but we do need to make it part of our understanding of civic virtue that disease prevention is a collective responsibility, not for some to take care of while others merely reap the benefits.

Contributing to public projects we implicitly support is not especially onerous, when it's a matter of staying to the end of the talent show, or paying bills for unrequested but appreciated services. The obligation to vaccinate our kids falls into the same general category as the obligation to do these other things, but it's one that's much harder to fulfill. It's hard to take a perfectly healthy, much-loved little child to the doctor and watch her scream as she's injected with a vial of viral or bacterial proteins. Of course we want to get all the disease protection we can from others' efforts, and lower our own child's risks as much as we possibly can while sparing her pain. But here as elsewhere, taking advantage of other people is unethical. It doesn't make it right that in this instance we want to do so out of the special love we have for our own children. It just makes it more understandable.

Chapter 14

Lies, Lies, Lies

Should we ever lie to our children . . . or for them?

The ethics of lying comes up over and over again in the normal course of parenthood. We're often tempted to lie to our children, and most of us do so, for lots of different reasons. We also occasionally feel tempted to lie *for* our children, to help them manage various sticky situations. And then we have to deal with *their* lies, based on how bad we think it is for a child to lie in some specific situation.

Lies tend to *feel* bad. That's why it's possible for a lie detector test to be at least fairly reliable. Feeling bad, our hearts beat faster, we breathe differently, we tense up. But why the reluctance to lie? Why do we need to justify ourselves, instead of allowing lying to be just one of those things we do now and again?

Lying to someone gives you power over them, but a special kind of power—power over the information they have access to. Lying to someone is like putting a blindfold on him, so that he loses access to a body of information, or like putting a drug in her drink, so she suddenly sees things inaccurately. Being lied to diminishes your capacity to orient yourself to the real world, and diminishing someone's capacities is generally frowned upon. That at least begins to explain why lying seems bad, but it doesn't quite explain why lying seems *so* bad.

Perhaps the reason it seems so bad is that the capacity that is diminished by lying is one we value so much: the capacity to find out the truth. Plus, the way the capacity gets diminished exploits something we particularly value and depend on—the trust that allows us all to get information from each other through speech. It feels bad to betray someone's trust in that way, especially when the trusting person is as completely trusting as a child. Lying also moves us a little closer to a world in which the trust underlying communication is completely eroded. In such a world, we couldn't get our thoughts across to others or know their thoughts. That would be a world vastly worse than our own. For many good reasons, there's a high premium placed on truth-telling in most cultures, and a proscription against lying.

Lying is always tainted, but presumably it's not always wrong, all things considered (regardless of what a few stern moralists have said). Take the classic case of the inquiring murderer. Nazis came to the door of the building where Anne Frank and her family were hiding, and their protectors lied repeatedly—"No Jews are living here." Of course, the lies we tell to children aren't usually going to be as overwhelmingly justifiable as that lie. But if lying is not always wrong, then our lies could sometimes be justifiable.

What are the defensible lies we tell to children?

ENTERTAINING LIES

Many of the lies we tell to young children are extensions of storytelling and make-believe. Kids are incessantly told, read, and shown stories about nonexistent people, places, and things. Their lives are inundated with stuff that never happened, or even worse, couldn't have happened. There are no disclaimers like "This never happened," or even stronger, "This couldn't possibly have happened." Children's lives are particularly suffused with fiction because kids like to bring fictions into the real world through pretense ("Look, I'm a horse!"). Psychologist Alison Gopnik points out that kids pretend in a sustained way, talking to the same imaginary friend day after day or year after year. Some kids create imaginary places or schools that they keep returning to. Yet there is a line between fiction and fact, even for young kids. They do know the difference, according to Gopnik.

It's into this enriched but delineated children's world that parents insert some extra personae, just for fun: Santa Claus, the Easter Bunny, the Tooth Fairy, and the like. These characters are much like the ones kids encounter in books and movies, but they are presented to kids as if they were palpable figures in the real world. Santa comes down your chimney and places real presents under the tree that you can really open. The Easter Bunny gives you real, edible chocolate, and the Tooth Fairy gives you bona fide currency.

These figures fit in as denizens of a child's world, considering the magical beings that are already a part of it. So there's that defense of lying to kids. But if this is the defense, it matters how we do it. Parents would be wrong to tell their child about Santa Claus in exactly the same tone they use when explaining about the president or Grandma. If we tell our kids about magical beings to expand their imaginative worlds, then we ought to adopt something at least close to the tone of make-believe.

What throws kids, making them seriously believe in Santa Claus and all his ilk, is the purported way that these figures interact with the real world, an impossibility in the case of fictions. As parents, we can play up the bizarreness of the interaction, thereby making that seem to come out of the realm of fiction too ("You see, Santa Claus squeezes through a billion chimneys, leaving presents for a billion kids, all in one night"). You can say this to a child with a twinkle in your eye just like the one kids themselves have when they prance around saying "I'm a horse!" (Gopnik says there is a typical look and giggle when kids are pretending.) Sure, there's a bunny who hauls around a ton of chocolate and puts it in baskets on Easter morning (twinkle). Yes, there's a fairy who knows what's under every single child's pillow (twinkle).

The advantage of adopting this winking tone is that we're not betraying the trust of children so much. We're actually giving them the tools to answer their own questions, if they want the answers. We can have fun with make-believe even if we don't take it to the limit, making kids believe in Santa Claus in exactly the way they believe in the moon or Grandma.

PROTECTIVE LIES

A lot of the lies we tell to children are meant to protect them. Philosopher Amy Kind says she used to try to help her son avoid nightmares by spraying "bad-dream spray" into his bedroom before bed. She would imply that a special substance was in the bottle, not merely water, and this ruse helped him go to sleep. With this kind of lie, effectiveness requires a poker face. You can't play around, speaking in the tone of make-believe and planting seeds of doubt, if you want your lie to have its intended benefit. You have to either go all in on the lie or not tell it.

You *could* do the same thing for adults. Suppose your husband is having trouble with insomnia. You go to your local natural food emporium and buy him a vial of Groggy, with claims on the label about its value as a sleep aid. In addition, you tell him you did a Google search and learned that Groggy is quite effective. (In reality, you did a Google search and read that it's ineffective.) You know the placebo effect is powerful, so know his beliefs about Groggy could actually make taking it helpful.

Many of us are going to say "yes" to the bad-dream spray lie and "no" to the Groggy lie. In the case of Groggy, there's something condescending about the lie. You're approaching an adult as if he didn't have the wherewithal to solve his own problems, and couldn't thrive in the world as it really is. This deliberate diminishing of his understanding might be well-intentioned, but it underestimates him.

By contrast, bad-dream spray doesn't underestimate your child, if at age three he truly can't get over the tendency to have nightmares in any reality-based fashion. But imagine this strategy continues until the child is five, and then eight, and then ten, and then thirteen. At some point, clearly you're underestimating the child's personal resources. Or, even worse, you're failing to help the child develop those resources. So the age of the child *does* matter. In an article about lying to children, Amy Kind defends lying to her son this way:

> Children, especially young children, are not yet fully persons; they have not yet exercised the full potential of their rationality. Even when we're being entirely honest with them, parental conversations with children can never be the mutual engagements of personhood that take place in conversations between adults. Thus, we can't violate this mutuality by lying to them.

The Groggy lie *would* violate the mutuality between my husband and me.

It's hard to say when we need to tell our children protective lies. When do we need to invent things that make life more pleasant, or deny things that make life difficult? Should we tell them exactly where babies come from, as soon as they ask? Should we let them know about life's horrors? I very much doubt anyone takes one consistent approach, whatever the issues. I found telling kids where babies come from easy, even when my son asked how exactly sperm got into a woman's uterus. How to discuss the end of life was much less clear.

TALKING ABOUT DEATH

Death never came up until my kids were about three: no pet died, no grandparent passed away, no president was shot. Soon after they turned three, we faced the phenomenon of death for the first time. A sickening smell had seeped into the kids' bathroom. We speculated and investigated, and after many months, a plumber came to the house and discovered the cause—a squirrel had gotten trapped inside a wall and died. I explained about the squirrel. Then, with her twin brother at her side, my daughter asked, "Animals die, but people don't die, do they?"

At this point I was a pro-truth mother. I couldn't imagine that the basic facts of life could be terribly difficult to digest. I couldn't remember a time when I didn't know them and didn't feel reasonably comfortable with them. In the split second I had to think about it, I figured my children would take the news reasonably calmly if I explained that people do die, just like animals. And so I pressed on, explaining that our lives do come to an end, after a long, long, long time. It was a complete surprise when my daughter burst into tears, with her brother quickly joining in. This was not a brief bout of upsetness either. They cried on and on and on.

A few days after the initial debacle, the children spent the evening with their Catholic babysitter. When we reconnected in the morning, they were in good cheer. They had been relieved to hear from her that death isn't actually the end. After you die, you go to heaven.

This is a very nice alternative to lying, when it works. Instead of saying what you believe to be false, to make your child feel better, you can just let someone else's views into the room. You're not even indirectly lying, if you think there's at least a little room for disagreement on the topic. Generally speaking, it's good for kids to have many different sources of information instead of getting everything from one source. In principle, this could have been a good way out of our predicament.

The problem, though, is that children this young want to know what their parents think. They see their parents, not their babysitters, as authorities. Soon my kids asked whether the babysitter was right about death not being the end of us. I had already pronounced that death *is* the end of us and thought it would seem strange to change my mind ("Yes, my darlings, there *is* a heaven!"). It also felt wrong to lie about something so basic. All I could muster was a waffle: for all we know, there *might* be life after death. In other words, what I said originally might be true and what the babysitter said might be true.

The subject continued to come up, and the tears continued to flow. I tried to more firmly insist that we don't know for sure what happens after death, and that there *might* be an afterlife. But my daughter sensed that I wasn't being straight with her (in fact, I am almost positive there is no afterlife) and soon demanded plain answers: "But what do you really think?" she implored.

I tried to stress the things I really believe to be true. "Our lives go on for a very, very long time. You can't imagine how long—it feels like forever! There's so much wonderful stuff to do in our lives, there's no reason to dwell on the end. When it comes, we'll look back on our lives and feel content." (Granted, not every life is a long one; but I certainly wasn't going to mention *that*.)

These discussions did little good. My children had latched on to something that is disturbing: the ultimate "THE END." I really didn't have a way to make it much less disturbing. Despite attempts to divert them, for six months after the squirrel incident the subject of death came up again and again. Finally, one night, my daughter cried so hard that she threw up. My husband and I were pained to see her in such distress, and felt completely helpless. But as it turned out, that was the last episode. We stopped talking about it and over time both kids got used to the idea that life does come to an end.

Maybe I did the wrong thing. I could have let my kids believe the comforting story about a fluffy place called "heaven" until they were old enough to absorb the truth—or what I regard as the truth. There is a time and a place for protective lies. But in fact, I just did not realize death was going to be such a difficult topic.

EXPEDIENT LIES

Some of the lies parents tell are neither protective nor entertaining— they are simply told to make life go more smoothly. A case in point is the so-called Christmas "tradition" of the Elf on the Shelf (season-ally available at stores near you). This might be seen as a fun bit of make-believe in the same spirit as Santa Claus, but it's also a substi-tute for expensive surveillance cameras! You're supposed to set the elf figurine on a high shelf and tell the children that they're being watched, and the elf will report any naughty behavior to Santa. That way, even when you're in another room, the child won't take the candy canes off the Christmas tree, pull the cat's tail, or do anything else naughty. The lie about the watchful elf has to be told with a straight face, or the child won't take it seriously and will misbehave anyway.

Because this lie is so preposterous, I imagine when children believe it parents think it's very funny. This sets up a kind of interaction that's very common in the lives of children, and bothersome to many of them. Kids often know adults find them amusing and many of them detest not knowing why. As kids get older and more self-conscious, I think this becomes increasingly aggravating. They start to be bothered in just the way an adult is bothered when he or she is the object of inexplicable laughter.

So as for the preposterous expedient lie, my verdict is "no." But what about the nonpreposterous expedient lie? Would it be okay to say the mall is closed even if it isn't, simply to avoid a protracted argument about why there won't be a trip to the mall today? It would seem a little too moralistic to condemn every exhausted parent who has ever resorted to this sort of a shortcut, but this type of lie is harder to justify than the protective lie.

LYING FOR CHILDREN

Once my kids were teenagers, the issue about lying that came up most often was not whether to lie *to* them, but whether to lie *for* them. This sometimes comes up in the context of school-excuse writing.

The public schools in our community take a hard-and-fast approach to absences. Administrators will excuse an absence for any school field trip, even the orchestra trip to Florida that involves days off for sheer entertainment—trips to beaches, malls, and Disney World. But they won't excuse adding a day to Thanksgiving vacation so you can visit museums in Washington, DC with your family. Students are excused for any religious holiday, no matter how minor. But they won't be excused if a presidential candidate comes to town and you think they would get something out of attending the rally. It's excusable to miss school when you're physically under the weather to the smallest degree, but not excusable when you're overwhelmed with homework. To make it worse, unexcused absences can have serious repercussions; for example, some teachers waive final exams only for students who have unexcused absences under some number.

What's a parent to do? It's easy, if you're prepared to lie. You can have the educational trip to Washington excused if you just write a note saying "My child was ill," even though she wasn't, and likewise with all the other justifiable but unexcused absences. Assuming that lying is not *always* wrong, there's at least room for considering this option.

One way to think about it is to home in on the fact that lying in this context is not just lying for anyone, but lying for your child. This is a special case, because you have special prerogatives when it comes to your child's whereabouts and well-being. It would be different if one student was lying for another, or one employee was lying for another. Parents have a little more leeway to lie for their children than they have to lie on behalf of others. But parents don't have unlimited freedom to lie. It would be wrong of a parent to lie on immunization forms so that an unimmunized child could go to school or avoid being quarantined. So the special prerogatives of parents don't settle every question about lying for kids. We need to think about the lies parents want to tell one by one, considering which are justified and which are not.

In the classic case of justifiable lying, lying to the Nazis was permissible (in fact, obligatory) because though disrespectful, it prevented a much greater act of disrespect. Of course the stakes are vastly lower in our school-excuse example, but it's also true here that, however disrespectful it may be to lie, doing so can in some cases prevent a greater act of disrespect. Though it's bad to lie in an excuse, it seems worse for a child to be punished by the school for missing school when there was an objectively good reason for the absence. So what should we do?

Whatever the choice, it complicates matters that we'll carry it out with our children's knowledge. If we do send them to school with false excuses, we teach them to lie (but only in the kind of situation in question). If we don't send them to school with false excuses, we teach them to succumb to mistreatment. We could avoid the dilemma by not letting them take any days off to begin with, but that could mean missing out on some educational opportunities, or enduring too much stress.

Should we lie for our children in any case where the lie prevents something even worse than the lie? Some will say lies are pretty bad, so it's not common to be in that situation. Things worse than lying can happen if you don't lie, but often it's not so clear that's the right assessment. It's hard to be confident that a lie is "worth it" because of the comparative badness of what it prevents, except in extreme cases.

I find myself feeling uncertain in these situations, so I tend to look for escape routes. I may write an excuse that doesn't actually lie, but may nevertheless achieve the desired result. For example, the trip to Washington and the political rally are presented vaguely—as an "educational trip" or a "family occasion"—in the hope this will somehow sound like a legitimate excuse. The child bombarded with homework who needs a day to catch up is typically a sleep-deprived emotional wreck. It's true she "isn't feeling well," though I grant that's not the whole truth and nothing but the truth. Nevertheless, I have written letters saying my child wasn't feeling well under such conditions.

Writing an excuse that's more misleading than outright false at least gives a nod to the imperative to tell the truth. Judge my misleading school excuses if you wish. Just as I may have erred in the direction of too much truth when discussing death with toddlers, I may have told a bit too little truth when it comes to school excuses for teenagers. (If you have done the same thing, perhaps we'll meet in hell some day and we can discuss it some more!)

CHILDREN'S LIES

And then there are the lies that children tell. A strange thing about censuring someone for lying—even a child—is that the accusation burns so much. Paradoxically, it's often a more calamitous thing to call a lie a "lie" than to tell a lie. Yet we do have to encourage truth-telling and teach kids to avoid lying.

One way to frame the message is to say this: lying should be avoided unless necessary for something important that can't be achieved in any other way. Lying is a tool not to be thrown out altogether, but to be used sparingly and uncomfortably (since the discomfort is part of what makes us lie only as a last resort).

But the message will need to be even more nuanced. When a child lies to his parents, that undermines future communication, and we need to be able to trust our children when they tell us what went on or what their plans are. It's another matter when kids lie to their friends—perhaps telling an expedient or protective lie about why getting together this weekend will not work, rather than telling the truth. There's much more at stake in preserving a trusting relationship with your parents than with friends who come and go, let alone strangers in a bureaucratic setting.

Is this the right way to impart moral lessons to children—by presenting a complicated story about when, why, and to whom a seemingly bad action may be performed? Perhaps we actually have a better alternative. My children's elementary school used a "life skills" curriculum with a lot of appeal. Every week there was another life skill—another virtue—to learn about and practice. One week it was integrity, which the kids learned to define (tricky one!). Another week it was courage. In addition to discussing the virtues, kids were given awards for displaying them.

One of the life skills was truthfulness. Children should aspire to it, as should we all. Setting up truthfulness as a basic virtue (with no qualifications) imparts the main thing kids need to know. It's always bad to some degree to deviate from truthfulness—it feels bad, tastes bad, looks bad. We feel ashamed when we're caught lying, even if we had a good reason to lie. Once a child has acquired that life skill—and it may take years to acquire it—*then* we can start talking about special circumstances and exceptions.

Parents are just very grown-up kids, and hopefully retain the virtue of truthfulness they learned early on in their own lives. But then, parenthood is one of those special circumstances that require extra reflection. Interacting with a child gives a parent special reasons to bend or alter the truth—to make the world more magical for children (Santa Claus), or more safe (bad-dream spray), or more comfortable (what happens when we die?), or more fair (writing false school excuses). Once kids are old enough to see us as truthful or not, it all gets trickier, because they may take us as a model. They need to see us esteeming truthfulness as an important value, even when we do reluctantly give something else higher priority.

Chapter 15

Passing on Religion

Should we raise children in our own image?

Richard Dawkins became a hero to many people after he published *The God Delusion*, but a villain in the eyes of many others. He had rejected and lampooned belief in a deity, but perhaps he was most vilified for a point he made about parenthood. Religious education is a form of child abuse, he seemed to say: if you are sending your kids to Sunday school, you are abusing them.

Now, he didn't really say exactly that, but he did say something close. He wrote that as bad as sexual abuse can be, it's not always terribly scarring (Dawkins recounted being abused by a priest himself as a child), and in fact religious indoctrination is often even worse. In particular, it's even worse to fill a child's head with the idea that he's going to burn in hell for eternity if he doesn't behave himself or doesn't have all the right religious beliefs. That's a horrible idea that stays with many kids, requiring some to be treated by therapists later in life.

Another memorable passage in Dawkins's chapter on religious education demands that we stop putting religious labels on children. "A child is not a Christian child, not a Muslim child, but a child of Christian parents or a child of Muslim parents." He thinks it's as silly for my child to be regarded as a Jewish child as for him or her to be counted as a Democratic child. If parents became persuaded of this, then religious education would lose much of its point; parents often give their children a religious education precisely so that they will identify as Jewish children, Muslim children, and so on.

I wrestled with these issues myself for several years, because I did want my children to share my sense of Jewish identity. I wanted to have two Jewish children. At first, I didn't think this meant I would need to enroll them in formal classes. After all, I never had any religious education as a child myself, and I don't subscribe to a Jewish theology of any sort. After some time, though, I started to think it would be better if my kids had the religious education I never did. Hopefully they would feel more comfortable in Jewish settings than I did in the first few decades of my life. Perhaps they'd even have bar and bat mitzvahs.

I have two errors to answer for, from Dawkins's perspective: wanting to have Jewish children to begin with, and trying to achieve that by putting them in religious school. At least on the first score, I think I can defend myself. On the second, I'm not so sure.

BEYOND STEWARDSHIP

Dawkins thinks we must be merely stewards for our kids. We should teach them how to think for themselves; and we should instill whatever notions we think they'll be glad for, once they're old enough to have preferences. But steward-parents will give children an inadequate education, as I argued in chapter 9. Many beliefs probably have to be instilled early on, if they're going to "take." Kids need to hear early messages about honesty and respect, not just acquire the tools to philosophize about honesty and respect. Otherwise they may not develop the deep-rooted thoughts and emotions that are needed for virtues to become habitual.

Another problem is that parental restraint gives the surrounding culture more power to fill children's heads with whatever the majority believes or whatever is fashionable. Being a neutral steward in San Francisco is different from being a neutral steward in a small town in West Texas. Depending on where I live, if I imagine a child twenty years hence having been shaped more by the surrounding culture than by me, the answer to "What will my future child be glad she has been taught?" may be downright unacceptable to me.

Generally speaking, the steward model doesn't capture the real relationship that exists between parents and children. Parents and children are self-like to each other, and want to preserve that continuity. At first, the direction of influence is inevitably parent-to-child. Because his children are self-like to him, it's not wrong for Richard Dawkins to deliberately prepare them for a highly educated, Western, affluent type of life instead of trying to maintain neutrality, leaving equally open the paths to becoming an Oxford student, a shepherd, or a mechanic. We each try to give our child the life we see as desirable and the core beliefs we see as correct. At least, that's a reasonable starting point, barring special reasons we may have not to share our own lives with our children.

As avid readers and music lovers, my husband and I wanted our kids to be avid readers and music lovers—and they are. My husband wanted our kids to grow up with a sense of being British, because he is British; hence, our kids have had many trips to England and feel semi-British. We wanted them to feel connected to social justice causes and to liberal politics, so we brought them along to rallies and the like. They are liberals now, though of course that could change some day. We are vegetarians and they are vegetarians. If all that sharing is innocent, there doesn't seem to be anything inherently worse about sharing the sense of being Jewish.

It can seem to be a matter of asymmetrical dominance for parents to treat kids as second selves, but it doesn't have to be. As I said in chapter 9, the influence can go both ways. Even when kids are very young, parents are constantly altering themselves in order to stay connected to them. Surely I would never have been fond of Thomas the Tank Engine's world if my kids didn't love it so much. And I *would* have loved The Muppets if my kids had loved them (they didn't). There are limits, of course (nothing's going to make me fond of the Yu-Gi-Oh card game!), but it's through mutual accommodation that the bond between parent and child is sustained.

Later on, it can turn out that the only way to preserve a self-to-self connection is for parents to let themselves be influenced by their children. A religious, antigay parent who winds up having a gay atheist child can either open up to being influenced or feel estranged. I believe many a parent would rather be influenced than estranged. A Jewish friend whose son became a fervent Christian certainly remained Jewish, but seemed more open to seeing the commonalities between the two religions.

When kids are very young, the direction of influence on complicated matters like religion and politics will mostly be parent-to-child, but that can change with time. All things considered, the hope of passing on Jewishness seems fine, despite what Dawkins claims. But what about having children formally educated in Jewish beliefs and customs as a means of passing on that identity? Dawkins's doubts about this are multiple.

WHAT'S THE PROBLEM?

At its simplest, the complaint against a religious education may be that it is an education in falsehoods. Whatever your religion, you will probably accept this as a description of education into many or most other religions. Jews think Christians teach their kids false-hoods; Christians think Jews teach their kids falsehoods. Atheists are distinct only because they think all religions teach falsehoods.

For good reason, this isn't Dawkins's complaint. Of course, pass-ing along false beliefs will mean the next generation is afflicted with false beliefs, and that's undesirable. But we wouldn't find fault with parents as parents just because they propagated falsehoods. People were not being bad *parents* when they taught their kids the earth was flat, back when everyone thought the earth was flat. The parenting problem, if there is one, has to relate to how the sharing is accom-plished, or when, or with what results.

One of Dawkins's points is about the emotional damage done by religious education—which initially seems compelling. Telling kids that hell awaits them if they transgress can be psychologically hurt-ful to children, and we shouldn't hurt our children. However, this isn't a knock-out objection. Educating kids in ways that are clearly legitimate can be emotionally disturbing too. My own kids were very distressed by the fact that people die, as I discussed in chapter 14, but I would be reluctant to say people should keep death a secret from young children. If you tell kids about the world of microscopic viruses, bacteria, and parasites, and how their own bodies are full of them, they could be distressed, but those are the facts, and know-ing about them can be useful. They might be disturbed by the facts about 9/11, or the Holocaust. It could be upsetting to read the

Diary of Anne Frank and realize what torments a person could be subjected to, just for being Jewish. It's no simple thing to say that parents shouldn't pass on beliefs that cause a child emotional pain.

And then again, if skeptics do rest their case on hurtful effects, they must also take into account beneficial effects (while Dawkins only focuses on the potential negatives). The story I told in chapter 14 about our Catholic babysitter and her message about heaven is just one case in point. Positive psychologists tell us that, on the whole, there are more emotional benefits than harms involved in being religious.

Another objection some have to religious education is that a young child can't possibly make up his mind independently to accept religious claims or reject them. Again, this is not a knock-out blow. When my kids were just five, I decided that they should be inoculated against the creationists who are all too numerous in our state, so we spent a good deal of time talking about the age of the universe, the age of the earth, and the basic facts of evolution. Of course, it was completely beyond them to know how to assess all this information. But surely I did no wrong. In fact, Dawkins has authored a lovely book introducing kids to basic science, including the science of evolution. Much of what kids learn in school they have to take on trust, rather than functioning as independent, self-sufficient truth-seekers. If they can't think about religious claims independently, that's not remarkable.

Dawkins might respond that *someone* has done the serious, rational, empirical research that can back up science education, but nobody has done this for any body of religious beliefs. That may be true—in my view it *is* true—but we're going to have a hard time insisting on rational provability, or anything close, as a test that must be passed by everything we teach to children. I think moral education is a good idea, and we don't have that sort of research backing up what we teach to children. Like I argued in chapter 14, we need to impart "life skills" (or virtues) to children early on, so they have strong instincts with respect to honesty, integrity, respect for others, and so on.

It's starting to look like there's *nothing* wrong with religious education. That is what I thought when I decided to have my kids religiously educated when they were seven. But then things got more complicated. At that point I had never myself had any religious education and didn't know what to expect. It's when I gained some first-hand knowledge that I did start to see some problems.

TEACHING RELIGION

It makes perfect sense that we want to share our religious identities with our children, given that they are like second selves. However, our children are also separate from us. To share my present beliefs and values with my future self—literally myself—it's usually enough to simply keep thinking in the same way. But to get all that from my head into my child's head is another matter. Some of the effort is easy and uncontroversial: if I want to share a fondness for Hanukkah latkes, for example, all I've got to do is enlist my kids in making latkes once a year. This is no different from trying to share my love of the Beatles by playing Beatles songs. But if I want to get Jewish *beliefs* into my kids' heads, it takes a different approach. In fact, it's a particular challenge to share religious beliefs, no matter what the religion, because religious beliefs are typically hard-to-fathom beliefs about distant and seemingly impossible events.

Because of the odd content of the beliefs being taught, my kids started asking questions just as soon as their first year of religious school began, when they were seven. They wanted to know if the teacher was telling the truth. Having had no religious education myself, I couldn't picture the scene, so I attended a few classes. What was I expecting? I guess I thought the kids would be taught Bible stories, and that it would be left vague whether these were stories in the fiction sense or in the newspaper sense. What I discovered was not vagueness at all: Bible stories were presented as stories in the newspaper sense.

In the first class I attended, the teacher spoke about God as if he were a real person with whom the children were in regular contact. At one point she asked them, "What do you do when you want to feel close to God?" This seemed to be a bewildering question, and not just to my kids. The other kids also went silent and looked puzzled. But interestingly, they knew not to express their bewilderment. One brave child said he got in the car to be close to God. Wrong! The teacher corrected him and said, "We come to Temple when we want to feel close to God." Another question was "What does God want us to do?" More silence.

If you want kids to believe that an invisible being is available for close encounters and that this being thinks it's imperative that they behave in a certain way, it may take a certain amount of suppression of doubt and debate. This makes religious education distinctive. Though we can't give kids all the evidence we have for the science we teach them, and can't prove to them that any ethical precepts are indubitable, the way we teach those things doesn't involve the same prohibition on skepticism and debate. We don't ask kids to turn off their critical faculties, but instead answer questions as best we can. It *is* objectionable, I think, to teach the improbable and then disallow what naturally comes of the improbability: questioning, doubting, debating, challenging. It's not unfair to call this a process of indoctrination.

Another worry I had was that the religious school taught kids to believe things that the adults in charge didn't even consider true. For example, in one lesson a teacher spoke about Abraham. "You mean Abraham Lincoln?" said a child. The teacher allowed that Abraham from the Bible inhabited the same dimension of reality as Abraham the president; he was just a different Abraham. Which one? The teacher answered: the one who almost killed his son. This was not presented to children as an instructive story about faith, but as a historical sequence of events. Do the adults believe the story of Abraham and Isaac is true? In my experience of the clergy at this liberal temple, I get the impression the answer is no. They know the difference between history and myth.

When I asked the religious school director about these issues, he couldn't have been more supportive and understanding, but his explanation didn't make much sense to me. He explained that young children had to be taught simple ideas—they weren't ready for complexities. I suspect the real reason for keeping it simple at a young age and discouraging questions is that young children are thought to be especially trusting and receptive. If we impart a body of doctrine to them when they are at that trusting stage of life, it's more likely to sink in and take root.

Perhaps both are true: kids are trusting, and they are capable of doubting and questioning. But it's disturbing to think their trust is being exploited for purposes of inculcating beliefs the adults don't even have. But then, who was I to complain? I had enrolled my kids in this school knowing they would be taught at least *some* things I don't believe—like the basic idea that there is a god who created the world and cares about us. I had to be complicit in this exploitation of their trust.

Now, lies are not all bad, as I argued in chapter 14, so religious-education lies could, in principle, be defensible lies. The category of the lie is the lie that shores up identity, for that really is the goal, for many teachers and parents involved in religious education. (Another example of an identity-supporting lie is "My country is the greatest country in the world.") Is the identity-supporting lie another class of sometimes-defensible lies, like entertaining lies, protective lies, and expedient lies? I can't say for sure, but I was starting to feel quite uncomfortable with my children's religious education.

After visiting several classes and also visiting some other religious schools, I decided I had to give up on religious education. Not only did I have the worries about indoctrination and lying, but the effort to forge a Jewish identity in my children by imparting beliefs wasn't working. My kids thought these beliefs were ridiculous. They didn't believe the story about Moses receiving laws from God on a mountain top. They didn't think there was an Abraham who was told by God to sacrifice his son. One day my daughter said, "If this is what being Jewish is, then I'm not Jewish." These beliefs felt very foreign to her, not familiar and appealing, like Hanukah latkes. At that point we switched to a different mode of being Jewish, one that involves activities, rituals, music, and social justice causes, but no formal religious education.

THE DEVOUT

The objections I have made so far may be particularly applicable when parents are more liberal, not more conservative. It's in a liberal setting that parents and teachers may be lying to kids when they tell them about Moses meeting God on the mountain top. It's in a liberal setting that kids may respond with doubts they are not supposed to articulate. In a conservative setting, these very ideas will have been conveyed and reinforced more firmly and consistently.

Kids in that setting are probably more prepared to think Moses really did meet God on the mountain top—literally. So doubts are not being suppressed. And the adults teaching these things are not lying, but really believe them.

There's another objection that particularly pertains to religious education in the most conservative settings. Liberal Jews don't encourage doubt in a religious school classroom, but neither do they punish it. When I went to see the religious school director, there was no drama, no rejection. Around that time I also talked to a parent involved in curriculum development for the school, and she declared herself an agnostic. I had even attended a bat mitzvah during which the girl's father had declared himself an atheist. By contrast, doubt is more aggressively suppressed in certain conservative settings.

One method is to build mechanisms of doubt-suppression into the religion itself. A tenet of some Christian denominations is that hell awaits the nonbeliever. In some religions, religious faith is set up as a virtue, whereas religious doubt is set up as a vice. You are a bad person if you question what your coreligionists believe. A religion may prescribe terrible punishments for the apostate, even death itself. In other religions, permanent shunning is the punishment for the person who stops believing and living as the religion requires.

I suggested earlier that the problem with religious education is not the basic aim of sharing beliefs and customs with our children, but rather how that sharing is accomplished. Now it's becoming clear that there isn't always a clear line between *what* is shared and *how* it is shared. The content of a religion can be, in part, a method of transmission. If you can first transmit "Faith is a virtue, doubt is a vice," then all the rest of religious education will go much more smoothly. "Doubters will burn in hell for eternity" is another viral tenet, as you might call it, a tenet that tends to multiply adherents. Likewise, "Doubters will be sent away forever" and "Doubters have to be killed." To transmit viral tenets of a religion *is* to transmit the religion in a manipulative way that undermines a child's powers of thought.

There is nothing inherently wrong with parents wanting to pass on their religious identity or beliefs or customs, but now we have uncovered three problems, all to do with how the sharing is done, and thus three norms. The sharing should be accomplished without dampening a child's powers of thought; the sharing should be honest (the lie to shore up identity is a problematic lie); and we shouldn't teach viral tenets (that is, those intended to make the child unable to resist other tenets of the religion).

NORMALIZING RELIGIOUS EDUCATION

These three norms are easy to respect, when it comes to other aspects of educating our children. We can share the Beatles with kids without first saying "Loving the Beatles is a virtue, not loving the Beatles is a vice." We can encourage our kids to see issues as Democrats do or as Republicans do without saying they will burn in hell for having the wrong political standpoint. We can get kids to be vegetarians or to be pro-hunting without saying we'll shun them for going over to the other side. In all these matters, we can say what we really think, instead of transmitting simplistic falsehoods. We won't make our kids perfect copies of ourselves, but that's fine: parents do typically succeed in sharing some of the way they see the world, and we wouldn't want our kids to be perfect clones of ourselves. After all, it's to be expected that the next generation will have their own ideas, tastes, and so on.

Unlike Dawkins, I think at least *some* bodies of religious belief and custom are coherent and appealing enough that they can be shared with children in an ethical fashion, without parents becoming liars, manipulators, or suppressors of doubt. Not all of religion is palpably absurd and delusional, transmissible only through the dishonest manipulation of trusting children. There are people who honestly believe in God and share that belief with their children, without suppressing their propensity to doubt. But it does seem questionable that every religious belief can be passed on to the next generation in an honest, open, nonmanipulative fashion. Some religious doctrines are just too unbelievable to be embraced by many people without being heard very early on by children who have been discouraged from doubting. If we do use the methods of sharing that we use for other matters, we can't expect any more success. Kids will not always have the religious views we would like, any more than they'll have the tastes and opinions we would like in other areas of life.

So, what's a parent to do? Let children go their own way, believing only some of what their parents do? Or achieve more complete indoctrination, through manipulative, semihonest means? It's pretty clear what the good parent will do: avoid dishonesty and manipulation. The problem is that the good parent may have to be a bad religionist, doing less than others to keep the religious community populous and devout, going into the future. Should we be more committed to doing right by our children, or by the religious community into which we were born? That dilemma is only acute when religions are static things, committed to the very same doctrines in perpetuity. Perhaps we can do both, if religious communities allow themselves to evolve.

Chapter 16

Letting Go

What should we do for our grown children?

As a parent of two college-age children, I need to control a tendency to be nostalgic. To feel nostalgia is not merely to fondly recall the past, but rather to feel painfully cut off from it. Looking at pictures of my seven-year-olds posing on a beach in Cornwall, England in 2004, my first impulse is to want to go back to that beach and have some more fun with them. Indulging in those thoughts, I can feel as if those were children other than the ones I have now, children to whom I no longer have access. I have to remind myself that the kids on the beach are still fully accessible; they have just changed a lot, and we are no longer on the beach.

In fact, for most of the past year they have been away—the culmination of several years of planning. They turned eighteen, becoming adults in the eyes of the world—ready to vote, to join the army, to be ID'ed at airports. And then they went and turned nineteen. In the lead-up to their departure for college, I was intensely focused on where they would go and what our lives would be like without them. All the parents I know have had the same focus—on the "Which college?" question, and then on the fact of imminent separation, and then on their own lives as empty (or increasingly empty) nesters.

Of course, parents of college-bound kids have the anxieties associated with a certain kind of privilege. Parents experience separation from their grown-up children in many other ways. Some eighteen-year-olds dropped out of high school years earlier and went on to employment, unemployment, or even parenthood. Some eighteen-year-olds enlist in the military, or emigrate to the other side of the globe. It would be understandable if parents found the latter circumstances challenging, but they also find sending their kids off to college challenging. Why?

THE OBSESSION

William Deresiewicz offers many theories about the college obsession in his energetic polemic, *Excellent Sheep.* He hypothesizes that parents hover over their kids' higher-education plans, or insert themselves into them, or downright manage them, partly because the parent overidentifies with the child: "The child is made to function as an extension of somebody else." When parents treat children as a self-extension, he claims, children form a false self. They are happy with themselves when they achieve what their parents want for them. They are depressed when they fail at what their parents want for them. But they have no self of their own, pleased and displeased by whatever genuinely matters to them. Years of being pushed and packaged so that Yale might say "Yes, we want you" prevents the development of genuine goals and interests.

That's Deresiewicz's main diagnosis, but there's more. The intense involvement of parents in the college application process "bespeaks a misguided belief that you can make the world safe for your children: that if you only do everything right, nothing will ever impede or harm them." In addition, parents are driven by "status competition within extended families; peer pressure within communities; the desire to measure up to your own parents, or to best them; 'family branding.'" Ultimately, their child's admission to college will be the grade a parent gets for the past eighteen years. "When your kid gets into a prestigious college, it's as if you got an A in being a parent. And nothing less than that, of course, will do."

What's the solution? Children should fire their parents and invent their own lives. They can best do that, says Deresiewicz, if they get off the elite college track (if they were on it) and go to big public universities where they won't continue being pressured into relentless striving for superficial success. If you can get your parents off your back enough to land in that freeing environment, the next step is to limit contact.

> Don't talk to your parents more than once a week, or even better, once a month. Don't tell them your grades on papers or tests, or anything else about how you're doing during the term. Don't ask them for help of any kind. If they try to interfere with course selection or other aspects of your life, ask them politely to back off. If they don't, ask them impolitely. Make it clear to them that this is your experience, not theirs.

Freed of parental influence and overbearing pressure to succeed, you will now be in a position to find yourself. And that's actually what Deresiewicz thinks college is for—that's its true purpose.

Reading Deresiewicz when I'd already written most of this book, and when I was quite seriously immersed in helping my kids choose and get into good colleges, I felt a pang of guilt when I got to the part about parents treating kids as self-extensions. In this book, I am arguing that children *are*, in a sense, self-extensions. But they are also separate—a fact that's critical to good parenting from the earliest days onward. Plus, the self-like quality of kids decreases with time, as children start "coming from" many other sources besides their parents and directly from themselves as well. But I do say the self-like quality matters, giving parents prerogatives others don't have. Could the overbearing parent derided in Deresiewicz's book be an indictment of just the approach to parenting I've supported here? Would Aristotle's picture of our children as "second selves but separate," if taken seriously, turn us into bad parents?

OVERIDENTIFYING

No, that isn't the upshot. We can criticize parents who overidentify with their children without saying they shouldn't identify with them at all. In fact, understanding identification as inherent in parenthood helps us explain and anticipate the tendency to overidentify. Consider, by analogy, the tendency to overprotect. Recognizing this as a common parental vice doesn't mean parents shouldn't protect their children at all. In fact, their role as protectors makes it more explicable that overprotecting is a common parental vice.

Identifying with kids as they negotiate the complicated task of transitioning to college is actually vital. Recall some of the attitudes that go into regarding your child as a second self: generosity is easy, unlike the full-blown altruism we sometimes extend to others; there is pride in their accomplishments (and shame in their failures); we feel noncompetitive with our children; we have a tendency to inflate their strengths. These are attitudes that are helpful to parents of young adults, at least up to a point. Nonaltruistic generosity and pride help the parent foot the bill for what can be an extraordinarily expensive four years. Shame sounds entirely negative, but feeling vicariously bad about a child's low grades can motivate parents to hold kids to standards—reasonable ones—day after day, year after year. Noncompetition makes it possible to rejoice when our kids excel, rather than feeling intimidated by them. It also rules out rivalry; for example, it's unusual for a mother to resent a daughter for being the recipient of her father's financial largesse. Even inflation of a child's strengths has its benefits, to the extent that parents' overconfidence in their children can make up for a child's lack of confidence. The identifying parent is helpful up to a point—until he or she starts to overidentify.

Overidentifying means . . . what? Wanting for your children exactly what you would want for yourself. Being overinvolved in their successes to make up for the absence of your own. Caring about them primarily based on their achievements. Feeling devastated by their failures to the point that you can't intervene constructively. Taking over the whole process, so kids can't learn self-sufficiency or take pride in themselves. Treating a child too much as a second self and not enough as separate.

Deresiewicz's advice to students—get rid of your parents!—will make many a parent flinch. We want our children to come into their own selves and achieve self-sufficiency, but we also want to have an ongoing relationship with them. The same alarming message can be found in "Don't Pick Up: Why Kids Need to Separate from Their Parents," a funny and profound essay by Stanford English professor Terry Castle. She notes how many protagonists of great novels are orphans and says that's indicative of the fact that children can't really begin interesting lives of their own as long as their parents are hanging around, keeping them safe. "[W]e often know them by a single name or nickname: Moll, Tom, Fanny, Becky, Heathcliff,

Jane, Pip, Oliver, Ishmael, Huck, Dorothea, Jude, Isabel, Milly, Lily, Lolly, Sula." Children's literature is also brimming with orphans and unsupervised children. The Boxcar Children come to mind, as does Sarah Crewe in *The Little Princess*, Pippi Longstocking, and Harry Potter. It's typical that the fun begins in *The Cat in the Hat* when Mom leaves the house, and all the fun is over on the last page, when Mom's leg comes into view. Castle expresses her own "twisty, fraught, and disloyal" view this way:

> Parents, in my opinion, have to be finessed, *thought around*, even as we love them: They are so colossally wrong about so many important things. And even when they are not, paradoxically, *even when they are 100 percent right*, the imperative remains the same: To live an "adult" life, a meaningful life, it is necessary, I would argue, to engage in a kind of symbolic self-orphaning.

The ubiquitous orphan story teaches a lesson to budding adults and their parents:

> [I]t is indeed the self-conscious abrogation of one's inheritance, the "making strange" of received ideas, the cultivation of a willingness to defy, debunk, or just plain old *disappoint* one's parents, that is the absolute precondition, now more than ever, for intellectual and emotional freedom.

For panicked parents reading this passage, the crucial word is "willingness." I think I can agree that a child does have to cultivate a *willingness* to defy, debunk, disappoint. To live an adult, meaningful life, you have to be prepared to go where you must, even at the cost of self-orphaning, but why must that be the cost?

ORPHANING

Self-orphaning has its value. But all those fictional characters were *orphaned*, not self-orphaned—they didn't do the job of separating from their parents by themselves. Is it still good to shed your parents when parents are the ones who bring that about? It seems to very much matter how kids become orphaned. Harry Potter is orphaned in just the right way. His parents love him deeply and lay down memories that stay with him throughout this life. Despite their deaths at the hands of Voldemort, Harry's archenemy, he carries a sense of himself as wanted and loved. That's important, according to extensive research in anthropology and psychology, which shows that it's universally, cross-culturally true that children are damaged when parents don't give them the sense of being loved.

Most of the fictional orphans are orphaned due to forces beyond the control of their parents, like death, but parents can deliberately leave their children, in both fiction and real life. It happens all the time—especially when it comes to fathers. Barack Obama's father, for example, left his wife and child in Hawaii when his son was just two years old, first getting a doctorate at Harvard and then moving back to Kenya and on to other wives and other children. Obama talks about living with a painful sense of having been abandoned in his memoir *Dreams from My Father*. Disappearing altogether is at least better than cutting off children in response to their traits, choices, or viewpoints; there are Christians who reject their atheist kids, Amish people who reject their mainstream kids; parents who disown children for reasons of sexual orientation or gender identity.

In fact, parents can leave simply to find themselves, just as Deresiewicz and Castle would have young adults leave to find themselves. A character who does this, in recent fiction, is Gauri in Jumpha Lahiri's novel *The Lowlands*. Dissatisfied with her marriage to a man who was once her brother-in-law, and feeling haunted by ghosts from the past, she suddenly leaves her husband and her ten-year-old daughter in Rhode Island, taking up a position (as a philosophy professor) on the West Coast. There's no explanation, no communication. Decades pass before there's any contact. "She had never written to Bela. Never dared reach out, to reassure her." Deliberately abandoning a ten-year-old, with all the emotional injury that implies, seems completely indefensible. But what about deliberately orphaning an adult child? What if Bela had been thirty instead of ten?

There are better and worse ways to orphan your child, but (come on!) I doubt there's really any good way to do it. Once you have established yourself as the mother or father of a child, disappearing has many emotional costs for the child, not to mention economic costs. In real life, the abandoned child probably will not get to live in a house called Villa Villekula with a horse on the porch and eat pancakes for every meal, like Pippi Longstocking. Even the abandoned adult child is probably worse off, not better off, outside the pages of fiction, though it's difficult to find hard evidence on the subject.

SEPARATION

Enough about orphaning our children or our children self-orphaning. All metaphor and hyperbole aside, we do have to let go and allow our children to create their own lives. I can only imagine letting go as it was experienced by parents hundreds of years ago, when adventurous children embarked for distant lands, possibly never to be seen again, and to be heard from rarely, at best. Today as well, parents can have much bigger challenges than seeing a child move across the country to get a college education. There is still the possibility of a child emigrating to some distant location, an eventuality eased, but not completely erased, by the availability of email and Skype. When children join the military instead of going to college, a parent has to cope with a much different and more worrisome range of dangers.

The fact that children are self-like can make separation painful, but it can also help ease the pain of separation. If you identify strongly with the child who adventurously embarks for some place far away, some of the child's thrills will be yours as well, at least vicariously. I hope it was with this sort of identification that my grandparents watched my father leave Istanbul for America in the late 1940s, so he could study physics at the University of Wisconsin. With strong identification, his parents would have experienced his widening horizons as their own widening horizons. No doubt it grew harder when he decided to stay in the United States for graduate school, and harder still when he married and got a job here. Nevertheless, identification *can* help us let go instead of holding tight.

My own parents opted for identification, not vice-grip possession, when they let me take all sorts of risks as a teenager—including hiking in the Alps and bicycling all over England and Scotland with my younger brother. And as my own kids get older and demand more freedom, it strikes me that what makes it possible for me to relinquish control is not only respecting their autonomy—certainly a necessity, if you want your child to live a good life—but identifying with them. It's partly because I identify that I want them to experience the exhilaration of the open road, the late-night party, the unknown.

Whether your child is spreading her wings in a college environment, on a battlefield, or in other new territory, it's gratifying to see her do so, far beyond what it would be if she were just anyone's child, and not your own. But then—let's be honest—there is also particularly excruciating pain when things do not go well, and a child is too distant and too independent to be helped, let alone if our worst fears come true and we lose our children to one of the many things that can shorten life. There is no getting away from the fact that the unique connection we have to our children opens us to profound pleasures, but also to profound dismay and loss.

With the right effort and attitude, perhaps we can have children who are merely *willing* to defy, debunk, and disappoint. No parent can be anything but saddened by a child who feels obligated to actually "self-orphan." But even with the best of intentions all around, separation is always a possibility, considering that a child is a second self—but separate.

Chapter 17

Going Home

What should our grown children do for us?

As I come close to finishing this book, two roles take up a lot of my time and energy. I am a parent to children in college. I am also a child of elderly parents, called on often to be helpful to them (especially my father). When I think about what grown children should do for their parents, I find myself thinking about what I do for my parents and about what I hope my kids will one day do for me. But I also think about the matter as a philosophical parent. What do we really *have* to do for our parents?

FILIAL PIETY

The Confucian ethical tradition regards filial piety as the key virtue—one that not only enters into the parent-child relationship, but makes us live rightly in other contexts as well. Honoring, respecting, and obeying our parents is incumbent on us starting at an early age, and *of course* we can never orphan ourselves, breaking off contact. Filial piety will mean different things at different ages, with the child finally becoming a caregiver to his parents when they are very old. But why? Why is filial piety a virtue?

In the *Xiaojing* ("Classic of Filial Piety") filial piety is explained as follows: "The son derives his life from his parents, and no greater gift could possibly be transmitted. His ruler and parent (in one), his father deals with him accordingly, and no generosity could be greater than this. Hence, he who does not love his parents, but loves other men, is called a rebel against virtue, and he who does not revere his parents, but reveres other men, is called a rebel against propriety." The root of our duties to our parents is the fact that they created us.

In my view, it doesn't really make good sense for children to think they are indebted to their parents for giving them life. For one thing, parents almost never pick a particular child to create; a specific embryo forms by sheer accident. Furthermore, it would be a mistake to think that creating a child saves him from anything that would have been worse for *him*. A merely potential child is not doomed to languish in some cosmic orphanage, as I argued in chapter 2, because merely potential children simply don't exist. We usually make the *world* a little better by creating a child, but we don't make the child better off than he otherwise would have been. On the first day of a child's life, a child has not yet accumulated any debt of gratitude to his parents.

Now, having given them life, the things we do for our children *do* make them better off than they otherwise would have been. The child could have been hungry, but we fed him; he could have been cold, but we clothed him; he could have been illiterate, but we educated him. So now there is at least the potential to speak of a debt of gratitude. But should we?

NO DEBT TO PARENTS

In the 1970s, the philosopher Jane English wrote a now-famous article arguing that children can't be indebted to their parents for all their years of caregiving. Why not? Because while children certainly receive benefits from their parents, they don't ask for those benefits. She offers a simple analogy. If your neighbor mows your lawn for you while you're on vacation, that's very nice of him, but you don't owe him anything in return. If, on the other hand, you requested that he mow the lawn, you do wind up indebted to him if he complies. For lack of requesting the benefits they receive, children reach adulthood owing their parents nothing at all.

But fear not, English does think there's an alternative to talk of "owing." Adult children have "duties of friendship" to their parents. We all know what those are like; we think our friends should act in certain ways, and not act in certain ways, for the simple reason that we are friends. Parents and children are very good friends—or at least "affiliates"—and so should treat each other well.

English gives up on the "owing" talk rather quickly. We saw in the discussion of free riding in chapter 13 that it doesn't take an explicit request to be indebted to the person who gives something to you. True, we're not indebted to benefactors each and every time they offer us something unbidden; but we are indebted when we welcome what we are given, or when we alter our course of conduct so we deliberately become dependent on the gift, and especially when any rational person *would* welcome the gift. Recall the example in which elves fix your shoes, so you cancel your regular cobbler appointments. In that situation, there's indebtedness even without an explicit request for aid, because you're "all in" as far as the aid goes, you're on board with it, even though you didn't ask for it.

Children passively receive what their parents give them for many years, but as they near adulthood, it starts to be true that they have a choice whether to welcome assistance or reject it. You don't have to let your parents buy you a car, for example. You don't have to let them pay for four years of college. And on the other hand, much of what parents provide for their children—food, shelter, medical care, and so on—*would* be welcomed by any rational person. It's fair to say that children are on board with most of what's given to them by their parents, despite never having verbally requested their parents' help. If a child simply walks away after that, it's fair to say that she owed her parents better.

We *can* coherently speak of children owing something to their parents, but do we want to? It sounds so crass, so commercial, as if parents ran a hotel and at the end of a very long stay children must pay their bill. The language of love and friendship, recommended by English, is in some ways more appealing than that. The idea is that there are things we must do for our friends and loved ones, as long as we do consider them our friends and loved ones. For example, you visit a friend in the hospital not because you owe it to them, but simply because that person is your friend.

Thinking about children's obligations in those terms does have advantages. If twenty years of being cared for leaves the child in a state of outright indebtedness (the view English rejects), the debt isn't discharged until the child has given the parent a great deal—probably in the parent's old age. The parent's behavior in the intervening years can't cancel the debt, which means parents are free to act like jerks toward their children, while also expecting to eventually receive what they are owed. On the friendship view, on the other hand, acting like a jerk can change the relationship so that the friendship vanishes, and all obligations with it. With that understanding of the relationship, parents and adult children certainly have a greater incentive to treat each other respectfully and kindly over the years.

The friendship view has its advantages, but is it really entirely apt? Friends and lovers pair up freely, out of an appreciation of each other's character, talents, and appearance. If the affection and admiration wither away, the relationship may end. But parents and children are linked in a less deliberate manner, and the bond doesn't have to be accompanied by straightforward affection. A parent-child relationship can be quite fraught, but no less committed.

OUR PARENTS, OUR SELVES

A third way of thinking about our duties to our parents (not considered by English) focuses on the fact that children come from their parents. The extended identity of each includes the other. Nobody wonders why I am prepared to pay for my own life-saving operation. It's just obvious that I care about myself enough to do so. Likewise, we really don't wonder why a parent is willing to pay for a child's operation, or why an adult child is willing to pay for a parent's. We know implicitly that their identity is fused, so that the problems of the child are the parent's and the problems of the parent are the child's.

Duties to parents are thus duties to the self, in an expanded, extended sense. This description is consistent with the way we think about kids who walk away from their parents, failing to call, visit, or help. The distant, uninvolved child of a needy elderly parent seems appalling—strange, unnatural, freaky. Cutting off a parent in that way seems nearly as odd as cutting off one's own arm. There's something tragic about the child who self-orphans, a fact not captured by the idea that he simply hasn't paid off a debt or the idea that he's doing something akin to getting a divorce.

So what is the truth here? Do we have duties to our parents based on indebtedness to them, based on friendship with them, or based on sharing an extended identity with them? It's not out of the question that all three descriptions are partially correct. We have some degree of indebtedness, after decades of receiving benefits from our parents, whether we requested the benefits or not. Our parents are also (ideally) our friends, and so we have duties to them that come under that heading. At the same time, there is a fusion of identity that makes us feel entangled with our parents for a lifetime, and unable *not* to see their problems as our problems. It's appalling to cut them off, we think, as observers do as well.

All three of these possible explanations tell us what most of us already know: we should be good to our parents. But all three options also allow for exceptions. If we can owe our parents a debt of gratitude, they can also deserve just the opposite—condemnation for the way they *didn't* take good care of us. At some point, negative desert presumably cancels out the entire debt of gratitude. Abusive parents can't reasonably expect care from their children in old age. Likewise, if parents aren't good friends, but instead relentlessly critical and unsupportive, we stop having duties of friendship toward them.

Finally, even if we have a fused identity with our parents, it can occasionally make sense to cut them off. The real-life case of Aron

Ralston, dramatized in the movie *127 Hours*, makes it clear that you might have to amputate your own arm to save your whole life. (He had been trapped in a remote Utah canyon for all those hours, with his arm pinned under a fallen boulder.) Likewise, it's not impossible to have to break off your relationship with an abusive parent, in order to live a healthy, happy life. The adult child who self-orphans may do what's necessary but probably won't feel entirely whole—this view of the relationship predicts—just as Aron Ralston presumably feels less whole without his arm.

Chapter 18

Parenthood and Meaning

Does parenthood make us better off?

Having a child makes another person matter to you as much as you matter to yourself. Parenthood also enlarges us by connecting us to a wider community. Before kids come along, our circle of friends is usually based on shared interests. After kids, we can find ourselves sitting at the park or in a playgroup or in a school auditorium with a much wider assortment of people. We become more involved in the public life of the community we live in than we once were.

Being enlarged sounds positive, but it's not an *obvious* life good—like happiness, or well-being. By enlarging us and by altering our lives in myriad other ways, does having kids make our lives happier or better?

THE HAPPINESS PARADOX

If research in positive psychology is to be believed, parenthood does not make people happier. As economist Richard Layard puts it, "There is indeed great rejoicing when children are born. Yet within two years parents revert on average to their original level of happiness." Actually, when I read the footnotes associated with these sentences, I discovered the situation is even more dire. Andrew Clark and three other psychologists studied a large quantity of German survey data and found that reported levels of life satisfaction go up on average upon the birth of your first child, but subsequently go back down, and eventually dip *below* what they were before the child was born. Both men and women wind up with about a half-point less life satisfaction (out of a possible total of eleven points) by the time their child is four years old, compared to what they experienced before having children. (Women experience a bigger initial surge when the baby is born.)

Reported overall life satisfaction seems to dip as a result of becoming parents, but what about the time we spend in the company of our wonderful children? Is that at least enjoyable, even if appraisal of our lives as a whole is a little more negative, after children? That's not so clear either. In much-reported research done by Daniel Kahneman and several colleagues, roughly a thousand employed women created a retrospective diary of their activities in the previous twenty-four hours, noting how they felt during each activity. The researchers' goal was actually to develop a new tool— the day-reconstruction method—for the study of all aspects of well-being, but they stumbled on some surprising data about how women feel while doing the hands-on work of childcare. Ratings of positive affect showed that these women were happiest during intimate relations, followed by socializing, relaxing, and praying (or worshipping or meditating). Then came eating, exercising, watching TV . . . the list goes on and on. You have to descend all the way to the twelfth line on the list before you come to "taking care of my children." Even more surprising, taking care of their children generated more negative feelings than any activity besides working. Since Kahneman was really just developing the retrospective diary as a research tool, he didn't take pains to make sure his sample of women was representative of all women, or even all American women, but the study is still suggestive and puzzling.

It may come as a surprise that parenthood isn't a cause of greater happiness, especially to parents who think of their children as their greatest joy. What's going on here? One factor must be that many of the activities on Kahneman's list are undertaken voluntarily, whereas parenthood can just happen to us. We voluntarily and deliberately choose intimacy, socializing, worshipping, and exercise, whereas people can fall into parenthood when they were looking for sex, or maybe a relationship. To see whether parenthood boosts happiness in the way that these other experiences do, based on an apples-to-apples comparison, we would have to look at the subgroup that chooses parenthood, instead of the whole class of people with children, and I am not aware of any research on that subgroup.

Another worry is that these researchers are focused on the time of life when parenting is most labor-intensive. The Clark study only follows parents until their children are age four, and in the Kahneman study the only child-oriented activity is "taking care of my children." What if a study compared midlife men who have no children and midlife men who have teenagers they spend time with—watching their sporting events or going running together or attending concerts? Would this sort of recreation really be low on the list of enjoyable activities? I would be extremely surprised if that were the case.

And of course, being a parent continues, past the point when children require any taking care of at all. My obstetrician had to have a colleague deliver my children because she'd gone to Los Angeles to visit her college-age daughter. She beamed while telling me how much fun they were going to have shopping together. In fact, parents do an awful lot of beaming, if they're not having much fun. My friends and siblings *seem* genuinely elated when they talk about visits with their grownup children.

And then there is the last stage of the parent–child relationship. My father, at age ninety, resides in a senior-living facility and spends time on Skype every day with me and my two brothers. Unless he is an amazing fake, the time he spends with us is some of the most enjoyable time in his day. Residents in the facility who don't have children visiting them shouldn't be assumed to get equal enjoyment from other visitors, because aside from spouses and children, there aren't many other visitors, from what I can see. In the fullness of time, children can be an irreplaceable blessing.

But focusing again on the first five or ten years of childhood, when having children is most labor intensive, it's worth asking *why* childcare makes us less happy—assuming it really does. Berit Brogaard hypothesizes that the crux of the matter is that a parent's autonomy is reduced by a demanding infant. It's not only the feeling of fatigue that is unpleasant (recall Anne Lamott's description of her son's first year, which I quoted in chapter 11), but also the sense of not being able to control your own days and hours. When the grating sound of your baby's crying grabs your attention, you have to stop what you were doing and meet the baby's needs. When an eight-year-old has to be coaxed into finishing a homework assignment that's due tomorrow, the showdown must take place *now*, whatever else you have on your plate.

Some people are happier than others while doing the work of caregiving, and that deserves an explanation too. Partly it might be because they find ways to avoid autonomy deprivation—they let themselves not respond immediately to a crying infant, and they let the eight-year-old deal with his own homework. There is another factor at play here as well, which also has to do with a parent's sense of who is in charge. Once people have children, they can feel like leaders of their own very small country, with its own distinctive culture, values, and traditions. Growing up in my family of origin, our little country was extremely different from the ones in neighboring houses. We ate different food, ate at different times, went different places for vacations, had different books on our shelves. My mother was the show-runner for our household, more than anyone else, and I believe that was a source of enjoyment for her. My hypothesis—granted, I have no proof for it—is that people enjoy parenting more the more they play that sort of executive role, or at least share it with their partner. A mother will not feel like the leader of a tiny country if her husband insists on complete control, and vice versa. Likewise, mothers living within an extended family might find themselves under the control of a mother-in-law, instead of enjoying an executive role. Some parents will feel they must be completely obedient to a church or another institution, doing just as the school dictates with respect to homework, for example, or just as the church asserts with respect to sex education, for another example.

There is also the possibility of feeling like a slave to so-called experts. Parenthood will not give you an increased sense of governing—that is, governing both yourself and your family—if you are nervously consulting your favorite childcare guru at every turn, looking for the one right way of handling the many dilemmas parents encounter. It seems at least possible that personal satisfaction can be increased if parents choose a more independent, self-sufficient approach to parenting—though it would be unwise for parents to insulate themselves entirely from all external norms and advice.

Even in the best of cases, the first years of parenthood are often stressful and sometimes boring. I don't want to paint an overly rosy picture, but based on first-person experience and anecdotal evidence, I'd say a parent of young children is a bit like someone hiking up a mountain. The view from all the lookout points is thrilling, but some of the climb is tedious or even excruciating. One of the dynamics accounting for the lower total happiness of parents is that one enjoyable activity can interfere with others. Avid mountain climbers can find other areas of their lives going less well: spouses grow resentful; professional responsibilities can be neglected; the sport is expensive. Something similar can be said about avid parents. Parenthood has a tendency to crowd out other powerful sources of life satisfaction—like career advancement (especially for women) and the satisfactions of an adult relationship. Still, with few exceptions, mountain climbers are glad to be mountain climbers, and parents are glad to be parents.

MEANING

More than adding happiness, both mountain climbers and parents add something nebulous but highly valued to their lives: they add more meaning. But philosophers have tended not to notice how having children adds meaning to life. When they talk about the meaning of life—if they talk about it at all—they usually talk about grander things, like God and eternity and large-scale benevolence. Or they despair that nothing can eliminate the meaninglessness, or the absurdity, of life.

The meaning of life has become a respected topic in philosophy only fairly recently. Before the nineteenth century it wasn't a topic at all, surprisingly enough, and it was a fairly marginal topic in the eyes of academic philosophers until as recently as the 1970s. Most philosophers even today see the humor in the question "What is the meaning of life?"—somehow it's just too big and unanswerable. But a literature has blossomed in the past several decades, thanks partly to an essay entitled "The Absurd," which the influential philosopher Thomas Nagel published in 1971. Does Nagel affirm the notion that parenthood can give our lives meaning?

Well, actually, no. Nagel identifies two ways of looking at ourselves and our activities. We can take the "inside" view, and feel engaged, absorbed, and committed to our undertakings. From that standpoint, just about anything can be taken seriously. We can also step back and take the "outside" view and find any of our activities transitory and pointless. The absurdity of life, writes Nagel, lies in the fact that any activity is always open to both interpretations. Any engaged moment can be disrupted by a painful sense of meaninglessness, or (best-case scenario) a moment of laughter about how ridiculous it all is. We can't escape the oscillation between the two standpoints.

Isn't anything doubt-proof? No, says Nagel. Even if we dedicated ourselves to grand things like God, science, truth, or saving lives, we could always ask "What's the point?" If I'm making scientific discoveries, why does it matter, really? If I'm saving lives, my efforts are just a drop in the ocean—there are millions more to be saved. Even someone who thinks she's glorifying God can always wonder why it's important for God to be glorified. All that *may* be true, but what's striking is that Nagel overlooks the activity that's most self-evidently worthwhile to most people: raising their children. In fact, we don't oscillate between Nagel's inside and outside views when we're sitting with a sick child, taking his temperature, mopping his brow, and cheering him up with silly nothings. At such times, who even fleetingly wonders "What's the point?" Caring for a beloved child—at least for most parents—is utterly doubt-proof.

Peter Singer is another influential ethicist who is willing to tackle questions about meaningfulness, but he also doesn't notice the meaning-giving potential of parenthood. In his 1995 book *How Are*

We to Live?, he describes the sense of emptiness that people suffer if they invest all their energy in making money, getting promoted, watching sports, or going shopping. Parenthood comes into the picture, but only adds to its bleakness. Singer relies on Betty Friedan's *The Feminine Mystique* to capture the plight of the "suburban housewife": "Her only role is to bring up a family, and her children soon spend all day at school, and most of the rest of their time watching television. Nothing else seems worth achieving." Singer's paragons of the meaningful life are people like animal activist Henry Spira. Self-transcendence, he says, involves a shift from one's small, personal world to the world at large. The person who achieves this shift does good for thousands or even millions, and feels deeply fulfilled as a result. There is no recognition of the ordinary, small-scale self-transcending of a parent who develops an extended identity that includes his or her children.

Parenthood has a more positive valence in one of Singer's more recent books, *The Life You Can Save,* which includes a chapter on the conflict between caring for one's own children, and making large-scale contributions to the good of others. The dilemma is illustrated with a profile of Paul Farmer, the extraordinary doctor and global health leader so fascinatingly described in the beautiful book *Mountains Beyond Mountains,* by Tracy Kidder. At the time that he was interviewed by Kidder, Farmer had a young daughter who lived in Paris with her mother, but Farmer seldom saw her, opting instead to spend most of his time in Haiti providing much-needed healthcare to the poor. Singer frames the family–philanthropy conflict in a revealing way. There is admittedly a duty associated with family, and there is a special love we feel toward family members, but the opportunities for *meaning* lie in large-scale philanthropy. He promises that "taking part in a collective effort to help the world's poorest people"—not taking care of your own children—"would give your life greater meaning and fulfillment."

Yes, that might very well be true for some people; in fact, I hope it's true. But is there no meaning to be found in the simple business of having and raising children?

BEING SURE

When my children were babies, my circle of friends frequently talked about how raising children gave them a sense of purpose they had never found as clearly in anything else. They felt enlarged and expanded and fulfilled. I heard the same thing from my husband and other fathers I knew. It could be that the parents I know are especially enthusiastic because most of them came to parenthood relatively late, or because they are relatively affluent (compared to the women in the Kahneman survey). But certainty has been a recurrent theme whenever I've heard parents talking about the experience of having children. It's puzzling that philosophers have been slow to make a connection between parenthood and meaning.

Part of the explanation, no doubt, is that throughout the Western tradition, children have always been on the other side of the house—that is, far from the (male) philosopher's study—if they were in the house at all (some of the most famous philosophers were childless). One of the first in-depth treatments of questions about the meaning of life was written by Leo Tolstoy in 1879. Though an acclaimed novelist and essayist, and a very wealthy man, he had sunk to the depths of despair, finding a complete absence of meaning in his life, until he had a religious conversion. It has always struck me as astonishing that he went through this crisis when he was living on his estate not alone, but with a wife who loved him, and with their nine children. Presumably the children were off in the distance, under the care of his wife and the servants, and not a focal point for Tolstoy himself.

But there is more behind the tendency for philosophers not to think of parenthood when they think about what makes life meaningful. For many thinkers in the Western tradition, a source of meaning must be unchanging—there always, and impossible to lose. Meaning isn't supposed to be "fragile" (to use Martha Nussbaum's perfect term). But what we get by having children *is* fragile. There are good days and bad days. Our kids can turn out badly, or—a parent's worst fear—die. If all goes as well as possible, children grow up and become independent, and parenting can no longer be a mother's or father's primary focus in life.

Not only is meaning supposed to be "forever," and impossible to lose, but it's supposed to be available to all, and always available. You get to have it whoever you are, and at every stage of life. Everyone who succeeds in living meaningfully is expected to converge on *the* meaning of life, for some one meaning. Parenthood isn't a meaning-maker like that, so (it's been assumed) it can't be a source of meaning at all. But arguably, an activity *can* be meaningful, yet not permanently or universally available.

The meaning-of-life literature has blossomed since the publication of Nagel's 1971 article, and there is certainly more reference to parenthood in that literature than before. There has also been a considerable effort to articulate specific conditions under which life, or at least parts of life, can be meaningful. Borrowing elements from a number of different authors, but especially from Susan Wolf's book *Meaning in Life and Why it Matters,* I suggest that to have meaning in your life, first of all you have to have overarching goals that organize your time and energy, so that life is *not* just one damned day after another. When activities have this sort of larger significance, they point beyond themselves. In fact, they point beyond themselves like words do (the squiggle "DOG" points to dogs). Thus, the talk of "meaning," for both lives and words, is not coincidental. To have meaning in your life, your activities must point beyond themselves to larger goals, but (second) you also need to be wholeheartedly committed to those goals—durably, and without constant doubt. To avoid doubt (and this is the third condition), those goals have to be well enough grounded in reality to survive reflection.

Obviously, meaning *in* life is not the same thing as the meaning *of* life—some cosmic purpose possessed by life itself. If all of life points beyond to some grand goal, perhaps the goal of a deity, then life is not just meaningful, but transcendently meaningful. Having meaning in one's life is also not exactly the same thing as living a good life. A life could be very good, overall—amply endowed with necessities like happiness and autonomy—even if it was devoid of overarching goals. That would not make it bad overall—just lacking a certain virtue that most of us (at least after obtaining the basic elements of a good life) strive for.

So much for what meaning is (roughly and briefly). Can parenthood really supply it? It's obvious that parenthood structures our days, months, and years. It takes a long time to usher a child from infancy to adulthood, and there are lots of goals and plans involved. Parenthood also gives us wholeheartedness, as Harry Frankfurt explains eloquently in his book *The Reasons of Love.* Frankfurt makes a surprising comparison. Love gives us something comparable to mathematical certainty, he claims.

> Mathematical certainty, like other modes of certainty that are grounded in logically or conceptually necessary truths, is restful because it relieves us from having to contend with disparate

tendencies in ourselves concerning what to believe. The issue is settled. We need no longer struggle to make up our minds. . . . Similarly, the necessity with which love binds the will puts an end to indecisiveness concerning what to care about.

Love for anything produces restful certainty, but Frankfurt sees (rightly, I think) that love of one's own children is especially pure and constant.

Why do we feel such unalloyed love for our children? Here also, Frankfurt is helpful. It's not a response to their intrinsic value—as real and enormous as that may be. It's love itself that makes the child seem to us so extremely valuable, not independently existing value that makes us love a child so deeply.

But what is the nature of that love? Where does it come from? At different points in his book, Frankfurt calls the love we feel for our children the purest form of love, and also calls self-love the purest form of love. Is there a reason why both types of love seem so similar in their certainty, clarity, and constancy and come in for highest praise? He doesn't offer an explanation, but we have one ready to hand: if children are "second selves but separate," it's no wonder that love for children shares many features with self-love.

For some, that assimilation will seem like a curse, putting parental love in a bad light. What narcissists we are! But Frankfurt wisely says otherwise:

When all is said and done, what is so embarrassing or so unfortunate about our propensity to love ourselves? Why should we regard it with any sort of righteous sorrow or distaste, or presume that it is somehow a dreadful obstacle to the attainment of our most proper goals? Why should we think of self-love as being at all an impediment to the sort of life at which we ought reasonably to aim?

As Frankfurt sees it, self-love turns out to be a sort of wholehearted-ness about our own cares, concerns, and interests, and not a matter of selfishness or indifference to the rest of the world, beyond our-selves. The wholeheartedness of self-love makes our lives meaning-ful, Frankfurt claims. When we have more selves to love—because we have children—it stands to reason that we have even more access to meaning.

THE ULTIMATE

The case for parenthood as a source of meaning certainly doesn't turn on judging that nothing else makes life as meaningful, or that finding meaning in other ways can't make people just as happy. In fact, everything I have said about why parenting can make life meaningful supports meaning-pluralism. Some people get the rest-fulness of love from other pursuits—from loving music, or loving a partner, or loving sports, or loving endless study and debate. There are other big projects that can give structure to life, generate whole-heartedness, and survive reflection. There are meaning-boosters of many kinds.

But is parenthood preeminent? A team of psychologists led by Douglas Kenrick recently proposed a revision to Abraham Maslow's famous hierarchy of needs, which pictures self-actualization at the top of a pyramid. Maslow, the influential twentieth-century inven-tor of humanistic psychology, thought the consummately mature human being found his or her calling, whether it be art or music or poetry (his examples), after taking care of more basic needs (for food and sex, safety, love, and esteem). The ultimate activity, the end of the line, was creative self-expression. In that pyramid, parenthood doesn't have its own specific level. It's part sex, part love, but lower in importance than finding your personal calling. In Kenrick's revised pyramid, parenthood is at the top, with mate selection and retention right below. What happened to art, music, and poetry? They have become a means to mate selection and mate retention. The old pyramid favored a creative elite, while the new makes parenting "the ultimate."

The elevation of parenthood to the pinnacle of the pyramid creates a far less elitist pyramid than the old one. Most people become parents, but most people don't create art, music, and poetry. But the truth is even more inclusive. Voluntarily childless people can have consummate meaning and can claim full and complete development too. What Kenrick and his collaborators have missed is what parenthood and finding one's calling (artistic or otherwise) have in common. Both give people long-lasting and life-structuring goals, wholeheartedness, and projects that survive reflection. In fact, there's even a felt similarity: people talk about their books, their businesses, their pets—whatever absorbs them, long-term—as their children.

We don't all have to make procreation a part of our life plan to live meaningful lives, but what about a weaker thesis? Perhaps, to live meaningfully, you don't have to have your own children, but *somebody* needs to be having children. Without *somebody* having them, childless people would eventually find themselves in a world solely populated by the elderly. At the most basic level, they would be deprived of all sorts of products and services they need to survive, but looking ahead *now* to a childless future world, they would also have an existential problem. As Samuel Scheffler points out in the book *Death and the Afterlife,* some of our current pursuits would be drained of significance if we were all going to die without being outlived by the next generation. The afterlife we need, for meaningful existence—Scheffler claims—is not a heavenly afterlife for us personally, but simply the continuation of life as we know it, with a new cast of characters. It's only with new people continuing to be created that I can think the seeds I sow today—in the course of my various projects and activities—will keep making at least some difference in the far future.

If Scheffler is right, we don't all have to be parents for our lives to be meaningful, but we do all need there to be parenthood for life to be meaningful. And parents need other parents too. The continuity we have with our own children will not carry us into the far, far future. For that degree of continuity, parents and nonparents alike need parenthood as an ongoing practice. We also need the ability to identify not only with our own children (which is easy), but with other people's children. We could even try to identify *equally* with our own child and other people's, present and future, avoiding partiality and selective identification. Wouldn't that give us equanimity in the face of possible loss and maximize our sense of survival into the far future?

It sounds good, and this strategy for coping with finitude has support from some quarters—see Mark Johnston's book *Surviving Death*—but I've argued throughout this book that we do in fact identify in a special way with people who come from us directly, and doing this makes parenthood more fulfilling and makes us better parents. The identification parents almost always feel with their own children is something far more vivid, complete, certain, and animating. That identification is something to aspire to, when it comes to neighbors, friends, colleagues, students, and others, but something we can almost certainly have just by being parents.

Parents are necessary because children need them in order to grow up safely, happily, and well-prepared for the future. But having children also benefits the parents. It creates continuities that enlarge us, so that we completely identify with others instead of seeing our own solitary selves as uniquely important. It also defeats the skeptic inside each of us—the person who wakes up in the middle of the night thinking "What's the point?" At a blog I once wrote for, a new mother once commented that *she* would lay in bed after a tiring day of dealing with work and caring for her new baby, and feel—no, not a sense of the absurdity of life—but waves of euphoric love for her child. Whatever the payoff in terms of total satisfaction, parenthood does give us such moments of perfect meaningfulness and certainty, and those are awfully precious.

ACKNOWLEDGMENTS

I am very grateful to two readers for Oxford University Press who gave me extensive and extremely helpful comments. Many chapters of this book are more nuanced as a result of their critical scrutiny and generosity. I'm also grateful to OUP editor Lucy Randall for her careful reading of the manuscript and her many wise suggestions.

My colleague at Southern Methodist University, Justin Fisher, read the whole manuscript at two stages. This book is better thanks to his detailed and challenging feedback; I'm especially in his debt for a number of points about embryonic metaphysics in chapter 5. I'm also indebted to Justin for inviting me to discuss the manuscript with the Dallas Fellowship of Freethought's philosophy club. Members of the group made me see where new points had to be added, anecdotes added or subtracted, arguments tightened. Thanks very much to you all!

I'm also grateful to two delightful groups of students who took my class on procreation and parenthood at SMU, giving me a chance to try out ideas and offering me their own insights and examples.

I appreciate Lucas Heinrich's amusing interpretation of my title on the cover. Of course philosophical parents don't have to be a mother and a father, or white, or affluent enough to have a nice baby carriage and flowing togas. Philosophical parents can be all sorts of people, raising children in all sorts of circumstances.

Parts of chapters 11 and 18 started life as parts of three essays published in *The Philosophers' Magazine*: "The Good Life and the Mommy Wars" (2007); "Family Ties" (2011); and "Our Children, Ourselves" (2015). Passages from chapter 15 started off as an essay published in *Free Inquiry*: "People Don't Die, Do They?" (2007).

ACKNOWLEDGMENTS

The personal anecdotes in this book are true stories, or at least as accurate as I could make them, writing many years after the original events or conversations; names have been changed and personal details slightly altered. To friends whose stories I tell: I'm grateful to you for the wonderful times and great conversations we've had as parents. I'm also grateful to the smart babysitter discussed in chapter 14.

Thank you most of all to my husband, Peter, for making so many things possible and for being a great editor. And thank you also to our children, Becky and Sam, for putting up with this book.

ANNOTATED BIBLIOGRAPHY

Chapter 1. Children Come from Us

Aristotle. *Nicomachean Ethics*. 2nd ed. Translated by Terrence Irwin. Indianapolis: Hackett, 1999.
> The discussion of parenthood is in Book 8, chapter 12. All source quotes are on p. 133 (my versions are very slightly modified). Aristotle discusses friendship throughout Books 8 and 9.

Bartholet, Elizabeth. *Family Bonds: Adoption, Infertility, and the New World of Child Production*. Boston: Beacon, 1993.
> "I am the complete rationalist . . .": see p. 22. I discuss Bartholet's views on adoption in chapter 8.

Conn, Peter. *Adoption: A Brief Social and Cultural History*. New York: Palgrave, 2013.
> For discussion of adoption in Ancient Greece, see pp. 30–34.

Fried, Charles. *Right and Wrong*. Cambridge, MA: Harvard College, 1978.
> Fried's discussion of parenthood is on pp. 150–55. "Parenthood is a kind of . . .": see p. 155.

Hrdy, Sarah Blaffer. *Mother Nature: Maternal Instincts and How They Shape the Human Species*. New York: Ballantine, 2000.

Huxley, Aldous. *Brave New World*. New York: Harper Perennial, 2006.

Jones, J. "Adoption Experiences of Women and Men and Demand for Children to Adopt by Women 18–44 Years of Age in the United States, 2002." National Center for Health Statistics. Vital Health Stat Series 23, no. 27 (2008).
For fertility status of women seeking to adopt, see p. 15, figure 9.

Krazit, Tom. "The Backstory of Steve Jobs' Quote About Parenthood." Gigaom.com. October 11, 2011. http://bit.ly/1ruKHkm.
The origin of the Elizabeth Stone "heart outside the body" quote is explained here.

Nozick, Robert. *The Examined Life: Philosophical Meditations*. New York: Touchstone, 1989.
Nozick's discussion of parents and children is in chapter 3. The quote about children is on p. 28.

Plato. *The Republic*. Translated by G. M. A. Grube and C. D. C. Reeve. Indianapolis: Hackett, 1992.
The reproduction of Guardians is discussed in Book 5.

Simon, Scott. *Baby, We Were Meant for Each Other: In Praise of Adoption*. New York: Random House, 2010.

Simon, Scott. "'Meant for Each Other': Scott Simon's Adoption Story." *National Public Radio*. August 20, 2010. http://n.pr/29Mlslc.
Quotes from Simon's book *Baby, We Were Meant for Each Other* are in the book excerpt that can be found here.

Vandivere, S., K. Malm, and L. Radel. *Adoption USA: A Chartbook Based on the 2007 National Survey of Adoptive Parents*. Washington, DC: The U.S. Department of Health and Human Services, Office of the Assistant Secretary for Planning and Evaluation, 2009.
For data on adoption satisfaction, see p. 35. This survey found that the vast majority who adopt would make the same adoption decision all over again.

Chapter 2. Life Is Good

Adiga, Aravind. *Last Man in Tower*. New York: Alfred A. Knopf, 2011.
"I was never born . . .": see p. 7. The author characterizes this as "adapted from *The Bhagavad Gita*."

Benatar, David. *Better Never to Have Been: The Harm of Coming into Existence*. Oxford: Oxford University Press, 2008.

Caplan, Bryan. *Selfish Reasons to Have More Kids: Why Being a Great Parent Is Less Work and More Fun than You Think*. New York: Basic Books, 2006.
"To deny the gift of life . . .": see p. 12.

Dawkins, Richard. *Unweaving the Rainbow: Science, Delusion and the Appetite for Wonder.* New York: Mariner Books, 1998.
"We are going to die . . .": see p. 1.

Overall, Christine. *Why Have Children? The Ethical Debate.* Cambridge, MA: The MIT Press, 2012.

Parfit, Derek. *Reasons and Persons.* Oxford: Oxford University Press, 1984.

Smilansky, Saul. "Is There a Moral Obligation to Have Children?" *Journal of Applied Philosophy* 12 (1995): 41–53.

Wittgenstein, Ludwig. *Philosophical Investigations.* Malden, MA: Wiley- Blackwell, 2009.

Chapter 3. Quantity Control

Adams, Lisa Ramsey. "Eternal Progression." In *Encyclopedia of Mormonism*, edited by Daniel H. Ludlow. New York: MacMillan, 1992. http://bit.ly/1PzT7wX.

Boulding, Kenneth. *The Meaning of the Twentieth Century: The Great Transition.* London: George Allen and Unwin Ltd., 1964.
The cap-and-trade system is described on pp. 135–36.

Caplan, Bryan. *Selfish Reasons to Have More Kids: Why Being a Great Parent Is Less Work and More Fun than You Think.* New York: Basic Books, 2011.
"the good effects . . .": see p. 136.

De la Croix, David, and Axel Gosseries. "Population Policy through Tradable Procreation Entitlements." *International Economic Review* 50, no. 2 (2009): 507–42.

Joyce, Kathryn. *Quiverfull: Inside the Christian Patriarchy Movement.* Boston: Beacon Press, 2009.

Ord, Toby. "Overpopulation or Underpopulation?" Presentation delivered at the Oxford Martin School at Oxford University, October 2011. http://bit.ly/1Sbfk47.

Pew Research Center. *America's Changing Religious Landscape.* May 12, 2015. http://pewrsr.ch/21sCEB2.
The fertility statistics are on p. 64.

Roberts, Sam. "A Village with the Numbers, Not the Image, of the Poorest Place." *New York Times*, April 20, 2011. http://nyti.ms/1yQ3RmN.

Sachs, Kenneth. *The End of Poverty: Economic Possibilities for Our Time.* New York: Penguin, 2005.

See pp. 323–26 (and throughout chapter 16) for a discussion of the relationship between fertility and variables like poverty, infant mortality rates, and
gender equality.

Scheffler, Samuel. *Death and the Afterlife*. Oxford: Oxford University Press, 2013.
To Scheffler I owe the idea that life for our survivors is tantamount to an afterlife for us.

Wikipedia, s. v. "Endangered species." Last modified May 19, 2016. http://en.
wikipedia.org/wiki/Endangered_species.

Wikipedia, s. v. "Population growth." Last modified May 3, 2016. http://en.
wikipedia.org/wiki/Population_growth.

Chapter 4. Quality Control

"Bare Branches, Redundant Males." *The Economist*, April 18, 2015. Source for sex
ratios in India and China.

California Cryobank Reproductive Tissue Services. "Look-A-Likes." http://www.
cryobank.com/Donor-Search/Look-A-Likes/.

Egg Donation, Inc. https://www.eggdonor.com/.

Glover, Jonathan. *Choosing Children: The Ethical Dilemmas of Genetic Intervention*.
Oxford: Oxford University Press, 2006.
"Cheerful moral anarchy . . . ": see p. 54.

iPledge: Committed to Pregnancy Prevention. http://www.ipledgeprogram.com.
This is the online version of the isotretinoin booklet.

Kamm, Francis. "What Is and Is Not Wrong with Enhancement?" In *Human
Enhancement*, edited by Julian Savulescu and Nick Bostrom, 91–130.
Oxford: Oxford University Press, 2009.
"One can know . . .": see p. 113.

Parfit, Derek. *Reasons and Persons*. Oxford: Oxford University Press, 1984.
My Accutane example is inspired by the medical programs scenario on p. 367.
My distinction between protecting and selecting is meant to capture the
distinction Parfit draws between making a reproductive decision based on
a person-affecting principle, and based on an impersonal principle.

Sandel, Michael. *The Case against Perfection: Ethics in the Age of Genetic Engineering*.
Cambridge, MA: Belknap Press of Harvard University Press, 2007.
"openness to the unbidden": see p. 45. Sandel credits the phrase to the theolo-
gian William F. May.

Savulescu, Julian. "Procreative Beneficence: Why We Should Select the Best Children." *Bioethics* 15, no. 5/6 (2001): 413–25.

Savulescu, Julian, and Guy Kahane. "The Moral Obligation to Create Children with the Best Chance of the Best Life." *Bioethics* 23, no. 5 (2009): 274–90.

Tantibanchachai, Chanapa. "Isotretinoin as a Teratogen." *The Embryo Project Encyclopedia.* http://bit.ly/1SbfDMh.

Thernstrom, Melanie. "Meet the Twiblings." *The New York Times Magazine*, December 29, 2010.
This article is the source of the quote from a mother-to-be who says that egg donation is akin to blood donation.

Velleman, David. "Family History." *Philosophical Papers* 34, no. 3 (2005): 357–78.

Weinberg, Rivka. "The Moral Complexity of Sperm Donation." *Bioethics* 22, no. 3 (2008): 166–78.

Chapter 5. In the Beginning

Baird, Robert M., and Stuart E. Rosenbaum. *The Ethics of Abortion: Pro-Life vs. Pro-Choice.* Amherst: Prometheus, 2001.
When I write "there's no simple, direct route from the status of the fetus to the permissibility or impermissibility of ending pregnancy," I have in mind the well-known articles by Judith Jarvis Thomson and Don Marquis that are reprinted in this volume. Thomson assumes for the sake of argument that the fetus is a person, but makes an impressive case that abortion is nevertheless defensible under certain conditions; Marquis assumes the fetus is not a person, and yet makes a thought-provoking case that abortion is nevertheless just as problematic as killing a person.

Baker, Lynne Rudder. *Persons and Bodies: A Constitution View.* Cambridge: Cambridge University Press, 2000.

Baker, Lynne Rudder. "When Does a Person Begin?" *Social Philosophy and Policy* 22, no. 2 (2005): 25–48.
"rudimentary first person perspective": see pp. 30–36. "just an ontologically insignificant . . .": see p. 40. In this article (see pp. 26–27), Rudder makes the twinning argument against asserting that the fetal organism comes into existence prior to implantation.

Brogaard, Berit. "The Moral Status of the Human Embryo." In *Biomedical Ethics: Humanist Perspectives of Humanism Today*, edited by Howard B. Rades, 81–90. Amherst: Prometheus Books, 2006.

Brogaard surveys a number of ways of understanding the metaphysics of twinning. She argues that even mere *potential* for twinning blocks the identity of any early embryo, and a later fetus or baby.

Eliot, Lise. *What's Going on in There? How the Brain and Mind Develop in the First Five Years of Life.* New York: Bantam, 1999.
"250,000 neurons are born per minute": see p. 26.

Ford, Norman. *When Did I Begin? Conception of the Human Individual in History, Philosophy, and Science.* Cambridge: Cambridge University Press, 1991.

Koch, Christof. "When Does Consciousness Arise?" *Scientific American Mind*, September 1, 2009. http://bit.ly/1OwIPSO.
Source for the view that consciousness is not present until the third trimester, when the fetus has a normal EEG.

Lagercrantz, Hugo, and Jean-Pierre Changeux. "The Emergence of Human Consciousness: From Fetal to Neonatal Life." *Pediatric Research* 65 (2009): 255–60.
Source for the view that different aspects of consciousness emerge at different points, and for timing of olfaction and hearing.

Lee, Susan J., Henry J. Ralston, Eleanor A. Drey, John Colin Partridge, and Mark A. Rosen. "Fetal Pain: A Systematic Review of the Evidence." *Journal of the American Medical Association* 294, no. 8 (2005): 947–54.
A detailed investigation of fetal consciousness, with emphasis on fetal pain.

Olson, Eric T. *The Human Animal: Personal Identity without Psychology.* Oxford: Oxford University Press, 1997.
This very clear and readable book is the place to start if you are interested in Olson's account of when Larry's life begins. Olson's support for Norman Ford is on p. 91.

Olson, Eric T. *What Are We? A Study in Personal Ontology.* Oxford: Oxford University Press, 2007.

Pearson, Helen. "Your Destiny, from Day One." *Nature* 418 (July 4, 2002): 14–15.
This short, clear article is the source for my discussion of the early embryo's axes, and for the claim that 85 percent of a blastocyst becomes support structures and 15 percent becomes fetus.

Smith, Barry, and Berit Brogaard. "Sixteen Days." *Journal of Medical Philosophy* 28, no. 1 (2003): 45–78.
The argument about the lack of a defense system for maintaining stability is on p. 60.

The Visible Embryo. http://www.visembryo.com/.
Great source for information about fetal development.

Chapter 6. A Child Is Born

Brody, Jane. "As Cases of Induced Labor Rise, So Do Experts' Concerns." *New York Times*, January 14, 2003. http://nyti.ms/1YzkGxy.

Epstein, Randi Hutter. *Get Me Out: A History of Childbirth*. New York: W. W. Norton, 2010.

Moyer, Melinda Wenner. "The Truth about Epidurals: Are They Really So Bad?" *Slate*, January 11, 2012. http://slate.me/1C7LCqt.

Nozick, Robert. *Anarchy, State, and Utopia*. Cambridge, MA: Harvard University Press, 1974.
  The experience machine thought experiment is on pp. 42–45.

Chapter 7. Whose Child Is This?

Archard, David. *Children: Rights and Childhood*. 2nd ed. Milton Park, UK: Routledge, 2004.
  See pp. 144–45 for his claim that Charles Fried and Robert Nozick, who both speak of children as self-like, are both under the influence of the owner-property model of the parent-child relationship. The quotes about friends, colleagues, etc., are on p. 145.

Boswell, John. *The Kindness of Strangers: The Abandonment of Children in Western Europe from Late Antiquity to the Renaissance*. New York: Pantheon, 1988.
  On Romans who abandoned their children, see pp. 75–78. On Rousseau's abandonment of his children, see p. 20 (note 42). *The quote from Emile* is in note 42. On recovery of abandoned children as a theme in Roman literature, see chapter 2 (pp. 95–137).

Fessler, Ann. *The Girls Who Went Away: The Hidden History of Women Who Surrendered Children for Adoption in the Decades before Roe. V. Wade*. New York: Penguin, 2006.

Glass, Ira. "Unconditional Love, Act One. Love Is a Battlefield." (Episode 317) *This American Life*, 2006.
  Radio show about astonishingly dedicated adoptive parents of an emotionally disturbed boy.

Glass, Ira. "Switched at Birth." (Episode 360) *This American Life*, 2008.
  Radio show about children accidentally switched at birth.

Homes, A. M. *The Mistress's Daughter*. New York: Viking, 2007.
  A memoir about growing up adopted, and about one adult child's perplexity.

Jacobs, Margaret D. *A Generation Removed: The Fostering and Adoption of Indigenous Children in the Postwar World*. Lincoln: University of Nebraska, 2014.

Locke, John. *Second Treatise of Government*. In *Political Writings of John Locke*, edited by David Wooton. New York: Mentor, 1993.
Discussion of labor and the phrase "as much and as good" are in paragraph 27 (p. 274).

Richards, Norvin. *The Ethics of Parenthood*. Oxford: Oxford University Press, 2010.

Sedlak, Andrea J., and Diane D. Broadhurst. "Executive Summary of the Third National Incidence Study of Child Abuse and Neglect." US Department of Health and Human Services, 1996. http://bit.ly/28NdAtX.

Solomon, Andrew. *Far from the Tree: Parents, Children, and the Search for Identity*. New York: Scribner, 2012.

Chapter 8. Nobody's Child

Bartholet, Elizabeth. *Family Bonds: Adoption, Infertility, and the New World of Child Production*. Boston: Beacon, 1999.
"My point is not that ...": see p. 181. "The sense that a child ... ": see pp. 181–82. "Some presumption ..." and the quotes that follow are on pp. 181–82.

Bartholet, Elizabeth. "International Adoption: The Child's Story." Harvard Law School Faculty Scholarship Series, Paper 27, 2007. http://lsr.nellco.org/harvard_faculty/27.
"Wrong ideas about children": see p. 28. "Those who believe in children's rights ...": see p. 30.

Bartholet, Elizabeth. *Nobody's Children: Abuse and Neglect, Foster Drift, and the Adoption Alternative*. Boston: Beacon Press, 1999.
The "blood bias" quote is on p. 7.

Bartholet, Elizabeth, and David M. Smolin. "The Debate." In *Intercountry Adoption: Policies, Practices, and Outcomes*, edited by Judith L. Gibbons and Karen Smith Rotabi, 233–51. Williston, VT: Ashgate, 2012.

Boo, Katharine. *Behind the Beautiful Forevers: Life, Death, and Hope in a Mumbai Undercity*. New York: Random House, 2012.

Brake, Elizabeth. "Willing Parents: A Voluntarist Account of Parental Role Obligations." In *Procreation and Parenthood: The Ethics of Bearing and Rearing*

Children, edited by David Archard and David Benatar, 151–77. Oxford: Oxford University Press, 2011.

Brighouse, Harry, and Adam Swift. *Family Values: The Ethics of Parent-Child Relationships.* Princeton, NJ: Princeton University Press, 2014.
"We doubt that the adult interest . . . ": see p. 107. "Adoptive parents need not model . . .": p. 107.

Conn, Peter. *Adoption: A Brief Social and Cultural History.* New York: Palgrave MacMillan, 2013.
Conn discusses the natural order on p. 11; Aristotle on women on p. 12; and Aristotle's defense of slavery on p. 14.

Jacobs, Margaret D. *A Generation Removed: The Fostering and Adoption of Indigenous Children in the Postwar World.* Lincoln: Nebraska University Press, 2014.
This book covers removal of indigenous children from their biological parents in the United States, Canada, and Australia.

Joyce, Kathryn. *The Child Catchers: Rescue, Trafficking, and the New Gospel of Adoption.* New York: Public Affairs-Perseus, 2013.

LeBlanc, Adrian Nicole. *Random Family: Love, Drugs, Trouble, and Coming of Age in the Bronx.* New York: Scribner, 2004.

Page, Edgar. "Parental rights." *Journal of Applied Philosophy* 1 (1984): 187–203.
"For most people . . .": see p. 201.

Prusak, Bernard. *Parental Obligations and Bioethics: The Duties of a Creator.* New York: Routledge, 2013.

Shanley, Mary Lyndon. *Making Babies, Making Families: What Matters Most in an Age of Reproductive Technologies, Surrogacy, Adoption, and Same-Sex and Unwed Parents.* Boston: Beacon Press, 2001.

Sixsmith, Martin. *Philomena: A Mother, Her Son, and a Fifty-Year Search.* New York: Penguin, 2009.

Smith, Janet Farrell. "A Child of One's Own: A Moral Assessment of Property Concepts in Adoption." In *Adoption Matters: Philosophical and Feminist Essays,* edited by Sally Haslanger and Charlotte Witt, 112–31. Ithaca, NY: Cornell University Press, 2005.

Chapter 9. Parenthood's Aim

Brighouse, Harry, and Adam Swift. *Family Values: The Ethics of Parent-Child Relationships.* Princeton, NJ: Princeton University Press, 2014.

Chua, Amy. *Battle Hymn of the Tiger Mother.* New York: Penguin, 2011.

Feinberg, Joel. "The Child's Right to an Open Future." In *Whose Child? Children's Rights, Parental Authority, and State Power,* edited by William Aiken and Hugh LaFollette, 124–53. Totowa, NJ: Littlefield, Adams & Co., 1980.

Harris, Judith Rich. *The Nurture Assumption: Why Children Turn Out the Way They Do.* New York: Free Press, 1998 (revised in 2009).

Irvine, William B. *Doing Right by Children.* St. Paul, MN: Paragon House, 2001. The stewardship model of parenting is discussed on pp. 213–27.

Kazez, Jean. *The Weight of Things: Philosophy and the Good Life.* Oxford: Blackwell, 2007.

Kristof, Nicholas D., and Sheryl WuDunn. *Half the Sky: Turning Oppression into Opportunity for Women Worldwide.* New York: Knopf, 2009.

Macleod, Colin M. "Conceptions of Parental Autonomy." *Politics and Society* 25 (1997): 117–40.

Slote, Michael. *Goods and Virtues.* Oxford: Oxford University Press, 1983.
See chapter 1 of this book for a defense of the view that childhood successes and misfortunes are less important than later successes and misfortunes. Slote writes, "Within a very wide range, the facts of childhood simply don't enter with any great weight into our estimation of the (relative) goodness of total lives" (p. 14).

Chapter 10. First Decisions

American Academy of Pediatrics, Committee on Fetus and Newborn, Committee on Drugs, Section on Anesthesiology, Section on Surgery. "Neonatal Anesthesia." *Pediatrics* 80 (1987): 446.
The AAP position on management of newborn pain is stated here. I owe this reference to Stang (1998).

American Academy of Pediatrics, Task Force on Circumcision. "Circumcision Policy Statement." *Pediatrics* 130, no. 3 (2012): 585–86.

American Academy of Pediatrics, Task Force on Circumcision. "Technical Report: Male Circumcision." *Pediatrics* 130, no. 3 (2012): e756–85.
Source for most of the information about costs and benefits of circumcision, but see Gray, McNeil, Smith et al., and UNFPA et al. articles for discussion of circumcision and HIV-AIDS.

Benatar, Michael, and David Benatar. "Between Prophylaxis and Child Abuse: The Ethics of Neonatal Male Circumcision." In *Cutting to the Core: Exploring the Ethics of Contested Surgeries*, edited by David Benatar, 23–46. Lanham, MD: Roman & Littlefield, 2006.

Boorstein, Michelle. "A Small but Growing Number of Jews Is Questioning the Ancient Ritual of Circumcision." *Washington Post*, December 28, 2013. http://wapo.st/1czTvL2.

Darby, Robert J. L. "The Child's Right to an Open Future: Is the Principle Applicable to Non-therapeutic Circumcision?" *Journal of Medical Ethics* 39 (2013): 463–68.

Diamant, Anita, with Karen Kushner. *How to Raise a Jewish Child: A Practical Handbook for Family Life*. New York: Schocken Books, 2008.
"The most compelling answer . . .": p. 163.

Campo-Flores, Arian. "Circumcision Coverage Comes Into Focus." *The Wall Street Journal*, January 20, 2014. http://on.wsj.com/2mbVsqY.
Source for information about Medicaid coverage.

Glick, Leonard. *Marked in Your Flesh: Circumcision from Ancient Judea to Modern America*. New York: Oxford University Press, 2005.
Glick discusses Genesis 17 on pp. 13–16. See p. 65 for the Maimonides quote.

Gray, Ronald. "Male Circumcision: The Shortcut to Sexually Transmitted Disease Prevention." Johns Hopkins 2010 Fall Provost's Lecture Series, December 7, 2010. http://bit.ly/2a0Nt9L.
My discussion of circumcision and HIV is largely based on this very clear and persuasive presentation.

JPS Tanakh: The Holy Scriptures. Philadelphia: The Jewish Publication Society, 1985.
Verses from Genesis, chapter 17, are on pp. 23–24.

Kunin, Samuel A. "A Non-Orthodox Physician-Mohel: Some Differences in Approach." InterFaithFamily. http://bit.ly/1YzjMRN.

McNeil, Donald G. "Cultural Attitudes and Rumors Are Lasting Obstacles to Safe Sex." *New York Times*, May 9, 2010. http://nyti.ms/2al6dma.
This article explains some of the cultural barriers to condom use in one African country with an HIV epidemic.

Neustadt, Rabbi Doniel. "The Yoledes in Halachah." http://bit.ly/2i8dxad.

Smith, Dawn, K., Allan Taylor, Peter H. Kilmarx, Patrick Sullivan, Lee Warner, Mary Kamb, Naomi Bock, Bob Kohmescher, Timothy D. Mastro. "Male Circumcision in the United States for the Prevention of HIV Infection and Other Adverse

Health Outcomes: Report from a CDC Consultation." *Public Health Reports* 125, Supplement 1 (2010): 72–82.
This article makes it clear how little research has been done on circumcision and HIV in the United States, but the authors nevertheless do affirm the likelihood of a benefit.

Stanford University Medical School. "Circumcision—Gomco Technique." http://stan.md/2idwXqo.

Stang, Howard J., and Leonard W. Snellman. "Circumcision Practice Patterns in the United States." *Pediatrics* 101, no. 6 (1998): e5.
This is the source for patterns of anesthesia usage among physicians who circumcise newborns.

Svoboda, J. Steven, and Robert S. Van Howe. "Out of Step: Fatal Flaws in the Latest AAP Policy Report on Neonatal Circumcision." *Journal of Medical Ethics* 39 (2013): 434–41.

UNFPA, WHO, and UNAIDS. "Position Statement on Condoms and the Prevention of HIV, other Sexually Transmitted Infections and Unintended Pregnancy." http://bit.ly/1JT9GT6.
Offers data on patterns of condom use and argues for the importance of condoms in preventing HIV–AIDS.

Ungar-Sargon, Eliyahu, director. *Cut: Slicing Through the Myths of Circumcision* (2005). http://www.cutthefilm.com/.

World Health Organization. *Male Circumcision: Global Trends and Determinants of Prevalence, Safety and Acceptability.* Geneva: WHO Press, 2007.
Source for US and global circumcision statistics.

Chapter 11. Still Life with Child

Aristotle. *The Nicomachean Ethics.* 2nd ed. Translated by Terence Irwin. Indianapolis: Hackett, 1999.
For Aristotle's account of virtue as a mean, see Book II, chapter 6. For Aristotle's initial concern with humans living differently from animals, see Book II, chapter 7. "We ought not to follow": Book X, chapter 7 (pp. 164–65).

Belkin, Lisa. "The Opt-Out Revolution." *New York Times Magazine*, October 26, 2003.
Much-discussed article about women at the high end of the economic spectrum choosing to leave successful careers.

Clarke-Stewart, Alison, and Virginia D. Allhusen. *What We Know About Childcare.* Cambridge, MA: Harvard University Press, 2005.
This is the source for the assertion that children in day care are not very different from children raised at home. This is not to say there are no differences. The authors claim (chapter 5) that children in day care are somewhat more aggressive and also somewhat ahead of their peers, socially and cognitively. They are no less attached to their mothers.

Cohany, Sharon R., and Emy Sok. "Trends in Labor Force Participation of Married Mothers of Infants." *Monthly Labor Review,* Bureau of Labor Statistics, February 2007. http://www.bls.gov/opub/mlr/2007/02/art2full.pdf.
See p. 15 for statistics about mothers at the two ends of the economic spectrum. Mothers with top-quintile husbands worked at a rate of 48 percent in 2005; those with bottom-quintile husbands worked at a rate of 47 percent. Those with middle-quintile husbands worked at a rate of 64 percent.

Cohn, D'Vera, Gretchen Livingston, and Wendy Wang. "After Decades of Decline, a Rise in Stay-at-Home Mothers." Washington, DC: Pew Research Center's Social and Demographic Trends Project, April 2014. http://pewrsr.ch/1mZ1sgq.
Source for statistics about the number of single mothers (p. 8) and on the reasons they give for staying home with their children (p. 14). Also the source for data about "opt-out" professional women (p. 6) and the common belief that children should be raised by a parent at home (p. 26).

Friedan, Betty. *The Feminine Mystique.* New York: W. W. Norton, 1963.

Hewlett, Sylvia Ann, and Carolyn Buck Luce. "Off-Ramps and On-Ramps: Keeping Talented Women on the Road to Success." *Harvard Business Review,* March 2005. http://bit.ly/2aeJ5U9.
Source for statics about women who succeed in returning to work.

Hirshman, Linda. *Get to Work: A Manifesto for Women of the World.* New York: Viking, 2006.
"Childcare and housekeeping . . .": see p. 2. "Although childrearing . . .": see p. 34. "doesn't remove decisions . . .": see p. 26.

Kazez, Jean. *The Weight of Things: Philosophy and the Good Life.* Malden, MA: Wiley-Blackwell, 2007.

Krakauer, Jon. *Into Thin Air: A Personal Account of the Mt. Everest Disaster.* New York: Villard, 1997.

Lamott, Anne. *Operating Instructions: A Journal of My Son's First Year.* New York: Anchor Books, 1993.
My favorite book about parenthood. Quotes are on pp. 19, 20, 60–61, and 48.

Nietzsche, Friedrich. *The Gay Science*. Translated by Walter Kaufmann. New York: Random House, 1974.
  "Become who you are": Book Three, section 270. More precisely, the quote is *"What does your conscience say?—'You shall become the person you are.'"*

Paul, L. A. *Transformative Experience*. Oxford: Oxford University Press, 2015.

Peters, Joan K. *When Mothers Work: Loving Our Children without Sacrificing Our Selves*. New York: Perseus, 1997.

Sandberg, Sheryl. *Lean In: Women, Work, and the Will to Lead*. New York: Knopf, 2013.
  Statistics about employment rates are on p. 202 (note 5) and p. 206 (note 23).

Saul, Jennifer. *Feminism: Issues and Arguments*. Oxford: Oxford University Press, 2003.
  Chapter 1, "The Politics of Work and Family," is particularly relevant.

Chapter 12. Boys and Girls

Angier, Natalie. *Woman: An Intimate Geography*. New York: Houghton Mifflin Harcourt, 1999.

Boylan, Jennifer Finney. *She's Not There: A Life in Two Genders*. New York: Broadway, 2013.

Butler, Judith. *Gender Trouble: Feminism and the Subversion of Identity*. New York: Routledge, 1990.

Churchland, Patricia. *Touching a Nerve: Our Brains, Our Selves*. New York: W. W. Norton, 2013.
  Most relevant is chapter 5, "Aggression and Sex."

Colapinto, John. *As Nature Made Him: The Boy Who Was Raised as a Girl*. New York: Harper Collins, 2000.

Davis, Bill, Fred Wolf, and Len Steckler (directors). *Free to Be You and Me*. Hen's Tooth Video (aired on television 1974, DVD released 2001).

Dawkins, Richard. *The Selfish Gene*. Oxford: Oxford University Press, 1976.
  The definition of sex is on pp. 140–42: "there is one fundamental feature of the sexes which can be used to label males and males, and females as females, throughout animals and plants. This is that the sex cells or 'gametes' of males are much smaller and more numerous than the gametes of females. This is true whether we are dealing with animals or plants."

Dreger, Alice. "The Social Construction of Sex." *Pacific Standard: The Science of Society*, March 21, 2014. http://bit.ly/1UhyfBZ.

Eliot, Lise. *Pink Brain/Blue Brain: How Small Differences Grow Into Troublesome Gaps—and What We Can Do About It.* New York: Mariner, 2009.
For data on skewed traits, see pp. 12–13.

Fausto-Sterling, Anne. *Sex/Gender: Biology in a Social World.* New York: Routledge, 2012.
For her very cautious, non-committal discussion of gender identity formation, see chapter 5. On p. 53, she explains some ingenious studies of how babies react to males and females in their environment. The estimate of the number of transgender kids is on p. 64. The terms "desist" and "persist" are on p. 65, but credited by Fausto-Sterling to other authors.

Fausto-Sterling, Anne. *Sexing the Body: Gender Politics and the Construction of Sexuality.* New York: Basic Books, 2000.
For the estimate that 1.7 percent of children are intersex, see p. 53. Chapter 3 is an excellent introduction to intersex conditions.

Fine, Cordelia. *Delusions of Gender: How Our Minds, Society, and Neurosexism Create Difference.* New York: W. W. Norton, 2010.

Hines, Melissa. *Brain Gender.* Oxford: Oxford University Press, 2005.
On sex and toy choice, see chapter 6, "Sex and Play."

Hyde, Janet Shibley. "The Gender Similarities Hypothesis." *American Psychologist* 60 (2005): 581–92.

Hyde, Janet Shibley. "New Direction in the Study of Gender Similarities and Differences." *Current Directions in Psychological Science* 16, no. 5 (2007): 259–63.
The meta-analysis of sex difference reports is on p. 260 (table 1). "within-gender variability is typically. . .": see p. 260.

Joel, Daphna. "Male or Female? Brains Are Intersex." *Frontiers in Integrative Neuroscience* 5, no. 57 (2011).

Jordan-Young, Rebecca. *Brain Storm: The Flaws in the Science of Sex Differences.* Cambridge, MA: Harvard University Press, 2010.

Kantor, Jodi. "Harvard Business School Case Study: Gender Equity." *New York Times*, September 7, 2013.

McCarthy, Margaret M., and Arthur P. Arnold. "Reframing Sexual Differentiation of the Brain." *Nature Neuroscience* 14, no. 6 (2011): 677–83.

Oprah Winfrey Network. *I Am Jazz: A Family in Transition* (documentary). http://bit.ly/1sLTOOQ.

Overall, Christine. "Sex/Gender Transitions and Life-Changing Aspirations." In *You've Changed: Sex Reassignment and Personal Identity*, edited by Laurie Shrage, 11–27. Oxford: Oxford University Press, 2009.

Pfaff, Donald. *Man and Woman: An Inside Story.* New York: Oxford University Press, 2011.
"Destroying the preoptic area . . .": see p. 75. "a wide variety of vertebrate species . . .": see p. 75. "in higher primates . . .": see p. 85. "Only the biologically-based . . .": see p. 68.

Poisson, Jayme. "Remember Storm? We Check In on the Baby Being Raised Gender-Neutral." *The Star*, November 15, 2013. http://on.thestar.com/1dsW5WI. Source for the Jane Ward quote.

Sax, Leonard. *Why Gender Matters: What Parents and Teachers Need to Know about the Emerging Science of Sex Differences.* New York: Three Rivers Press, 2005.
Sax advises parents of "anomalous" boys to send them to all-male summer camps that specialize in sports and outdoor activities. "Avoid computer science camps, arts camps, music camps, and the like," he counsels (p. 228).

Solomon, Andrew. *Far from the Tree: Parents, Children, and the Search for Identity.* New York: Scribner, 2012.
The chapter on transgender children is extremely illuminating.

Sveinsdóttir, Ásta. "The Metaphysics of Sex and Gender." In *Feminist Metaphysics: Explorations in the Ontology of Sex, Gender and the Self*, edited by Charlotte Witt, 47–65. New York: Springer, 2011.
For the two analogies, see p. 59. For the claim that sex is "conferred," see pp. 58–64.

Warnke, Georgia. *After Identity: Rethinking Race, Sex, and Gender.* Cambridge: Cambridge University Press, 2007.
The long quote is on p. 187.

Witt, Charlotte. *The Metaphysics of Gender.* Oxford: Oxford University Press, 2011.

Chapter 13. The One and the Many

Biss, Eula. *On Immunity: An Inoculation.* Minneapolis: Graywolf Press, 2014.

Centers for Disease Control and Prevention. "Polio Elimination in the United States." http://www.cdc.gov/polio/us/index.html.
Source for facts about polio incidence and the need for continued vaccination.

Cullity, Garrett. "Moral Free Riding." *Philosophy and Public Affairs* 24, no. 1 (1995): 3–34.
For the enterprising elves example, see p. 10.

Johns Hopkins Bloomberg School of Public Health, Institute for Vaccine Safety. "School Exemption Laws by State." http://www.vaccinesafety.edu/cc-exem.htm.

Lyten, Jeroen. "Vaccination Policy and Ethical Challenges Posed by Herd Immunity, Suboptimal Uptake and Subgroup Targeting." *Public Health Ethics* 4, no. 3 (2011): 280–91.
My classification of refusers follows this article closely, though I use different names.

National Conference of State Legislatures. "States with Religious and Philosophical Exemptions from School Immunization Requirements (August 23, 2016)." http://bit.ly/1yQZ0R9.

Nozick, Robert. *Anarchy, State, and Utopia.* New York: Basic Books, 1974.
For the public address system, see pp. 93–94.

Offit, Paul. *Deadly Choices: How the Anti-vaccine Movement Threatens Us All.* New York: Basic Books, 2011.

Oshinsky, David. *Polio: An American Story.* Oxford: Oxford University Press, 2005.
For polio statistics, see p. 161.

Reagan-Steiner, Sarah, David Yankey, Jenny Jeyarajah, Laurie D. Elam-Evans, James A. Singleton, C. Robinette Curtis, Jessica MacNeil, Lauri E. Markowitz, Shannon Stokley. "National, Regional, State, and Selected Local Area Vaccination Coverage Among Adolescents Aged 13–17—United States, 2014." *Morbidity and Mortality Weekly Report* 64, no. 29 (July 31, 2015): 784–92. http://bit.ly/2aqzhbh.
Source for HPV vaccination statistics.

Sears, Robert. *The Vaccination Book: Making the Right Decision for Your Child.* 2nd ed. New York: Little Brown, 2011.
For more on risk of polio, tetanus, diphtheria, and measles, see p. 197.

Stemwedel, Janet. "The Ethics of Opting Out of Vaccination." Scientific American Blogs: Doing Good Science, June 29, 2013. http://bit.ly/1UfLqOr.

Texas Department of State Health Services. "Vaccination Coverage Levels in Texas Schools." http://bit.ly/1Ow4Pha.

Texas Department of State Health Services. "Exclusions from Immunization Requirements." http://bit.ly/2mc4GDT.

Vestal, Christine. "In States with Looser Immunization Laws, Lower Rates." Pew Charitable Trusts, February 9, 2015. http://bit.ly/17b00p1.
Source for statistic that there are 2.5 times more exemptions when states allow personal belief exemptions as well as religious exemptions.

Chapter 14. Lies, Lies, Lies

Aebersold, Carol V., and Chanda A. Bell. *The Elf on the Shelf.* Atlanta: CCA and B Publishing, 2005.

Bok, Sissela. *Lying: Moral Choice in Public and Private Life.* New York: Vintage, 1999.
Includes an appendix with excerpts from classic discussions of lying by Augustine, Aquinas, Bacon, Grotius, Kant, Sidgwick, Harrod, Bonhoeffer, and Warnock.

Gopnik, Alison. *The Philosophical Baby: What Children's Minds Tell Us about Truth, Love, and the Meaning of Life.* New York: Picador, 2009.
For more on how children know the difference between real and imaginary companions, see pp. 53 and 71. For the look and giggle of pretense, see p. 31.

Kind, Amy. "Creative Mothering: Lies and the Lying Mothers Who Tell Them." In *Motherhood: The Birth of Wisdom (Philosophy for Everyone),* edited by Sheila Lintott, 29–40. Malden, MA: Wiley-Blackwell, 2010.
"Children, especially young children . . .": see p. 38.

Chapter 15. Passing on Religion

Dawkins, Richard. *The God Delusion.* New York: Mariner, 2006.
Discussion of religious education is in chapter 9. "A child is not a Christian child . . .": see p. 382. He subscribes to the stewardship view of parenting on p. 367.

Dennett, Daniel. *Breaking the Spell: Religion as a Natural Phenomenon.* New York: Penguin, 2006.
Dennett is insightful about mechanisms of doubt-suppression (see chapters 8 and 11).

Humphrey, Nicholas. "What Shall We Tell the Children?" Amnesty Lecture, Oxford, February 21, 1997. http://bit.ly/1UhxKrt.

Law, Stephen. *The War for Children's Minds.* Milton Park, UK: Routledge, 2006.

Chapter 16. Letting Go

Castle, Terry. "Don't Pick Up: Why Kids Need to Separate from Their Parents." *The Chronicle of Higher Education,* May 6, 2012.

Deresiewicz, William. *Excellent Sheep: The Miseducation of the American Elite and the Way to a Meaningful Life.* New York: Free Press, 2014.

"The child is made to function . . .": see p. 44. "bespeaks a misguided belief . . .": see p. 43. "status competition within . . .": see p. 43. "When your kids get into . . .": see p. 44. "Don't talk to your parents . . .": see p. 123.

Lahiri, Jumpha, *The Lowland*. New York: Random House, 2013. Quote is on p. 294.

Obama, Barack. *Dreams from My Father: A Story of Race and Inheritance*. New York: Three Rivers Press, 1995.

Rohner, Ronald P., Abdul Khaleque, and David E. Cournoyer. "Parental Acceptance-Rejection: Theory, Methods, Cross-Cultural Evidence, and Implications." *Ethos* 33, no. 3 (2005): 299–334.

Chapter 17. Going Home

Anonymous. *The Classic of Filial Piety (Xiao Jing)*. Translated by James Legge. http://bit.ly/2hY9gTG.
"The son derives his life . . .": see section IX.

English, Jane. "What Do Grown Children Owe Their Parents?" In *Having Children*, edited by Onora O'Neill and William Ruddick, 351–56. Oxford: Oxford University Press, 1979.

Chapter 18. Parenthood and Meaning

Brogaard, Berit. "Parental Love and the Meaning of Life." In *The Theory and Practice of Ontology*, edited by Leo Zaibert, 223–40. New York: Palgrave Macmillan, 2016.

Clark, Andrew E., Ed Diener, Yanni Georgellis, and Richard E. Lucas. "Lags and Leads in Life Satisfaction: A Test of the Baseline Hypothesis." Institute for the Study of Labor, Discussion Paper No. 2525, December 2006. http://bit.ly/1W5PTIf.
For impact of first child on life satisfaction, see the two figures on p. 23 and the discussion on p. 10.

Frankfurt, Harry. *The Reasons of Love*. Princeton, NJ: Princeton University Press, 2006.
For the quote about the mathematical certainty of love for children, see p. 65. He speaks of the purity of love for young children on p. 42. "When all is said and done . . . ": see p. 77. He calls self-love the purest form of love on p. 80.

Johnston, Mark. *Surviving Death*. Princeton, NJ: Princeton University Press, 2010.

Kahneman, Daniel, Alan B. Krueger, David A. Schkade, Norbert Schwarz, and Arthur A. Stone. "A Survey Method for Characterizing Daily Life Experience: The Day Reconstruction Method." *Science* 306, no. 5702 (2004): 1776–80.

Kenrick, Douglas. "Renovating the Pyramid of Needs: Contemporary Extensions Built Upon Ancient Foundations." *Perspectives in Psychological Science* 5, no. 3 (2010): 292–314.

Kidder, Tracy. *Mountains Beyond Mountains: The Quest of Dr. Paul Farmer, A Man Who Would Cure the World*. New York: Random House, 2004.

Layard, Richard. *Happiness: Lessons from a New Science*. New York: Penguin, 2005. "There is indeed great rejoicing . . . ": see p. 68.

Nagel, Thomas. "The Absurd." *Journal of Philosophy* 68, no. 20 (1971): 716–27.

Nussbaum, Martha. *The Fragility of Goodness: Luck and Ethics in Greek Tragedy and Philosophy*. Cambridge: Cambridge University Press, 1986.

Scheffler, Samuel. *Death and the Afterlife*. Oxford: Oxford University Press, 2013.

Senior, Jennifer. *All Joy and No Fun: The Paradox of Modern Parenthood*. New York: Ecco, 2014.

Singer, Peter. *How Are We to Live? Ethics in an Age of Self-Interest*. New York: Prometheus Books, 1993. "Her only role . . .": see p. 197.

Singer, Peter. *The Life You Can Save: Acting Now to End World Poverty*. New York: Random House, 2009. "taking part in a collective effort . . .": see p. 170.

Tolstoy, Leo. *The Death of Ivan Ilyich & Confession*. Translated by Peter Carson. New York: Liveright, 2014.

Wolf, Susan. *Meaning in Life and Why it Matters*. Princeton, NJ: Princeton University Press, 2012.

INDEX

South Huntington   SEP 25 2017